ABOUT THIS PUBLICATION

FOR SERVICE ASSISTANCE

Customer Service
1.704.898.0770

North Carolina General Statues is published by The Muliti-Media Group of Greater Charlotte in Charlotte, North Carolina. Copyright 2015 by the Multi-Media Group of Greater Charlotte. This book or parts thereof may not be reproduced in any form, stored in a retrieval system, or transmitted in any form by any means—electronic, mechanical, photocopy, recording or otherwise—without prior written permission of the publisher, except as provided by United States of America copyright law.

The records required by U.S. Code 2257(a) through (c) and the pertinent regulations 28 C.F.R. Cli. 1, Part 75 with respect to this publication and all materials associated with such records are maintained by The Multi-Media Group of Greater Charlotte, Publisher and available for review by Attorney General.

www.visionbooks.org

Copyright © 2015 by MMGGC
All rights reserved!

TID: 5105700
ISBN (10) digit: 1503228649
ISBN (13) digit: 978-1503228641

123-4-56789-01239-Paperback
123-4-56789-01239-Hardback

First Edition

090520140547

Printed in the United States of America

2015 EDITION

North Carolina Criminal Law And Procedure-Pamphlet # 71

Printed In conjunction with the Administration of the Courts

North Carolina Criminal Law and Procedure
Pamphlet Reference Guide

Chapters	Pamphlet
Chapter 1 Civil Procedure	1
Chapter 1 Civil Procedure (Continue)	2
Chapter 1A Rules of Civil Procedure	2
Chapter 1B Contribution.	2
Chapter 1C Enforcement of Judgments.	2
Chapter 1D Punitive Damages.	2
Chapter 1E Eastern Band of Cherokee Indians.	2
Chapter 1F North Carolina Uniform Interstate Depositions and Discovery Act.	2
Chapter 2 - Clerk of Superior Court [Repealed and Transferred.]	3
Chapter 3 - Commissioners of Affidavits and Deeds [Repealed.]	3
Chapter 4 - Common Law	3
Chapter 5 - Contempt [Repealed.]	3
Chapter 5A - Contempt	3
Chapter 6 - Liability for Court Costs	3
Chapter 7 - Courts [Repealed and Transferred.]	3
Chapter 7A – Judicial Department	3
Chapter 7A – Continuation (Judicial Department)	4
Chapter 7A – Continuation (Judicial Department)	5
Chapter 7B - Juvenile Code	5
Chapter 8 - Evidence	6
Chapter 8A - Interpreters for Deaf Persons [Recodified.]	6
Chapter 8B - Interpreters for Deaf Persons	6
Chapter 8C - Evidence Code	6
Chapter 9 - Jurors	6
Chapter 10 - Notaries [Repealed.]	6
Chapter 10A - Notaries [Recodified.]	6
Chapter 10B - Notaries	6
Chapter 11 - Oaths	6
Chapter 12 - Statutory Construction	6
Chapter 13 - Citizenship Restored	6
Chapter 14 - Criminal Law	7
Chapter 14 –Criminal Law (Continuation)	8
Chapter 15 - Criminal Procedure	9
Chapter 15A - Criminal Procedure Act (Continuation)	10
Chapter 15A - Criminal Procedure Act (Continuation)	11
Chapter 15B - Victims Compensation	11
Chapter 15C - Address Confidentiality Program	11
Chapter 16 - Gaming Contracts and Futures	11
Chapter 17 - Habeas Corpus	11

Chapter 17A - Law-Enforcement Officers [Recodified.]	11
Chapter 17B - North Carolina Criminal Justice Education and Training System [Recodified.] Chapter 17C - North Carolina Criminal Justice Education and Training Standards Commission	11
	11
Chapter 17D - North Carolina Justice Academy	11
Chapter 17E - North Carolina Sheriffs' Education and Training Standards Commission	11
Chapter 18 - Regulation of Intoxicating Liquors [Repealed.]	12
Chapter 18A - Regulation of Intoxicating Liquors [Repealed.]	12
Chapter 18B - Regulation of Alcoholic Beverages	12
Chapter 18C - North Carolina State Lottery	12
Chapter 19 - Offenses against Public Morals	12
Chapter 19A - Protection of Animals	12
Chapter 20 - Motor Vehicles	13
Chapter 20 - Motor Vehicles (Continuation)	14
Chapter 20 - Motor Vehicles (Continuation)	15
Chapter 20 - Motor Vehicles (Continuation)	16
Chapter 21 - Bills of Lading	17
Chapter 22 - Contracts Requiring Writing	17
Chapter 22A - Signatures	17
Chapter 22B - Contracts Against Public Policy	17
Chapter 22C - Payments to Subcontractors	17
Chapter 23 - Debtor and Creditor	17
Chapter 24 – Interest	17
Chapter 25 – Uniform Commercial Code	18
Chapter 25 – Uniform Commercial Code (Continuation)	19
Chapter 25A – Retail Installment Sales Act	20
Chapter 25B - Credit	20
Chapter 25C - Sales of Artwork	20
Chapter 26 - Suretyship	20
Chapter 27 - Warehouse Receipts [Repealed.]	20
Chapter 28 - Administration [Repealed.]	20
Chapter 28A - Administration of Decedents' Estates	20
Chapter 28B - Estates of Absentees in Military Service	20
Chapter 28C - Estates of Missing Persons	20
Chapter 29 - Intestate Succession	21
Chapter 30 - Surviving Spouses	21
Chapter 31 - Wills	21
Chapter 31A - Acts Barring Property Rights	21
Chapter 31B - Renunciation of Property and Renunciation of Fiduciary Powers Act	21
Chapter 31C - Uniform Disposition of Community Property Rights at Death Act	21
Chapter 32 - Fiduciaries	21
Chapter 32A - Powers of Attorney	21
Chapter 33 - Guardian and Ward [Repealed and Recodified.]	21

Chapter 33A - North Carolina Uniform Transfers to Minors Act	21
Chapter 33B - North Carolina Uniform Custodial Trust Act	21
Chapter 34 - Veterans' Guardianship Act	22
Chapter 35 - Sterilization Procedures	22
Chapter 35A - Incompetency and Guardianship	22
Chapter 36 - Trusts and Trustees [Repealed.]	22
Chapter 36A - Trusts and Trustees	22
Chapter 36B - Uniform Management of Institutional Funds Act [Repealed.]	22
Chapter 36C - North Carolina Uniform Trust Code	22
Chapter 36D - North Carolina Community Third Party Trusts, Pooled Trusts	23
Chapter 36E - Uniform Prudent Management of Institutional Funds Act	23
Chapter 37 - Allocation of Principal and Income [Repealed.]	23
Chapter 37A - Uniform Principal and Income Act	23
Chapter 38 - Boundaries	23
Chapter 38A - Landowner Liability	23
Chapter 39 - Conveyances	23
Chapter 39A - Transfer Fee Covenants Prohibited	23
Chapter 40 - Eminent Domain [Repealed.]	23
Chapter 40A - Eminent Domain	23
Chapter 41 - Estates	23
Chapter 41A - State Fair Housing Act	23
Chapter 42 - Landlord and Tenant	23
Chapter 42A - Vacation Rental Act	23
Chapter 43 - Land Registration	23
Chapter 44 - Liens	24
Chapter 44A - Statutory Liens and Charges	24
Chapter 45 - Mortgages and Deeds of Trust	24
Chapter 45A - Good Funds Settlement Act	24
Chapter 46 - Partition	24
Chapter 47 - Probate and Registration	25
Chapter 47A - Unit Ownership	25
Chapter 47B - Real Property Marketable Title Act	25
Chapter 47C - North Carolina Condominium Act	25
Chapter 47D - Notice of Settlement Act [Expired.]	25
Chapter 47E - Residential Property Disclosure Act	25
Chapter 47F - North Carolina Planned Community Act	25
Chapter 47G - Option to Purchase Contracts	25
Chapter 47H - Contracts for Deed	25
Chapter 48 - Adoptions +	26
Chapter 48A - Minors	26
Chapter 49 - Bastardy	26
Chapter 49A - Rights of Children	26
Chapter 50 - Divorce and Alimony	26
Chapter 50A - Uniform Child-Custody Jurisdiction and	

Enforcement Act	26
Chapter 50B - Domestic Violence	26
Chapter 50C - Civil No-Contact Orders	26
Chapter 51 - Marriage	26
Chapter 52 - Powers and Liabilities of Married Persons	27
Chapter 52A - Uniform Reciprocal Enforcement of Support Act [Repealed.]	27
Chapter 52B - Uniform Premarital Agreement Act	27
Chapter 52C - Uniform Interstate Family Support Act	27
Chapter 53 - Banks	27
Chapter 53A - Business Development Corporations and North Carolina Capital Resource Corporations	28
Chapter 53B - Financial Privacy Act	28
Chapter 54 - Cooperative Organizations	28
Chapter 54A - Capital Stock Savings and Loan Associations [Repealed.]	28
Chapter 54B - Savings and Loan Associations	29
Chapter 54C - Savings Banks	29
Chapter 55 - North Carolina Business Corporation Act	30
Chapter 55A - North Carolina Nonprofit Corporation Act	31
Chapter 55B - Professional Corporation Act	31
Chapter 55C - Foreign Trade Zones	31
Chapter 55D - Filings, Names, and Registered Agents for Corporations, Nonprofit Corporations, and Partnerships	31
Chapter 56 - Electric, Telegraph and Power Companies [Repealed.]	31
Chapter 57 - Hospital, Medical and Dental Service Corporations [Recodified.]	31
Chapter 57A - Health Maintenance Organization Act [Recodified.]	31
Chapter 57B - Health Maintenance Organization Act [Recodified.]	31
Chapter 57C - North Carolina Limited Liability Company Act.	31
Chapter 58 - Insurance.	32
Chapter 58 - Insurance (Continuation)	33
Chapter 58 - Insurance (Continuation)	34
Chapter 58 - Insurance (Continuation)	35
Chapter 58 - Insurance (Continuation)	36
Chapter 58 - Insurance (Continuation)	37
Chapter 58 - Insurance (Continuation)	38
Chapter 58A - North Carolina Health Insurance Trust Commission [Recodified.]	38
Chapter 59 - Partnership.	39
Chapter 59B - Uniform Unincorporated Nonprofit Association Act.	39
Chapter 60 - Railroads and Other Carriers [Repealed and Transferred.]	39
Chapter 61 - Religious Societies	39
Chapter 62 - Public Utilities	39

Chapter 62 - Public Utilities (Continuation)	40
Chapter 62A - Public Safety Telephone Service And Wireless Telephone Service	40
Chapter 63 - Aeronautics	40
Chapter 63A - North Carolina Global TransPark Authority	40
Chapter 64 - Aliens	40
Chapter 65 – Cemeteries	40
Chapter 66 - Commerce and Business	41
Chapter 67 - Dogs	41
Chapter 68 - Fences and Stock Law	41
Chapter 69 - Fire Protection	41
Chapter 70 - Indian Antiquities, Archaeological Resources and Unmarked Human Skeletal Remains Protection	42
Chapter 71 - Indians [Repealed.]	42
Chapter 71A - Indians	42
Chapter 72 - Inns, Hotels and Restaurants	42
Chapter 73 - Mills	42
Chapter 74 - Mines and Quarries	42
Chapter 74A - Company Police [Repealed.]	42
Chapter 74B - Private Protective Services Act [Repealed.]	42
Chapter 74C - Private Protective Services	42
Chapter 74D - Alarm Systems	42
Chapter 74E - Company Police Act	42
Chapter 74F - Locksmith Licensing Act	42
Chapter 74G - Campus Police Act	42
Chapter 75 - Monopolies, Trusts and Consumer Protection	42
Chapter 75A - Boating and Water Safety	43
Chapter 75B - Discrimination in Business	43
Chapter 75C - Motion Picture Fair Competition Act	43
Chapter 75D - Racketeer Influenced and Corrupt Organizations	43
Chapter 75E - Unlawful Activities in Connection With Certain Corporate Transactions	43
Chapter 76 - Navigation	43
Chapter 76A - Navigation and Pilotage Commissions	43
Chapter 77 - Rivers, Creeks, and Coastal Waters	43
Chapter 78 - Securities Law [Repealed.]	43
Chapter 78A - North Carolina Securities Act	43
Chapter 78B - Tender Offer Disclosure Act [Repealed.]	43
Chapter 78C - Investment Advisers	43
Chapter 78D - Commodities Act	43
Chapter 79 - Strays [Repealed.]	43
Chapter 80 - Trademarks, Brands, etc.	44
Chapter 81 - Weights and Measures [Recodified.]	44
Chapter 81A - Weights and Measures Act of 1975.	44
Chapter 82 - Wrecks [Repealed.]	44
Chapter 83 - Architects [Recodified.]	44

Chapter 83A - Architects	44
Chapter 84 - Attorneys-at-Law	44
Chapter 84A - Foreign Legal Consultants	44
Chapter 85 - Auctions and Auctioneers [Repealed.]	44
Chapter 85A - Bail Bondsmen and Runners [Recodified.]	44
Chapter 85B - Auctions and Auctioneers	44
Chapter 85C - Bail Bondsmen and Runners [Recodified.]	44
Chapter 86 - Barbers [Recodified.]	44
Chapter 86A - Barbers	44
Chapter 87 - Contractors	44
Chapter 88 - Cosmetic Art [Repealed.]	44
Chapter 88A - Electrolysis Practice Act	44
Chapter 88B - Cosmetic Art	45
Chapter 89 - Engineering and Land Surveying [Recodified.]	45
Chapter 89A - Landscape Architects	45
Chapter 89B - Foresters	45
Chapter 89C - Engineering and Land Surveying	45
Chapter 89D - Landscape Contractors	45
Chapter 89E - Geologists Licensing Act	45
Chapter 89F - North Carolina Soil Scientist Licensing Act	45
Chapter 89G - Irrigation Contractors	45
Chapter 90 - Medicine and Allied Occupations	45
Chapter 90 - Medicine and Allied Occupations (Continuation)	46
Chapter 90 - Medicine and Allied Occupations (Continuation)	47
Chapter 90 - Medicine and Allied Occupations (Continuation)	48
Chapter 90A - Sanitarians and Water and Wastewater Treatment Facility Operators	48
Chapter 90B - Social Worker Certification and Licensure Act	48
Chapter 90C - North Carolina Recreational Therapy Licensure Act	48
Chapter 90D - Interpreters and Transliterators	48
Chapter 91 - Pawnbrokers [Repealed.]	48
Chapter 91A - Pawnbrokers Modernization Act of 1989	48
Chapter 92 - Photographers [Deleted.]	48
Chapter 93 - Certified Public Accountants	48
Chapter 93A - Real Estate License Law	49
Chapter 93B - Occupational Licensing Boards	49
Chapter 93C - Watchmakers [Repealed.]	49
Chapter 93D - North Carolina State Hearing Aid Dealers and Fitters Board.	49
Chapter 93E - North Carolina Appraisers Act	49
Chapter 94 - Apprenticeship	49
Chapter 95 - Department of Labor and Labor Regulations	49
Chapter 95 - Department of Labor and Labor Regulations (Continuation)	50
Chapter 96 - Employment Security	50
Chapter 97 - Workers' Compensation Act	50
Chapter 97 - Workers' Compensation Act (Continuation)	51

Chapter 98 - Burnt and Lost Records	51
Chapter 99 - Libel and Slander	51
Chapter 99A - Civil Remedies for Criminal Actions	51
Chapter 99B - Products Liability	51
Chapter 99C - Actions Relating to Winter Sports Safety and Accidents	51
Chapter 99D - Civil Rights	51
Chapter 99E - Special Liability Provisions	51
Chapter 100 - Monuments, Memorials and Parks	51
Chapter 101 - Names of Persons	51
Chapter 102 - Official Survey Base	51
Chapter 103 - Sundays, Holidays and Special Days	51
Chapter 104 - United States Lands	51
Chapter 104A - Degrees of Kinship	51
Chapter 104B - Hurricanes or Other Acts of Nature	51
Chapter 104C - Atomic Energy, Radioactivity and Ionizing Radiation [Repealed and Recodified.]	51
Chapter 104D - Southern States Energy Compact	51
Chapter 104E - North Carolina Radiation Protection Act	51
Chapter 104F - Southeast Interstate Low-Level Radioactive Waste Management Compact [Repealed]	51
Chapter 104G - North Carolina Low-Level Radioactive Waste Management Authority Act of 1987 [Repealed]	51
Chapter 105 - Taxation	51
Chapter 105 - Taxation (Continuation)	52
Chapter 105 - Taxation (Continuation)	53
Chapter 105 - Taxation (Continuation)	54
Chapter 105A - Setoff Debt Collection Act	55
Chapter 105B - Defaulted Student Loan Recovery Act	55
Chapter 106 - Agriculture	55
Chapter 106 - Agriculture (Continue)	56
Chapter 106 - Agriculture (Continue)	57
Chapter 107 - Agricultural Development Districts [Repealed.]	57
Chapter 108 - Social Services [Repealed and Recodified.]	57
Chapter 108A - Social Services	57
Chapter 108B - Community Action Programs	58
Chapter 108C Medicaid and Health Choice Provider Requirements.	58
Chapter 108D Medicaid Managed Care for Behavioral Health Services.	58
Chapter 109 - Bonds [Recodified].	58
Chapter 110 - Child Welfare	58
Chapter 111 - Aid to the Blind	58
Chapter 112 - Confederate Homes and Pensions [Repealed.]	58
Chapter 113 - Conservation and Development	58
Chapter 113 - Conservation and Development (Continuation)	59

Chapter 113A - Pollution Control and Environment	59
Chapter 113A - Pollution Control and Environment (Continuation)	60
Chapter 113B - North Carolina Energy Policy Act of 1975	60
Chapter 114 - Department of Justice	60
Chapter 115 - Elementary and Secondary Education [Repealed.]	60
Chapter 115A - Community Colleges, Technical Institutes, and Industrial Education Centers [Repealed.]	60
Chapter 115B - Tuition and Fee Waivers	60
Chapter 115C - Elementary and Secondary Education	60
Chapter 115C - Elementary and Secondary Education (Continuation)	61
Chapter 115C - Elementary and Secondary Education (Continuation)	62
Chapter 115C - Elementary and Secondary Education (Continuation)	63
Chapter 115D - Community Colleges	63
Chapter 115E - Private Educational Facilities Finance Act [Recodified]	63
Chapter 116 - Higher Education	63
Chapter 116 - Higher Education (Continuation)	63
Chapter 116A - Escheats and Abandoned Property [Repealed.]	64
Chapter 116B - Escheats and Abandoned Property	64
Chapter 116C - Continuum of Education Programs	64
Chapter 116D - Higher Education Bonds	64
Chapter 116E - Education Longitudinal Data System	64
Chapter 117 - Electrification	64
Chapter 118 - Firemen's and Rescue Squad Workers' Relief and Pension Funds [Recodified.]	64
Chapter 118A - Firemen's Death Benefit Act [Repealed.]	64
Chapter 118B - Members of a Rescue Squad Death Benefit Act [Repealed.]	64
Chapter 119 - Gasoline and Oil Inspection and Regulation	64
Chapter 120 - General Assembly	65
Chapter 120 - General Assembly (Continuation)	66
Chapter 120 - General Assembly (Continuation)	67
Chapter 120C - Lobbying	67
Chapter 121 - Archives and History	67
Chapter 122 - Hospitals for the Mentally Disordered [Repealed.]	67
Chapter 122A - North Carolina Housing Finance Agency	67
Chapter 122B - North Carolina Agricultural Facilities Finance Act [Repealed.]	67
Chapter 122C - Mental Health, Developmental Disabilities, and Substance Abuse Act of 1985	67
Chapter 122C - Mental Health, Developmental Disabilities, and Substance Abuse Act of 1985 (Continuation)	68

Chapter 122D - North Carolina Agricultural Finance Act	68
Chapter 122E - North Carolina Housing Trust and Oil Overcharge Act	68
Chapter 123 - Impeachment	69
Chapter 123A - Industrial Development [Repealed.]	69
Chapter 124 - Internal Improvements	69
Chapter 125 - Libraries	69
Chapter 126 - State Personnel System	69
Chapter 127 - Militia [Repealed.]	69
Chapter 127A - Militia	69
Chapter 127B - Military Affairs	69
Chapter 127C - Advisory Commission on Military Affairs	69
Chapter 128 - Offices and Public Officers	69
Chapter 128 - Offices and Public Officers (Continuation)	70
Chapter 129 - Public Buildings and Grounds	70
Chapter 130 - Public Health [Repealed.]	70
Chapter 130A - Public Health	70
Chapter 130A - Public Health (Continuation)	71
Chapter 130A - Public Health (Continuation)	72
Chapter 130B - Hazardous Waste Management Commission [Repealed.]	72
Chapter 131 - Public Hospitals [Repealed.]	72
Chapter 131A - Health Care Facilities Finance Act	72
Chapter 131B - Licensing of Ambulatory Surgical Facilities [Repealed.]	72
Chapter 131C - Charitable Solicitation Licensure Act [Repealed.]	72
Chapter 131D - Inspection and Licensing of Facilities	72
Chapter 131E - Health Care Facilities and Services	72
Chapter 131E - Health Care Facilities and Services (Continuation)	73
Chapter 131F - Solicitation of Contributions	73
Chapter 132 - Public Records	73
Chapter 133 - Public Works	74
Chapter 134 - Youth Development [Recodified.]	74
Chapter 134A - Youth Services [Repealed.]	74
Chapter 135 - Retirement System for Teachers and State Employees; Social Security; Health Insurance Program for Children	74
Chapter 135 - Retirement System for Teachers and State Employees; Social Security; Health Insurance Program for Children	75
Chapter 136 - Transportation	75
Chapter 136 - Transportation (Continuation)	76
Chapter 137 - Rural Rehabilitation [Repealed.]	76
Chapter 138 - Salaries, Fees and Allowances	76
Chapter 138A - State Government Ethics Act	76

Chapter	Page
Chapter 139 - Soil and Water Conservation Districts	76
Chapter 140 - State Art Museum; Symphony and Art Societies	76
Chapter 140A - State Awards System	76
Chapter 141 - State Boundaries	76
Chapter 142 - State Debt	76
Chapter 143 - State Departments, Institutions, and Commissions	77
Chapter 143 - State Departments, Institutions, and Commissions (Continuation)	78
Chapter 143 - State Departments, Institutions, and Commissions (Continuation)	79
Chapter 143 - State Departments, Institutions, and Commissions (Continuation)	80
Chapter 143A - State Government Reorganization	80
Chapter 143B - Executive Organization Act of 1973	80
Chapter 143B - Executive Organization Act of 1973 (Continuation)	81
Chapter 143B - Executive Organization Act of 1973 (Continuation)	82
Chapter 143C - State Budget Act	83
Chapter 143D - The State Governmental Accountability and Internal Control Act	83
Chapter 144 - State Flag, Official Governmental Flags, Motto, and Colors	83
Chapter 145 - State Symbols and Other Official Adoptions.	83
Chapter 146 - State Lands	83
Chapter 147 - State Officers	83
Chapter 148 - State Prison System	84
Chapter 149 - State Song and Toast	84
Chapter 150 - Uniform Revocation of Licenses [Repealed.]	84
Chapter 150A - Administrative Procedure Act [Recodified.]	84
Chapter 150B - Administrative Procedure Act	84
Chapter 151 - Constables [Repealed.]	84
Chapter 152 - Coroners	84
Chapter 152A - County Medical Examiner [Repealed.]	84
Chapter 152A - County Medical Examiner [Repealed.] (Continuation)	84
Chapter 153 - Counties and County Commissioners [Repealed.]	84
Chapter 153A - Counties	84
Chapter 153A - Counties (Continue)	85
Chapter 153B - Mountain Resources Planning Act	85
Chapter 153C - Uwharrie Regional Resources Act	85
Chapter 154 - County Surveyor [Repealed.]	85
Chapter 155 - County Treasurer [Repealed.]	85

Chapter 156 - Drainage	85
Chapter 156 – Drainage (Continuation)	86
Chapter 157 - Housing Authorities and Projects	86
Chapter 157A - Historic Properties Commissions [Transferred.]	86
Chapter 158 - Local Development	86
Chapter 159 - Local Government Finance	86
Chapter 159 - Local Government Finance (Continuation)	87
Chapter 159A - Pollution Abatement and Industrial Facilities Financing Act [Unconstitutional.]	87
Chapter 159B - Joint Municipal Electric Power and Energy Act	87
Chapter 159C - Industrial and Pollution Control Facilities Financing Act	87
Chapter 159D - The North Carolina Capital Facilities Financing Act	87
Chapter 159E - Registered Public Obligations Act	87
Chapter 159F - North Carolina Energy Development Authority [Repealed.]	87
Chapter 159G - Water Infrastructure	87
Chapter 159H - [Reserved.]	87
Chapter 159I - Solid Waste Management Loan Program and Local Government Special Obligation Bonds	87
Chapter 160 - Municipal Corporations [Repealed And Transferred.]	87
Chapter 160A - Cities and Towns	88
Chapter 160A - Cities and Towns (Continuation)	89
Chapter 160B - Consolidated City-County Act	89
Chapter 160C - Baseball Park Districts [Repealed.]	90
Chapter 161 - Register of Deeds	90
Chapter 162 - Sheriff	90
Chapter 162A - Water and Sewer Systems	90
Chapter 162B Continuity of Local Government in Emergency.	90
Chapter 163 Elections and Election Laws.	90
Chapter 163 Elections and Election Laws. (Continuation)	91
Chapter 164 Concerning the General Statutes of North Carolina.	92
Chapter 165 Veterans.	92
Chapter 166 Civil Preparedness Agencies [Repealed.]	92
Chapter 166A North Carolina Emergency Management Act.	92
Chapter 167 State Civil Air Patrol [Repealed.]	92
Chapter 168 Persons with Disabilities.	92
Chapter 168A Persons With Disabilities Protection Act.	92

Article 9.

Solid Waste Management.

Part 1. Definitions.

§ 130A-290. Definitions.

(a) Unless a different meaning is required by the context, the following definitions shall apply throughout this Article:

(1) "Affiliate" has the same meaning as in 17 Code of Federal Regulations § 240.12b-2 (1 April 1996 Edition).

(1a) "Business entity" has the same meaning as in G.S. 55-1-40(2a).

(1b) "CERCLA/SARA" means the Comprehensive Environmental Response, Compensation, and Liability Act of 1980, Pub. L. No. 96-510, 94 Stat. 2767, 42 U.S.C. § 9601 et seq., as amended, and the Superfund Amendments and Reauthorization Act of 1986, Pub. L. No. 99-499, 100 Stat. 1613, as amended.

(1c) "Chemical or portable toilet" means a self-contained mobile toilet facility and holding tank and includes toilet facilities in recreational vehicles.

(1d) "Chlorofluorocarbon refrigerant" means any of the following when used as a liquid heat transfer agent in a mechanical refrigeration system: carbon tetrachloride, chlorofluorocarbons, halons, or methyl chloroform.

(2) "Closure" means the cessation of operation of a solid waste management facility and the act of securing the facility so that it will pose no significant threat to human health or the environment.

(2a) "Coal-fired generating unit" means a coal-fired generating unit, as defined by 40 Code of Federal Regulations § 96.2 (1 July 2001 Edition), that is located in this State and has the capacity to generate 25 or more megawatts of electricity.

(2b) "Combustion products" means residuals, including fly ash, bottom ash, boiler slag, mill rejects, and flue gas desulfurization residue produced by a coal-fired generating unit.

(2c) "Combustion products landfill" means a facility or unit for the disposal of combustion products, where the landfill is located at the same facility with the coal-fired generating unit or units producing the combustion products, and where the landfill is located wholly or partly on top of a facility that is, or was, being used for the disposal or storage of such combustion products, including, but not limited to, landfills, wet and dry ash ponds, and structural fill facilities.

(3) "Commercial" when applied to a hazardous waste facility, means a hazardous waste facility that accepts hazardous waste from the general public or from another person for a fee.

(4) "Construction" or "demolition" when used in connection with "waste" or "debris" means solid waste resulting solely from construction, remodeling, repair, or demolition operations on pavement, buildings, or other structures, but does not include inert debris, land-clearing debris or yard debris.

(4a) "Department" means the Department of Environment and Natural Resources.

(5) Repealed by Session Laws 1995 (Regular Session, 1996), c. 594, s. 1.

(6) "Disposal" means the discharge, deposit, injection, dumping, spilling, leaking or placing of any solid waste into or on any land or water so that the solid waste or any constituent part of the solid waste may enter the environment or be emitted into the air or discharged into any waters, including groundwaters.

(7) "Garbage" means all putrescible wastes, including animal offal and carcasses, and recognizable industrial by-products, but excluding sewage and human waste.

(8) "Hazardous waste" means a solid waste, or combination of solid wastes, which because of its quantity, concentration or physical, chemical or infectious characteristics may:

a. Cause or significantly contribute to an increase in mortality or an increase in serious irreversible or incapacitating reversible illness; or

b. Pose a substantial present or potential hazard to human health or the environment when improperly treated, stored, transported, disposed of or otherwise managed.

(8a) "Hazardous waste constituent" has the same meaning as in 40 Code of Federal Regulations § 260.10 (1 July 2006).

(9) "Hazardous waste facility" means a facility for the collection, storage, processing, treatment, recycling, recovery, or disposal of hazardous waste. Hazardous waste facility does not include a hazardous waste transfer facility that meets the requirements of 40 Code of Federal Regulations § 263.12 (1 July 2006).

(10) "Hazardous waste generation" means the act or process of producing hazardous waste.

(11) "Hazardous waste disposal facility" means any facility or any portion of a facility for disposal of hazardous waste on or in land in accordance with rules adopted under this Article.

(12) "Hazardous waste management" means the systematic control of the collection, source separation, storage, transportation, processing, treatment, recovery and disposal of hazardous wastes.

(13) "Hazardous waste management program" means the program and activities within the Department pursuant to Part 2 of this Article, for hazardous waste management.

(13a) "Hazardous waste transfer facility" means a facility or location where a hazardous waste transporter stores hazardous waste for a period of more than 24 hours but less than 10 days.

(13b) "Industrial solid waste" means solid waste generated by manufacturing or industrial processes that is not hazardous waste.

(14) "Inert debris" means solid waste which consists solely of material that is virtually inert and that is likely to retain its physical and chemical structure under expected conditions of disposal.

(15) "Land-clearing debris" means solid waste which is generated solely from land-clearing activities.

(16) "Landfill" means a disposal facility or part of a disposal facility where waste is placed in or on land and which is not a land treatment facility, a surface

impoundment, an injection well, a hazardous waste long-term storage facility or a surface storage facility.

(16a) "Leachate" means a liquid that has passed through or emerged from solid waste and contains soluble, suspended, or miscible materials removed from such waste. The term "leachate" does not include liquid adhering to tires of vehicles leaving a sanitary landfill and transfer stations.

(17) "Manifest" means the form used for identifying the quantity, composition and the origin, routing and destination of hazardous waste during its transportation from the point of generation to the point of disposal, treatment or storage.

(17a) "Medical waste" means any solid waste which is generated in the diagnosis, treatment, or immunization of human beings or animals, in research pertaining thereto, or in the production or testing of biologicals, but does not include any hazardous waste identified or listed pursuant to this Article, radioactive waste, household waste as defined in 40 Code of Federal Regulations § 261.4(b)(1) in effect on 1 July 1989, or those substances excluded from the definition of "solid waste" in this section.

(18) "Motor vehicle oil filter" means a filter that removes impurities from the oil used to lubricate an internal combustion engine in a motor vehicle.

(18a) "Municipal solid waste" means any solid waste resulting from the operation of residential, commercial, industrial, governmental, or institutional establishments that would normally be collected, processed, and disposed of through a public or private solid waste management service. Municipal solid waste does not include hazardous waste, sludge, industrial waste managed in a solid waste management facility owned and operated by the generator of the industrial waste for management of that waste, or solid waste from mining or agricultural operations.

(18b) "Municipal solid waste management facility" means any publicly or privately owned solid waste management facility permitted by the Department that receives municipal solid waste for processing, treatment, or disposal.

(19) "Natural resources" means all materials which have useful physical or chemical properties which exist, unused, in nature.

(20) "Open dump" means any facility or site where solid waste is disposed of that is not a sanitary landfill and that is not a facility for the disposal of hazardous waste.

(21) "Operator" means any person, including the owner, who is principally engaged in, and is in charge of, the actual operation, supervision, and maintenance of a solid waste management facility and includes the person in charge of a shift or periods of operation during any part of the day.

(21a) "Parent" has the same meaning as in 17 Code of Federal Regulations § 240.12b-2 (1 April 1996 Edition).

(22) "Person" means an individual, corporation, company, association, partnership, unit of local government, State agency, federal agency or other legal entity.

(22a) "Pre-1983 landfill" means any land area, whether publicly or privately owned, on which municipal solid waste disposal occurred prior to 1 January 1983 but not thereafter, but does not include any landfill used primarily for the disposal of industrial solid waste.

(23) "Processing" means any technique designed to change the physical, chemical, or biological character or composition of any solid waste so as to render it safe for transport; amenable to recovery, storage or recycling; safe for disposal; or reduced in volume or concentration.

(24) "Recovered material" means a material that has known recycling potential, can be feasibly recycled, and has been diverted or removed from the solid waste stream for sale, use, or reuse. In order to qualify as a recovered material, a material must meet the requirements of G.S. 130A-309.05(c).

(25) "RCRA" means the Resource Conservation and Recovery Act of 1976, Pub. L. 94-580, 90 Stat. 2795, 42 U.S.C. § 6901 et seq., as amended.

(26) "Recyclable material" means those materials which are capable of being recycled and which would otherwise be processed or disposed of as solid waste.

(27) "Recycling" means any process by which solid waste, or materials which would otherwise become solid waste, are collected, separated, or processed, and reused or returned to use in the form of raw materials or products.

(28) "Refuse" means all nonputrescible waste.

(28a) "Refuse-derived fuel" means fuel that consists of municipal solid waste from which recyclable and noncombustible materials are removed so that the remaining material is used for energy production.

(29) "Resource recovery" means the process of obtaining material or energy resources from discarded solid waste which no longer has any useful life in its present form and preparing the solid waste for recycling.

(30) "Reuse" means a process by which resources are reused or rendered usable.

(31) "Sanitary landfill" means a facility for disposal of solid waste on land in a sanitary manner in accordance with the rules concerning sanitary landfills adopted under this Article.

(31a) "Secretary" means the Secretary of Environment and Natural Resources.

(32) "Septage" means solid waste that is a fluid mixture of untreated and partially treated sewage solids, liquids, and sludge of human or domestic origin which is removed from a wastewater system. The term septage includes the following:

a. Domestic septage, which is either liquid or solid material removed from a septic tank, cesspool, portable toilet, Type III marine sanitation device, or similar treatment works receiving only domestic sewage. Domestic septage does not include liquid or solid material removed from a septic tank, cesspool, or similar treatment works receiving either commercial wastewater or industrial wastewater and does not include grease removed from a grease trap at a restaurant.

b. Domestic treatment plant septage, which is solid, semisolid, or liquid residue generated during the treatment of domestic sewage in a treatment works where the designed disposal is subsurface. Domestic treatment plant septage includes, but is not limited to, scum or solids removed in primary, secondary, or advanced wastewater treatment processes and a material derived from domestic treatment plant septage. Domestic treatment plant septage does not include ash generated during the firing of domestic treatment plant septage in an incinerator or grit and screenings generated during preliminary treatment of domestic sewage in a treatment works.

c. Grease septage, which is material pumped from grease interceptors, separators, traps, or other appurtenances used for the purpose of removing cooking oils, fats, grease, and food debris from the waste flow generated from food handling, preparation, and cleanup.

d. Industrial or commercial septage, which is material pumped from septic tanks or other devices used in the collection, pretreatment, or treatment of any water-carried waste resulting from any process of industry, manufacture, trade, or business where the design disposal of the wastewater is subsurface. Domestic septage mixed with any industrial or commercial septage is considered industrial or commercial septage.

e. Industrial or commercial treatment plant septage, which is solid, semisolid, or liquid residue generated during the treatment of sewage that contains any waste resulting from any process of industry, manufacture, trade, or business in a treatment works where the designed disposal is subsurface. Industrial or commercial treatment plant septage includes, but is not limited to, scum or solids removed in primary, secondary, or advanced wastewater treatment processes and a material derived from domestic treatment plant septage. Industrial or commercial treatment plant septage does not include ash generated during the firing of industrial or commercial treatment plant septage in an incinerator or grit and screenings generated during preliminary treatment of domestic sewage in a treatment works.

(33) "Septage management firm" means a person engaged in the business of pumping, transporting, storing, treating or disposing septage. The term does not include public or community wastewater systems that treat or dispose septage.

(34) "Sludge" means any solid, semisolid or liquid waste generated from a municipal, commercial, institutional or industrial wastewater treatment plant, water supply treatment plant or air pollution control facility, or any other waste having similar characteristics and effects.

(35) "Solid waste" means any hazardous or nonhazardous garbage, refuse or sludge from a waste treatment plant, water supply treatment plant or air pollution control facility, domestic sewage and sludges generated by the treatment thereof in sanitary sewage collection, treatment and disposal systems,

and other material that is either discarded or is being accumulated, stored or treated prior to being discarded, or has served its original intended use and is generally discarded, including solid, liquid, semisolid or contained gaseous material resulting from industrial, institutional, commercial and agricultural operations, and from community activities. The term does not include:

a.   Fecal waste from fowls and animals other than humans.

b.   Solid or dissolved material in:

1.   Domestic sewage and sludges generated by treatment thereof in sanitary sewage collection, treatment and disposal systems which are designed to discharge effluents to the surface waters.

2.   Irrigation return flows.

3.   Wastewater discharges and the sludges incidental to and generated by treatment which are point sources subject to permits granted under Section 402 of the Water Pollution Control Act, as amended (P.L. 92-500), and permits granted under G.S. 143-215.1 by the Environmental Management Commission. However, any sludges that meet the criteria for hazardous waste under RCRA shall also be a solid waste for the purposes of this Article.

c.   Oils and other liquid hydrocarbons controlled under Article 21A of Chapter 143 of the General Statutes. However, any oils or other liquid hydrocarbons that meet the criteria for hazardous waste under RCRA shall also be a solid waste for the purposes of this Article.

d.   Any source, special nuclear or byproduct material as defined by the Atomic Energy Act of 1954, as amended (42 U.S.C. § 2011).

e.   Mining refuse covered by the North Carolina Mining Act, G.S. 74-46 through 74-68 and regulated by the North Carolina Mining and Energy Commission (as defined under G.S. 143B-293.1). However, any specific mining waste that meets the criteria for hazardous waste under RCRA shall also be a solid waste for the purposes of this Article.

f.   Recovered material.

(36)   "Solid waste disposal site" means any place at which solid wastes are disposed of by incineration, sanitary landfill or any other method.

(37) "Solid waste generation" means the act or process of producing solid waste.

(38) "Solid waste management" means purposeful, systematic control of the generation, storage, collection, transport, separation, treatment, processing, recycling, recovery and disposal of solid waste.

(39) "Solid waste management facility" means land, personnel and equipment used in the management of solid waste.

(40) "Special wastes" means solid wastes that can require special handling and management, including white goods, whole tires, used oil, lead-acid batteries, and medical wastes.

(41) "Storage" means the containment of solid waste, either on a temporary basis or for a period of years, in a manner which does not constitute disposal.

(41a) "Subsidiary" has the same meaning as in 17 Code of Federal Regulations § 240.12b-2 (1 April 1996 Edition).

(41b) "Tire-derived fuel" means a form of fuel derived from scrap tires.

(42) "Treatment" means any method, technique or process, including neutralization, designed to change the physical, chemical or biological character or composition of any hazardous waste so as to neutralize such waste or so as to render such waste nonhazardous, safer for transport, amenable for recovery, amenable for storage or reduced in volume. "Treatment" includes any activity or processing designed to change the physical form or chemical composition of hazardous waste so as to render it nonhazardous.

(43) "Unit of local government" means a county, city, town or incorporated village.

(44) "White goods" includes refrigerators, ranges, water heaters, freezers, unit air conditioners, washing machines, dishwashers, clothes dryers, and other similar domestic and commercial large appliances.

(44a) "Wooden pallet" means a wooden object consisting of a flat or horizontal deck or platform supported by structural components that is used as a base for assembling, stacking, handling, and transporting goods.

(45) "Yard trash" means solid waste consisting solely of vegetative matter resulting from landscaping maintenance.

(b) Unless a different meaning is required by the context, the following definitions shall apply throughout G.S. 130A-309.15 through G.S. 130A-309.24:

(1) "Public used oil collection center" means:

a. Automotive service facilities or governmentally sponsored collection facilities, which in the course of business accept for disposal small quantities of used oil from households; and

b. Facilities which store used oil in aboveground tanks, which are approved by the Department, and which in the course of business accept for disposal small quantities of used oil from households.

(2) "Reclaiming" means the use of methods, other than those used in rerefining, to purify used oil primarily to remove insoluble contaminants, making the oil suitable for further use; the methods may include settling, heating, dehydration, filtration, or centrifuging.

(3) "Recycling" means to prepare used oil for reuse as a petroleum product by rerefining, reclaiming, reprocessing, or other means or to use used oil in a manner that substitutes for a petroleum product made from new oil.

(4) "Rerefining" means the use of refining processes on used oil to produce high-quality base stocks for lubricants or other petroleum products. Rerefining may include distillation, hydrotreating, or treatments employing acid, caustic, solvent, clay, or other chemicals, or other physical treatments other than those used in reclaiming.

(5) "Used oil" means any oil which has been refined from crude oil or synthetic oil and, as a result of use, storage, or handling, has become unsuitable for its original purpose due to the presence of impurities or loss of original properties, but which may be suitable for further use and is economically recyclable.

(6) "Used oil recycling facility" means any facility that recycles more than 10,000 gallons of used oil annually. (1969, c. 899; 1975, c. 311, s. 2; 1977, 2nd Sess., c. 1216; 1979, c. 464, s. 1; 1981, c. 704, s. 4; 1983, c. 795, ss. 1, 8.1; c. 891, s. 2; 1983 (Reg. Sess., 1984), c. 973, s. 2; 1985, c. 738, s. 1; 1987, c. 574,

s. 1; 1987 (Reg. Sess., 1988), c. 1020, s. 1; c. 1058, s. 1; 1989, c. 168, s. 11; c. 742, s. 5; c. 784, s. 1; 1991, c. 342, s. 7; c. 621, s. 1; 1991 (Reg. Sess., 1992), c. 1013, s. 7; 1993, c. 173, ss. 1-3; c. 471, ss. 1, 2; 1995 (Reg. Sess., 1996), c. 594, ss. 1-5; 1997-27, s. 1; 1997-330, s. 3; 1997-443, s. 11A.81; 2005-362, s. 1; 2007-107, ss. 1.1(c), 1.8(a), (b); 2007-550, ss. 7(a), 12(a), (b); 2012-143, s. 1(d); 2013-413, s. 59.3.)

Part 2. Solid and Hazardous Waste Management.

§ 130A-291. Division of Waste Management.

(a)   For the purpose of promoting and preserving an environment that is conducive to public health and welfare, and preventing the creation of nuisances and the depletion of our natural resources, the Department shall maintain a Division of Waste Management to promote sanitary processing, treatment, disposal, and statewide management of solid waste and the greatest possible recycling and recovery of resources, and the Department shall employ and retain qualified personnel as may be necessary to effect such purposes. It is the purpose and intent of the State to be and remain cognizant not only of its responsibility to authorize and establish a statewide solid waste management program, but also of its responsibility to monitor and supervise, through the Department, the activities and operations of units of local government implementing a permitted solid waste management facility serving a specified geographic area in accordance with a solid waste management plan.

(b)   In furtherance of this purpose and intent, it is hereby determined and declared that it is necessary for the health and welfare of the inhabitants of the State that solid waste management facilities permitted hereunder and serving a specified geographic area shall be used by public or private owners or occupants of all lands, buildings, and premises within the geographic area, and a unit of local government may, by ordinance, require that all solid waste generated within the geographic area and placed in the waste stream for disposal, shall be delivered to the permitted solid waste management facility or facilities serving the geographic area. Actions taken pursuant to this Article shall be deemed to be acts of the sovereign power of the State of North Carolina, and to the extent reasonably necessary to achieve the purposes of this section, a unit of local government may displace competition with public service for solid waste management and disposal. It is further determined and declared that no person, firm, corporation, association or entity within the geographic area shall engage in any activities which would be competitive with this purpose or with ordinances, rules adopted pursuant to the authority granted herein. (1969, c. 899; 1973, c. 476, s. 128; 1975, c. 311, s. 3; 1977, 2nd Sess., c. 1216; 1983, c. 795, ss. 2, 8.1; c. 891, s. 2; 1987, c. 574, s. 1; 1989, c. 727, s. 144; 1989 (Reg. Sess., 1990), c. 1004, ss. 7, 8; 1995 (Reg. Sess., 1996), c. 743, s. 4.)

§ 130A-291.1. Septage management program; permit fees.

(a) The Department shall establish and administer a septage management program in accordance with the provisions of this section.

(b) For the protection of the public health, the Commission shall adopt rules governing the management of septage. The rules shall include, but are not limited to, criteria for the sanitary management of septage, including standards for the transportation, storage, treatment, and disposal of septage; operator registration and training; the issuance, suspension, and revocation of permits; and procedures for the payment of annual fees.

(c) No septage management firm shall commence or continue operation that does not have a permit issued by the Department. The permit shall be issued only when the septage management firm satisfies all of the requirements of the rules adopted by the Commission. A septage management firm that commences operation without first having obtained a permit shall cease to operate until the firm obtains a permit under this section and shall pay an initial annual fee equal to twice the amount of the annual fee that would otherwise be applicable under subsection (e) of this section.

(d) Septage shall be treated and disposed only at a wastewater system that has been approved by the Department under rules adopted by the Commission or by the Environmental Management Commission or at a site that is permitted by the Department under this section. A permit shall be issued only if the site satisfies all of the requirements of the rules adopted by the Commission.

(e) A septage management firm that operates one pumper truck shall pay an annual fee of five hundred fifty dollars ($550.00) to the Department. A septage management firm that operates two or more pumper trucks shall pay an annual fee of eight hundred dollars ($800.00) to the Department.

(e1) An individual who operates a septage treatment or disposal facility but who does not engage in the business of pumping, transporting, or disposing of septage shall pay an annual fee of two hundred dollars ($200.00).

(e2) A properly completed application for a permit and the annual fee under this section are due by 1 January of each year. The Department shall mail a notice of the annual fees to each permitted septage management firm and each individual who operates a septage treatment or disposal facility prior to 1 November of each calendar year. A late fee in the amount equal to fifty percent (50%) of the annual permit fee under this section shall be submitted when a properly completed application and annual permit fee are not submitted by 1 January following the 1 November notice. The clear proceeds of civil penalties collected pursuant to this subsection shall be remitted to the Civil Penalty and Forfeiture Fund in accordance with G.S. 115C-457.2.

(e3) The Septage Management Account is established as a nonreverting account within the Department. Fees collected under this section shall be placed in the Septage Management Account and shall be applied only to the costs of the septage management program.

(e4) Permits for new septage management firm operators and permits for septage management firm operators that have not operated a septage management firm in the 24 months immediately preceding the submittal of an application shall be considered probationary for 12 months. The Department may revoke any probationary permit of a firm or an individual that violates any provision of this section, G.S. 130A-291.2, G.S. 130A-291.3, or any rule adopted under these sections. If the Department revokes a probationary permit issued to a firm or individual, the Department shall not issue another permit to that firm or individual, and the firm or individual may not engage in any septage management activity for a period of 12 months.

(e5) The Department shall provide technical and regulatory assistance to permit applicants and permit holders. Assistance may include, but is not limited to, taking soil samples on proposed and permitted septage land application sites and providing required training to permit applicants and permit holders.

(f) All wastewater systems designed to discharge effluent to the surface waters may accept, treat, and dispose septage from permitted septage management firms, unless acceptance of the septage would constitute a violation of the permit conditions of the wastewater system. The wastewater system may charge a reasonable fee for acceptance, treatment, and disposal of septage based on a fee schedule that takes into account septage composition and quantity and that is consistent with other charges for use of that system.

(g)   Production of a crop in accordance with an approved nutrient management plan on land that is permitted as a septage land application site is a bona fide farm purpose under G.S. 153A-340.

(h)   The Department shall inspect each septage land application site at least twice a year and shall inspect the records associated with each septage land application site at least annually. The Department shall inspect each pump truck used for septage management at least once every two years.

(h1)   The annual permit application shall identify the pumper trucks to be used by the septage management firm. A permitted septage management firm shall notify the Department within 10 days of placing a pumper truck in service that was not previously included in a permit issued to the firm and shall make the pumper truck available for inspection by the Department. A septage management firm is not prohibited from use of a pumper truck that meets the requirements of the rules adopted by the Commission prior to inspection by the Department.

(i)   The Department shall approve innovative or alternative septage treatment or storage methods that are demonstrated to protect the public health and the environment.

(j)   Septage generated by the operation of a wastewater system permitted under Article 11 of this Chapter may be managed as provided in this section and may be land applied at a septage land application site permitted under this section. (1987 (Reg. Sess., 1988), c. 1058, s. 2; 1991 (Reg. Sess., 1992), c. 1039, s. 8; 1993, c. 173, s. 4; 2001-505, s. 1.1; 2005-276, s. 6.37(t); 2006-255, s. 5.1(a); 2012-200, s. 15.)

§ 130A-291.2. Temporary domestic wastewater holding tanks.

When a permanent domestic wastewater collection and treatment system is not available at a construction site or a temporary special event, a temporary wastewater holding tank of adequate capacity to prevent overflow may be used under a mobile or modular office to accommodate domestic wastewater from a commode and sink. The wastewater shall be removed often enough to prevent the temporary domestic wastewater holding tank from overflowing. The owner or lessee of a temporary construction trailer shall contract with a registered septage management firm or registered portable toilet sanitation firm for the removal of domestic waste. The wastewater shall be removed from the temporary domestic wastewater holding tank by a septage management firm holding a current permit to operate a septage firm. (2001-505, s. 1.2.)

§ 130A-291.3. Septage operator training required.

(a) Each septage management firm operator shall attend a training course approved pursuant to subsection (d) of this section of no less than four hours of instruction per year. New septage management firm operators and those that have not operated a septage management firm in the 24 months preceding the submittal of an application shall complete the training before commencing operation.

(b) Each septage land application site operator shall attend a training course approved pursuant to subsection (d) of this section of no less than three hours of instruction per year. New septage land application site operators and those that have not operated a septage land application site in the 24 months preceding the submittal of an application shall complete the training before commencing operation.

(c) Upon the completion of the permit requirements under G.S. 130A-291.1 and the training requirements under this section, the Department shall issue the septage management firm a certificate to operate as a registered portable sanitation firm or a registered septage management firm, or both.

(d) The Department shall establish educational committees to develop and approve a training curriculum to satisfy the training requirements under this section. A training committee shall be established to develop a training program for portable sanitation waste; a training committee shall be established to develop a training program for septic tank waste and grease septage; and a training committee shall be established to develop a training program for land application of septage. Each committee shall consist of four industry members, one public health member, two employees of the Department, and one representative of the North Carolina Cooperative Extension Service. (2001-505, s. 1.2.)

§ 130A-292. Conveyance of land used for commercial hazardous waste disposal facility to the State.

(a) No land may be used for a commercial hazardous waste disposal facility until fee simple title to the land has been conveyed to this State. In consideration for the conveyance, the State shall enter into a lease agreement with the grantor for a term equal to the estimated life of the facility in which the State will be the lessor and the grantor the lessee. The lease agreement shall specify that for an annual rent of fifty dollars ($50.00), the lessee shall be allowed to use the land for the development and operation of a hazardous waste disposal facility. The lease agreement shall provide that the lessor or any person authorized by the lessor shall at all times have the right to enter without a search warrant or permission of the lessee upon any and all parts of the premises for monitoring, inspection and all other purposes necessary to carry out the provisions of this Article. The lessee shall remain fully liable for all damages, losses, personal injury or property damage which may result or arise out of the lessee's operation of the facility, and for compliance with regulatory requirements concerning insurance, bonding for closure and post-closure costs, monitoring and other financial or health and safety requirements as required by applicable law and rules. The State, as lessor, shall be immune from liability except as otherwise provided by statute. The lease shall be transferable with the written consent of the lessor and the consent will not be unreasonably withheld. In the case of a transfer of the lease, the transferee shall be subject to all terms and conditions that the State deems necessary to ensure compliance with applicable laws and rules. If the lessee or any successor in interest fails in any material respect to comply with any applicable law, rule or permit condition, or with any term or condition of the lease, the State may terminate the lease after giving the lessee written notice specifically describing the failure to comply and upon providing the lessee a reasonable time to comply. If the lessee does not effect compliance within the reasonable time allowed, the State may reenter and take possession of the premises.

(b) Notwithstanding the termination of the lease by either the lessee or the lessor for any reason, the lessee shall remain liable for, and be obligated to perform, all acts necessary or required by law, rule, permit condition or the lease for the permanent closure of the site until the site has either been permanently closed or until a substituted operator has been secured and has assumed the obligations of the lessee.

(c) In the event of changes in laws or rules applicable to the facility which make continued operation by the lessee impossible or economically infeasible, the lessee shall have the right to terminate the lease upon giving the State reasonable notice of not less than six months, in which case the lessor shall have the right to secure a substitute lessee and operator.

(d)   In the event of termination of the lease by the lessor as provided in subsection (a) of this section, or by the lessee as provided in subsection (c) of this section, the lessee shall be paid the fair market value of any improvements made to the leased premises less the costs to the lessor resulting from termination of the lease and securing a substitute lessee and operator. However, the lessor shall have no obligation to secure a substitute lessee or operator and may require the lessee to permanently close the facility. (1981, c. 704, s. 5; 1983, c. 891, s. 2; 1989, c. 168, s. 12.)

§ 130A-293. Local ordinances prohibiting hazardous waste facilities invalid; petition to preempt local ordinance.

(a)   It is the intent of the General Assembly to maintain a uniform system for the management of hazardous waste and to place limitations upon the exercise by all units of local government in North Carolina of the power to regulate the management of hazardous waste by means of special, local, or private acts or resolutions, ordinances, property restrictions, zoning regulations, or otherwise. Notwithstanding any authority granted to counties, municipalities, or other local authorities to adopt local ordinances, including but not limited to those imposing taxes, fees, or charges or regulating health, environment, or land use, any local ordinance that prohibits or has the effect of prohibiting the establishment or operation of a hazardous waste facility that the Secretary has preempted pursuant to subsections (b) through (f) of this section, shall be invalid to the extent necessary to effectuate the purposes of this Chapter. To this end, all provisions of special, local, or private acts or resolutions are repealed that:

(1)   Prohibit the transportation, treatment, storage, or disposal of hazardous waste within any county, city, or other political subdivision.

(2)   Prohibit the siting of a hazardous waste facility within any county, city, or other political subdivision.

(3)   Place any restriction or condition not placed by this Article upon the transportation, treatment, storage, or disposal of hazardous waste, or upon the

siting of a hazardous waste facility within any county, city, or other political subdivision.

(4)   In any manner are in conflict or inconsistent with the provisions of this Article.

(a1)   No special, local, or private act or resolution enacted or taking effect hereafter may be construed to modify, amend, or repeal any portion of this Article unless it expressly provides for such by specific references to the appropriate section of this Article. Further to this end, all provisions of local ordinances, including those regulating land use, adopted by counties, municipalities, or other local authorities that prohibit or have the effect of prohibiting the establishment or operation of a hazardous waste facility are invalidated to the extent preempted by the Secretary pursuant to this section.

(b)   When a hazardous waste facility would be prevented from construction or operation by a county, municipal, or other local ordinance, the operator of the proposed facility may petition the Secretary to review the matter. After receipt of a petition, the Secretary shall hold a hearing in accordance with the procedures in subsection (c) of this section and shall determine whether or to what extent to preempt the local ordinance to allow for the establishment and operation of the facility.

(c)   When a petition described in subsection (b) of this section has been filed with the Secretary, the Secretary shall hold a public hearing to consider the petition. The public hearing shall be held in the affected locality within 60 days after receipt of the petition by the Secretary. The Secretary shall give notice of the public hearing by:

(1)   Publication in a newspaper or newspapers having general circulation in the county or counties where the facility is or is to be located or operated, once a week for three consecutive weeks, the first notice appearing at least 30 days prior to the scheduled date of the hearing; and

(2)   First class mail to persons who have requested notice. The Secretary shall maintain a mailing list of persons who request notice in advance of the hearing pursuant to this section. Notice by mail shall be complete upon deposit of a copy of the notice in a post-paid wrapper addressed to the person to be notified at the address that appears on the mailing list maintained by the Board, in a post office or official depository under the exclusive care and custody of the United States Postal Service.

(c1) Any interested person may appear before the Secretary at the hearing to offer testimony. In addition to testimony before the Secretary, any interested person may submit written evidence to the Secretary for the Secretary's consideration. At least 20 days shall be allowed for receipt of written comment following the hearing.

(d) A local zoning or land-use ordinance is presumed to be valid and enforceable to the extent the zoning or land-use ordinance imposes requirements, restrictions, or conditions that are generally applicable to development, including, but not limited to, setback, buffer, and stormwater requirements, unless the Secretary makes a finding of fact to the contrary. The Secretary shall determine whether or to what extent to preempt local ordinances so as to allow for the establishment and operation of the facility no later than 60 days after conclusion of the hearing. The Secretary shall preempt a local ordinance only if the Secretary makes all of the following findings:

(1) That there is a local ordinance that would prohibit or have the effect of prohibiting the establishment or operation of a hazardous waste facility.

(2) That the proposed facility is needed in order to establish adequate capability to meet the current or projected hazardous waste management needs of this State or to comply with the terms of any interstate agreement for the management of hazardous waste to which the State is a party and therefore serves the interests of the citizens of the State as a whole.

(3) That all legally required State and federal permits or approvals have been issued by the appropriate State and federal agencies or that all State and federal permit requirements have been satisfied and that the permits or approvals have been denied or withheld only because of the local ordinance.

(4) That local citizens and elected officials have had adequate opportunity to participate in the siting process.

(5) That the construction and operation of the facility will not pose an unreasonable health or environmental risk to the surrounding locality and that the facility operator has taken or consented to take reasonable measures to avoid or manage foreseeable risks and to comply to the maximum feasible extent with applicable local ordinances.

(d1) If the Secretary does not make all of the findings under subsection (d) of this section, the Secretary shall not preempt the challenged local ordinance. The

Secretary's decision shall be in writing and shall identify the evidence submitted to the Secretary plus any additional evidence used in arriving at the decision.

(e) The decision of the Secretary shall be final unless a party to the action files a written appeal under Article 4 of Chapter 150B of the General Statutes, as modified by G.S. 7A-29 and this section, within 30 days of the date of the decision. The record on appeal shall consist of all materials and information submitted to or considered by the Secretary, the Secretary's written decision, a complete transcript of the hearing, all written material presented to the Secretary regarding the location of the facility, the specific findings required by subsection (d) of this section, and any minority positions on the specific findings required by subsection (d) of this section. The scope of judicial review shall be that the court may affirm the decision of the Secretary, or may remand the matter for further proceedings, or may reverse or modify the decision if the substantial rights of the parties may have been prejudiced because the agency findings, inferences, conclusions, or decisions are:

(1) In violation of constitutional provisions;

(2) In excess of the statutory authority or jurisdiction of the agency;

(3) Made upon unlawful procedure;

(4) Affected by other error of law;

(5) Unsupported by substantial evidence admissible under G.S. 150B-29(a) or G.S. 150B-30 in view of the entire record as submitted; or

(6) Arbitrary or capricious.

(e1) If the court reverses or modifies the decision of the agency, the judge shall set out in writing, which writing shall become part of the record, the reasons for the reversal or modification.

(f) In computing any period of time prescribed or allowed by this procedure, the provisions of Rule 6(a) of the Rules of Civil Procedure, G.S. 1A-1, shall apply.

(g) Repealed by Session Laws 1989, c. 168, s. 13. (1981, c. 704, s. 5; 1983, s. 891, s. 2; 1983 (Reg. Sess., 1984), c. 973, ss. 3-5; 1987, c. 827, s. 249;

1987 (Reg. Sess., 1988), c. 993, s. 28; c. 1082, s. 13; 1989, c. 168, s. 13; 1993, c. 501, s. 13; 2001-474, s. 17; 2007-107, s. 1.10(a).)

§ 130A-294. Solid waste management program.

(a)   The Department is authorized and directed to engage in research, conduct investigations and surveys, make inspections and establish a statewide solid waste management program. In establishing a program, the Department shall have authority to:

(1)   Develop a comprehensive program for implementation of safe and sanitary practices for management of solid waste;

(2)   Advise, consult, cooperate and contract with other State agencies, units of local government, the federal government, industries and individuals in the formulation and carrying out of a solid waste management program;

(3)   Develop and adopt rules to establish standards for qualification as a "recycling, reduction or resource recovering facility" or as "recycling, reduction or resource recovering equipment" for the purpose of special tax classifications or treatment, and to certify as qualifying those applicants which meet the established standards. The standards shall be developed to qualify only those facilities and equipment exclusively used in the actual waste recycling, reduction or resource recovering process and shall exclude any incidental or supportive facilities and equipment;

(4)   a.   Develop a permit system governing the establishment and operation of solid waste management facilities. A landfill with a disposal area of 1/2 acre or less for the on-site disposal of land clearing and inert debris is exempt from the permit requirement of this section and shall be governed by G.S. 130A-301.1. Demolition debris from the decommissioning of manufacturing buildings, including electric generating stations, that is disposed of on the same site as the decommissioned buildings, is exempt from the permit requirement of this section and rules adopted pursuant to this section and shall be governed by G.S. 130A-301.3. The Department shall not approve an application for a new permit, the renewal of a permit, or a substantial amendment to a permit for a sanitary landfill, excluding demolition landfills as defined in the rules of the Commission, except as provided in subdivisions (3) and (4) of subsection (b1) of this section. No permit shall be granted for a solid waste management facility

having discharges that are point sources until the Department has referred the complete plans and specifications to the Environmental Management Commission and has received advice in writing that the plans and specifications are approved in accordance with the provisions of G.S. 143-215.1. In any case where the Department denies a permit for a solid waste management facility, it shall state in writing the reason for denial and shall also state its estimate of the changes in the applicant's proposed activities or plans that will be required for the applicant to obtain a permit.

b. Repealed by Session Laws 2007-550, s. 1(a), effective August 1, 2007.

c. The Department shall deny an application for a permit for a solid waste management facility if the Department finds that:

1. Construction or operation of the proposed facility would be inconsistent with or violate rules adopted by the Commission.

2. Construction or operation of the proposed facility would result in a violation of water quality standards adopted by the Environmental Management Commission pursuant to G.S. 143-214.1 for waters, as defined in G.S. 143-213.

3. Construction or operation of the facility would result in significant damage to ecological systems, natural resources, cultural sites, recreation areas, or historic sites of more than local significance. These areas include, but are not limited to, national or State parks or forests; wilderness areas; historic sites; recreation areas; segments of the natural and scenic rivers system; wildlife refuges, preserves, and management areas; areas that provide habitat for threatened or endangered species; primary nursery areas and critical fisheries habitat designated by the Marine Fisheries Commission; and Outstanding Resource Waters designated by the Environmental Management Commission.

4. Construction or operation of the proposed facility would substantially limit or threaten access to or use of public trust waters or public lands.

5. The proposed facility would be located in a natural hazard area, including a floodplain, a landslide hazard area, or an area subject to storm surge or excessive seismic activity, such that the facility will present a risk to public health or safety.

6. There is a practical alternative that would accomplish the purposes of the proposed facility with less adverse impact on public resources, considering engineering requirements and economic costs.

7. The cumulative impacts of the proposed facility and other facilities in the area of the proposed facility would violate the criteria set forth in sub-sub-subdivisions 2. through 5. of this sub-subdivision.

8. Construction or operation of the proposed facility would be inconsistent with the State solid waste management policy and goals as set out in G.S. 130A-309.04 and with the State solid waste management plan developed as provided in G.S. 130A-309.07.

9. The cumulative impact of the proposed facility, when considered in relation to other similar impacts of facilities located or proposed in the community, would have a disproportionate adverse impact on a minority or low-income community protected by Title VI of the federal Civil Rights Act of 1964. This subdivision shall apply only to the extent required by federal law.

d. Management of land clearing debris burned in accordance with 15A NCAC 02D.1903 shall not require a permit pursuant to this section.

(4a) Repealed by Session Laws 2007-550, s. 1(a), effective August 1, 2007.

(5) Repealed by Session Laws 1983, c. 795, s. 3.

(5a) Designate a geographic area within which the collection, transportation, storage and disposal of all solid waste generated within said area shall be accomplished in accordance with a solid waste management plan. Such designation may be made only after the Department has received a request from the unit or units of local government having jurisdiction within said geographic area that such designation be made and after receipt by the Department of a solid waste management plan which shall include:

a. The existing and projected population for such area;

b. The quantities of solid waste generated and estimated to be generated in such area;

c. The availability of sanitary landfill sites and the environmental impact of continued landfill of solid waste on surface and subsurface waters;

d. The method of solid waste disposal to be utilized and the energy or material which shall be recovered from the waste; and

e. Such other data that the Department may reasonably require.

(5b) Authorize units of local government to require by ordinance, that all solid waste generated within the designated geographic area that is placed in the waste stream for disposal be collected, transported, stored and disposed of at a permitted solid waste management facility or facilities serving such area. The provisions of such ordinance shall not be construed to prohibit the source separation of materials from solid waste prior to collection of such solid waste for disposal, or prohibit collectors of solid waste from recycling materials or limit access to such materials as an incident to collection of such solid waste; provided such prohibitions do not authorize the construction and operation of a resource recovery facility unless specifically permitted pursuant to an approved solid waste management plan. If a private solid waste landfill shall be substantially affected by such ordinance then the unit of local government adopting the ordinance shall be required to give the operator of the affected landfill at least two years written notice prior to the effective date of the proposed ordinance.

(5c) Except for the authority to designate a geographic area to be serviced by a solid waste management facility, delegate authority and responsibility to units of local government to perform all or a portion of a solid waste management program within the jurisdictional area of the unit of local government; provided that no authority over or control of the operations or properties of one local government shall be delegated to any other local government.

(5d) Require that an annual report of the implementation of the solid waste management plan within the designated geographic area be filed with the Department.

(6) Charge and collect fees from operators of hazardous waste disposal facilities. The fees shall be used to establish a fund sufficient for each individual facility to defray the anticipated costs to the State for monitoring and care of the facility after the termination of the period during which the facility operator is required by applicable State and federal statutes, regulations or rules to remain responsible for post-closure monitoring and care. In establishing the fees, consideration shall be given to the size of the facility, the nature of the hazardous waste and the projected life of the facility.

(7)   Establish and collect annual fees from generators and transporters of hazardous waste, and from storage, treatment, and disposal facilities regulated under this Article as provided in G.S. 130A-294.1.

(a1)   A permit for a solid waste management facility may be transferred only with the approval of the Department.

(a2)   Permits for sanitary landfills and transfer stations shall be issued for (i) a design and operation phase of five years or (ii) a design and operation phase of 10 years. A permit issued for a design and operation phase of 10 years shall be subject to a limited review within five years of the issuance date.

(b)   The Commission shall adopt and the Department shall enforce rules to implement a comprehensive statewide solid waste management program. The rules shall be consistent with applicable State and federal law; and shall be designed to protect the public health, safety, and welfare; preserve the environment; and provide for the greatest possible conservation of cultural and natural resources. Rules for the establishment, location, operation, maintenance, use, discontinuance, recordation, post-closure care of solid waste management facilities also shall be based upon recognized public health practices and procedures, including applicable epidemiological research and studies; hydrogeological research and studies; sanitary engineering research and studies; and current technological development in equipment and methods. The rules shall not apply to the management of solid waste that is generated by an individual or individual family or household unit on the individual's property and is disposed of on the individual's property.

(b1)   (1)   For purposes of this subsection and subdivision (4) of subsection (a) of this section, a "substantial amendment" means either:

a.   An increase of ten percent (10%) or more in:

1.   The population of the geographic area to be served by the sanitary landfill;

2.   The quantity of solid waste to be disposed of in the sanitary landfill; or

3.   The geographic area to be served by the sanitary landfill.

b.   A change in the categories of solid waste to be disposed of in the sanitary landfill or any other change to the application for a permit or to the permit for a sanitary landfill that the Commission or the Department determines to be substantial.

(2) A person who intends to apply for a new permit, the renewal of a permit, or a substantial amendment to a permit for a sanitary landfill shall obtain, prior to applying for a permit, a franchise for the operation of the sanitary landfill from each local government having jurisdiction over any part of the land on which the sanitary landfill and its appurtenances are located or to be located. A local government may adopt a franchise ordinance under G.S. 153A-136 or G.S. 160A-319. A franchise granted for a sanitary landfill shall include all of the following:

a. A statement of the population to be served, including a description of the geographic area.

b. A description of the volume and characteristics of the waste stream.

c. A projection of the useful life of the sanitary landfill.

d. Repealed by Session Laws 2013-409, s. 8, effective August 23, 2013.

e. The procedures to be followed for governmental oversight and regulation of the fees and rates to be charged by facilities subject to the franchise for waste generated in the jurisdiction of the franchising entity.

f. A facility plan for the sanitary landfill that shall include the boundaries of the proposed facility, proposed development of the facility site in five-year operational phases, the boundaries of all waste disposal units, final elevations and capacity of all waste disposal units, the amount of waste to be received per day in tons, the total waste disposal capacity of the sanitary landfill in tons, a description of environmental controls, and a description of any other waste management activities to be conducted at the facility. In addition, the facility plan shall show the proposed location of soil borrow areas, leachate facilities, and all other facilities and infrastructure, including ingress and egress to the facility.

(2a) A local government may elect to award a preliminary franchise. If a local government elects to award a preliminary franchise, the preliminary franchise shall contain, at a minimum, all of the information described in sub-subdivisions a. through e. of subdivision (2) of this subsection plus a general description of the proposed sanitary landfill, including the approximate number of acres required for the proposed sanitary landfill and its appurtenances and a description of any other solid waste management activities that are to be conducted at the site.

(2b)   A local government may elect to include as part of a franchise agreement a surcharge on waste disposed of in its jurisdiction by other local governments located within the State. Funds collected by a local government pursuant to such a surcharge may be used to support any services supported by the local government's general fund.

(3)   Prior to the award of a franchise for the construction or operation of a sanitary landfill, the board of commissioners of the county or counties in which the sanitary landfill is proposed to be located or is located or, if the sanitary landfill is proposed to be located or is located in a city, the governing board of the city shall conduct a public hearing. The board of commissioners of the county or counties in which the sanitary landfill is proposed to be located or is located or, if the sanitary landfill is proposed to be located or is located in a city, the governing board of the city shall provide at least 30 days' notice to the public of the public hearing. The notice shall include a summary of all the information required to be included in the franchise, and shall specify the procedure to be followed at the public hearing. The applicant for the franchise shall provide a copy of the application for the franchise that includes all of the information required to be included in the franchise, to the public library closest to the proposed sanitary landfill site to be made available for inspection and copying by the public.

(4)   An applicant for a new permit, the renewal of a permit, or a substantial amendment to a permit for a sanitary landfill shall request each local government having jurisdiction over any part of the land on which the sanitary landfill and its appurtenances are located or to be located to issue a determination as to whether the local government has in effect a franchise, zoning, subdivision, or land-use planning ordinance applicable to the sanitary landfill and whether the proposed sanitary landfill, or the existing sanitary landfill as it would be operated under the renewed or substantially amended permit, would be consistent with the applicable ordinances. The request to the local government shall be accompanied by a copy of the permit application and shall be delivered to the clerk of the local government personally or by certified mail. In order to serve as a basis for a determination that an application for a new permit, the renewal of a permit, or a substantial amendment to a permit for a sanitary landfill is consistent with a zoning, subdivision, or land-use planning ordinance, an ordinance or zoning classification applicable to the real property designated in the permit application shall have been in effect not less than 90

days prior to the date the request for a determination of consistency is delivered to the clerk of the local government. The determination shall be verified or supported by affidavit signed by the chief administrative officer, the chief administrative officer's designee, clerk, or other official designated by the local government to make the determination and, if the local government states that the sanitary landfill as it would be operated under the new, renewed, or substantially amended permit is inconsistent with a franchise, zoning, subdivision, or land-use planning ordinance, shall include a copy of the ordinance and the specific reasons for the determination of inconsistency. A copy of the determination shall be provided to the applicant when the determination is submitted to the Department. The Department shall not act upon an application for a permit under this section until it has received a determination from each local government requested to make a determination by the applicant; provided that if a local government fails to submit a determination to the Department as provided by this subsection within 15 days after receipt of the request, the Department shall proceed to consider the permit application without regard to a franchise, local zoning, subdivision, and land-use planning ordinances. Unless the local government makes a subsequent determination of consistency with all ordinances cited in the determination or the sanitary landfill as it would be operated under the new, renewed, or substantially amended permit is determined by a court of competent jurisdiction to be consistent with the cited ordinances, the Department shall attach as a condition of the permit a requirement that the applicant, prior to construction or operation of the sanitary landfill under the permit, comply with all lawfully adopted local ordinances cited in the determination that apply to the sanitary landfill. This subsection shall not be construed to affect the validity of any lawfully adopted franchise, local zoning, subdivision, or land-use planning ordinance or to affect the responsibility of any person to comply with any lawfully adopted franchise, local zoning, subdivision, or land-use planning ordinance. This subsection shall not be construed to limit any opportunity a local government may have to comment on a permit application under any other law or rule. This subsection shall not apply to any facility with respect to which local ordinances are subject to review under either G.S. 104E-6.2 or G.S. 130A-293.

(5) As used in this subdivision, "coal-fired generating unit" and "investor-owned public utility" have the same meaning as in G.S. 143-215.107D(a). Notwithstanding subdivisions (a)(4), (b1)(3), or (b1)(4) of this section, no franchise shall be required for a sanitary landfill used only to dispose of waste generated by a coal-fired generating unit that is owned or operated by an investor-owned utility subject to the requirements of G.S. 143-215.107D.

(b2)   The Department shall require an applicant for a permit or a permit holder under this Article to satisfy the Department that the applicant or permit holder, and any parent, subsidiary, or other affiliate of the applicant, permit holder, or parent, including any joint venturer with a direct or indirect interest in the applicant, permit holder, or parent:

(1)   Is financially qualified to carry out the activity for which the permit is required. An applicant for a permit and permit holders for solid waste management facilities that are not hazardous waste facilities shall establish financial responsibility as required by G.S. 130A-295.2. An applicant for a permit and permit holders for hazardous waste facilities shall establish financial responsibility as required by G.S. 130A-295.04.

(2)   Has substantially complied with the requirements applicable to any activity in which the applicant or permit holder, or a parent, subsidiary, or other affiliate of the applicant, permit holder, or parent, or a joint venturer with a direct or indirect interest in the applicant has previously engaged and has been in substantial compliance with federal and state laws, regulations, and rules for the protection of the environment as provided in G.S. 130A-295.3.

(b3)   An applicant for a permit or a permit holder under this Article shall satisfy the Department that the applicant has met the requirements of subsection (b2) of this section before the Department is required to otherwise review the application.

(c)   The Commission shall adopt and the Department shall enforce rules governing the management of hazardous waste. These rules shall establish a complete and integrated regulatory scheme in the area of hazardous waste management, implement this Part, and shall:

(1)   Establish criteria for hazardous waste, identify the characteristics of hazardous waste, and list particular hazardous waste.

(1a)   Establish criteria for hazardous constituents, identify the characteristics of hazardous constituents, and list particular hazardous constituents.

(2)   Require record keeping and reporting by generators and transporters of hazardous waste and owners and operators of hazardous waste facilities.

(3)   Require proper labeling of hazardous waste containers.

(4) Require use of appropriate containers for hazardous waste.

(5) Require maintenance of a manifest system to assure that all hazardous waste is designated for treatment, storage or disposal at a hazardous waste facility to which a permit has been issued.

(6) Require proper transportation of hazardous waste.

(7) Develop treatment storage and disposal standards of performance and techniques to be used by hazardous waste facilities.

(8) Develop standards regarding location, design, ownership and construction of hazardous waste facilities; provided, however, that no hazardous waste disposal facility or polychlorinated biphenyl disposal facility shall be located within 25 miles of any other hazardous waste disposal facility or polychlorinated biphenyl disposal facility.

(9) Require plans to minimize unanticipated damage from treatment, storage or disposal of hazardous waste; and a plan or plans providing for the establishment and/or operation of one or more hazardous waste facilities in the absence of adequate approved hazardous waste facilities established or operated by any person within the State.

(10) Require proper maintenance and operation of hazardous waste facilities, including requirements for ownership by any person or the State, require demonstration of financial responsibility in accordance with this section and G.S. 130A-295.04, provide for training of personnel, and provide for continuity of operation and procedures for establishing and maintaining hazardous waste facilities.

(11) Require owners or operators of hazardous waste facilities to monitor the facilities.

(12) Authorize or require inspection or copying of records required to be kept by owners or operators.

(13) Provide for collection and analysis of hazardous waste samples and samples of hazardous waste containers and labels from generators and transporters and from owners and operators of hazardous waste facilities.

(14) Develop a permit system governing the establishment and operation of hazardous waste facilities.

(15) Develop additional requirements as necessary for the effective management of hazardous waste.

(16) Require the operator of the hazardous waste disposal facility to maintain adequate insurance to cover foreseeable claims arising from the operation of the facility. The Department shall determine what constitutes an adequate amount of insurance.

(17) Require the bottom of a hazardous waste disposal facility to be at least 10 feet above the seasonal high water table and more when necessary to protect the public health and the environment.

(18) Require the operator of a hazardous waste disposal facility to make monthly reports to the board of county commissioners of the county in which the facility is located on the kinds and amounts of hazardous wastes in the facility.

(d) The Commission is authorized to adopt and the Department is authorized to enforce rules where appropriate for public participation in the consideration, development, revision, implementation and enforcement of any permit rule, guideline, information or program under this Article.

(e) Rules adopted under this section may incorporate standards and restrictions which exceed and are more comprehensive than comparable federal regulations.

(f) Within 10 days of receiving an application for a permit or for an amendment to an existing permit for a hazardous waste facility, the Department shall notify the clerk of the board of commissioners of the county or counties in which the facility is proposed to be located or is located and, if the facility is proposed to be located or is located within a city, the clerk of the governing board of the city, that the application has been filed, and shall file a copy of the application with the clerk. Prior to the issuance of a permit or an amendment of an existing permit the Secretary or the Secretary's designee shall conduct a public hearing in the county, or in one of the counties in which the hazardous waste facility is proposed to be located or is located. The Secretary or the Secretary's designee shall give notice of the hearing, and the public hearing shall be in accordance with applicable federal regulations adopted pursuant to RCRA and with Chapter 150B of the General Statutes. Where the provisions of the federal regulations and Chapter 150B of the General Statutes are inconsistent, the federal regulations shall apply.

(g) The Commission shall develop and adopt standards for permitting of hazardous waste facilities. Such standards shall be developed with, and provide for, public participation; shall be incorporated into rules; shall be consistent with all applicable federal and State law, including statutes, regulations and rules; shall be developed and revised in light of the best available scientific data; and shall be based on consideration of at least the following factors:

(1) Hydrological and geological factors, including flood plains, depth to water table, groundwater travel time, soil pH, soil cation exchange capacity, soil composition and permeability, cavernous bedrock, seismic activity, slope, mines, and climate;

(2) Environmental and public health factors, including air quality, quality of surface and groundwater, and proximity to public water supply watersheds;

(3) Natural and cultural resources, including wetlands, gamelands, endangered species habitats, proximity to parks, forests, wilderness areas, nature preserves, and historic sites;

(4) Local land uses;

(5) Transportation factors, including proximity to waste generators, route safety, and method of transportation;

(6) Aesthetic factors, including the visibility, appearance, and noise level of the facility;

(7) Availability and reliability of public utilities; and

(8) Availability of emergency response personnel and equipment.

(h) Rules adopted by the Commission shall be subject to the following requirements:

(1) Repealed by Session Laws 1989, c. 168, s. 20.

(2) Hazardous waste shall be treated prior to disposal in North Carolina. The Commission shall determine the extent of waste treatment required before hazardous waste can be disposed of in a hazardous waste disposal facility.

(3) Any hazardous waste disposal facility hereafter constructed in this State shall meet, at the minimum, the standards of construction imposed by federal regulations adopted under the RCRA at the time the permit is issued.

(4) No hazardous waste disposal facility or polychlorinated biphenyl disposal facility shall be located within 25 miles of any other hazardous waste disposal facility or polychlorinated biphenyl disposal facility.

(5) Repealed by Session Laws 2001-474, s. 23, effective November 29, 2001.

(6) The following shall not be disposed of in a hazardous waste disposal facility: ignitables as defined in the RCRA, polyhalogenated biphenyls of 50 ppm or greater concentration, and free liquids whether or not containerized.

(7) Facilities for disposal or long-term storage of hazardous waste shall have at a minimum the following: a leachate collection and removal system above an artificial impervious liner of at least 30 mils in thickness, a minimum of five feet of clay or clay-like liner with a maximum permeability of $1.0 \times 10-7$ centimeters per second (cm/sec) below said artificial liner, and a leachate detection system immediately below the clay or clay-like liner.

(8) Hazardous waste shall not be stored at a hazardous waste treatment facility for over 90 days prior to treatment or disposal.

(9) The Commission shall consider any hazardous waste treatment process proposed to it, if the process lessens treatment cost or improves treatment over then current methods or standards required by the Commission.

(10) Prevention, reduction, recycling, and detoxification of hazardous wastes should be encouraged and promoted. Hazardous waste disposal facilities and polychlorinated biphenyl disposal facilities shall be detoxified as soon as technology which is economically feasible is available and sufficient money is available without additional appropriation.

(i) (Effective until December 31, 2017) The Department shall report to the Fiscal Research Division of the General Assembly, the Senate Appropriations

Subcommittee on Natural and Economic Resources, the House Appropriations Subcommittee on Natural and Economic Resources, and the Environmental Review Commission on or before January 1 of each year on the implementation and cost of the hazardous waste management program. The report shall include an evaluation of how well the State and private parties are managing and cleaning up hazardous waste. The report shall also include recommendations to the Governor, State agencies, and the General Assembly on ways to: improve waste management; reduce the amount of waste generated; maximize resource recovery, reuse, and conservation; and minimize the amount of hazardous waste which must be disposed of. The report shall include beginning and ending balances in the Hazardous Waste Management Account for the reporting period, total fees collected pursuant to G.S. 130A-294.1, anticipated revenue from all sources, total expenditures by activities and categories for the hazardous waste management program, any recommended adjustments in annual and tonnage fees which may be necessary to assure the continued availability of funds sufficient to pay the State's share of the cost of the hazardous waste management program, and any other information requested by the General Assembly. In recommending adjustments in annual and tonnage fees, the Department may propose fees for hazardous waste generators, and for hazardous waste treatment facilities that treat waste generated on site, which are designed to encourage reductions in the volume or quantity and toxicity of hazardous waste. The report shall also include a description of activities undertaken to implement the resident inspectors program established under G.S. 130A-295.02. In addition, the report shall include an annual update on the mercury switch removal program that shall include, at a minimum, all of the following:

(1) A detailed description of the mercury recovery performance ratio achieved by the mercury switch removal program.

(2) A detailed description of the mercury switch collection system developed and implemented by vehicle manufacturers in accordance with the NVMSRP.

(3) In the event that a mercury recovery performance ratio of at least 0.90 of the national mercury recovery performance ratio as reported by the NVMSRP is not achieved, a description of additional or alternative actions that may be implemented to improve the mercury switch removal program.

(4) The number of mercury switches collected and a description of how the mercury switches were managed.

(5) A statement that details the costs required to implement the mercury switch removal program, including a summary of receipts and disbursements from the Mercury Switch Removal Account.

(i) (Effective December 31, 2017) The Department shall report to the Fiscal Research Division of the General Assembly, the Senate Appropriations Subcommittee on Natural and Economic Resources, the House Appropriations Subcommittee on Natural and Economic Resources, and the Environmental Review Commission on or before January 1 of each year on the implementation and cost of the hazardous waste management program. The report shall include an evaluation of how well the State and private parties are managing and cleaning up hazardous waste. The report shall also include recommendations to the Governor, State agencies, and the General Assembly on ways to: improve waste management; reduce the amount of waste generated; maximize resource recovery, reuse, and conservation; and minimize the amount of hazardous waste which must be disposed of. The report shall include beginning and ending balances in the Hazardous Waste Management Account for the reporting period, total fees collected pursuant to G.S. 130A-294.1, anticipated revenue from all sources, total expenditures by activities and categories for the hazardous waste management program, any recommended adjustments in annual and tonnage fees which may be necessary to assure the continued availability of funds sufficient to pay the State's share of the cost of the hazardous waste management program, and any other information requested by the General Assembly. In recommending adjustments in annual and tonnage fees, the Department may propose fees for hazardous waste generators, and for hazardous waste treatment facilities that treat waste generated on site, which are designed to encourage reductions in the volume or quantity and toxicity of hazardous waste. The report shall also include a description of activities undertaken to implement the resident inspectors program established under G.S. 130A-295.02. In addition, the report shall include an annual update on the mercury switch removal program that shall include, at a minimum, all of the following:

(1) A detailed description and documentation of the capture rate achieved.

(2) Repealed by Session Laws 2012-200, s. 21(b), effective December 31, 2017.

(3) In the event that a capture rate of at least ninety percent (90%) is not achieved, a description of additional or alternative actions that may be implemented to improve the mercury minimization plan and its implementation.

(4) The number of mercury switches collected, the number of end-of-life vehicles containing mercury switches, the number of end-of-life vehicles processed for recycling, and a description of how the mercury switches were managed.

(5) A statement that details the costs required to implement the mercury minimization plan.

(j) Repealed by Session Laws 2007-107, s. 1.1(e), effective October 1, 2007.

(k) Each person who generates hazardous waste who is required to pay a fee under G.S. 130A-294.1, and each operator of a hazardous waste treatment facility which treats waste generated on-site who is required to pay a fee under G.S. 130A-294.1, shall submit to the Department at the time such fees are due, a written description of any program to minimize or reduce the volume and quantity or toxicity of such waste.

(l) Disposal of solid waste in or upon water in a manner that results in solid waste entering waters or lands of the State is unlawful. Nothing herein shall be interpreted to affect disposal of solid waste in a permitted landfill.

(m) Demolition debris consisting of used asphalt or used asphalt mixed with dirt, sand, gravel, rock, concrete, or similar nonhazardous material may be used as fill and need not be disposed of in a permitted landfill or solid waste disposal facility. Such demolition debris may not be placed in the waters of the State or at or below the seasonal high water table.

(n) The Department shall encourage research and development and disseminate information on state-of-the-art means of handling and disposing of hazardous waste. The Department may establish a waste information exchange for the State.

(o) The Department shall promote public education and public involvement in the decision-making process for the siting and permitting of proposed hazardous waste facilities. The Department shall assist localities in which facilities are proposed in collecting and receiving information relating to the suitability of the proposed site. At the request of a local government in which facilities are proposed, the Department shall direct the appropriate agencies of State government to develop such relevant data as that locality shall reasonably request.

(p) The Department shall each year recommend to the Governor a recipient for a "Governor's Award of Excellence" which the Governor shall award for outstanding achievement by an industry or company in the area of waste management.

(q) The Secretary shall, at the request of the Governor and under the Governor's direction, assist with the negotiation of interstate agreements for the management of hazardous waste.

(r) The Commission shall, in accordance with the procedures set forth in G.S. 160A-211.1 and G.S. 153A-152.1, review upon appeal specific privilege license tax rates that localities may apply to waste management facilities in their jurisdiction.

(s) The Department is authorized to enter upon any lands and structures upon lands to make surveys, borings, soundings, and examinations as may be necessary to determine the suitability of a site for a hazardous waste facility or hazardous waste disposal facility. The Department shall give 30 days notice of the intended entry authorized by this section in the manner prescribed for service of process by G.S. 1A-1, Rule 4. Entry under this section shall not be deemed a trespass or taking; provided, however, that the Department shall make reimbursement for any damage to land or structures caused by these activities. (1969, c. 899; 1973, c. 476, s. 128; 1975, c. 311, s. 4; c. 764, s. 1; 1977, c. 123; 1977, 2nd Sess., c. 1216; 1979, c. 464, s. 2; c. 694, s. 2; 1981, c. 704, s. 6; 1983, c. 795, ss. 3, 8.1; c. 891, s. 2; 1983 (Reg. Sess., 1984), c. 973, ss. 6, 7; c. 1034, s. 73; 1985, c. 582; c. 738, ss. 2, 3; 1985 (Reg. Sess., 1986), c. 1027, s. 31; 1987, c. 597; c. 761; c. 773, s. 1; c. 827, ss. 1, 250; c. 848; 1987 (Reg. Sess., 1988), c. 1111, s. 6; 1989, c. 168, ss. 15-22; c. 317; c. 727, s. 218(86); c. 742, s. 6; 1991, c. 537, s. 1; 1993, c. 86, s. 1; c. 273, s. 1; c. 365, s. 1; c. 473, ss. 1, 2; c. 501, s. 14; 1993 (Reg. Sess., 1994), c. 580, s. 1; c. 722, ss. 1, 2; 1995, c. 502, s. 1; c. 509, s. 70; 1995 (Reg. Sess., 1996), c. 594, ss. 6, 7; 1997-27, s. 2; 2001-357, s. 2; 2001-474, ss. 22, 23, 24, 25; 2002-148, s. 4; 2003-37, s. 1; 2006-256, ss. 1, 2, 3; 2007-107, ss. 1.1(b), 1.1(d), 1.1(e), 2.1(a); 2007-495, s. 14; 2007-550, s. 1(a); 2012-200, s. 21(a), (b); 2013-55, s. 1; 2013-408, s. 1; 2013-409, s. 8; 2013-413, ss. 28(e), 59(a), 59.4(e).)

§ 130A-294.1. Fees applicable to generators and transporters of hazardous waste, and to hazardous waste storage, treatment, and disposal facilities.

(a) It is the intent of the General Assembly that the fee system established by this section is solely to provide funding in addition to federal and State appropriations to support the State's hazardous waste management program.

(b) Funds collected pursuant to this section shall be used for personnel and other resources necessary to:

(1) Provide a high level of technical assistance and waste minimization effort for the hazardous waste management program;

(2) Provide timely review of permit applications;

(3) Insure that permit decisions are made on a sound technical basis and that permit decisions incorporate all conditions necessary to accomplish the purposes of this Part;

(4) Improve monitoring and compliance of the hazardous waste management program;

(5) Increase the frequency of inspections;

(6) Provide chemical, biological, toxicological, and analytical support for the hazardous waste management program; and

(7) Provide resources for emergency response to imminent hazards associated with the hazardous waste management program;

(8) Implement and provide oversight of necessary response activities involving inactive hazardous substance or waste disposal sites; [and]

(9) Provide compliance and prevention activities within the solid waste program to ensure that hazardous waste is not disposed in solid waste management facilities.

(c) It is the intent of the General Assembly that the total funds collected per year pursuant to this section not exceed thirty percent (30%) of the total funds budgeted from all sources for the hazardous waste management program. This subsection shall not be construed to limit the obligation of any person to pay any fee imposed by this section.

(d) The Hazardous Waste Management Account is established as a nonreverting account within the Department. All fees collected under this section shall be credited to the Account and shall be used for the purposes listed in subsection (b).

(e) A person who generates either one kilogram or more of any acute hazardous waste as listed in 40 C.F.R. § 261.30(d) or § 261.33(e) as revised 1 July 1987, or 1000 kilograms or more of hazardous waste, in any calendar month during the year beginning 1 July and ending 30 June shall pay an annual fee of one thousand four hundred dollars ($1,400).

(f) A person who generates 100 kilograms or more of hazardous waste in any calendar month during the year beginning 1 July and ending 30 June but less than 1000 kilograms of hazardous waste in each calendar month during that year shall pay an annual fee of one hundred seventy-five dollars ($175.00).

(g) A person who generates one kilogram or more of acute hazardous waste or 1000 kilograms or more of hazardous waste in any calendar month during the calendar year shall pay, in addition to any fee under subsections (e) and (f) of this section, a tonnage fee of seventy cents ($0.70) per ton or any part thereof of hazardous waste generated during that year up to a maximum of 25,000 tons.

(h) A person who generates less than one kilogram of acute hazardous waste and less than 100 kilograms of hazardous waste in each calendar month during the year beginning 1 July and ending 30 June shall not be liable for payment of a fee under subsections (e) and (f) of this section for that year.

(i) Hazardous waste generated as a result of any type of remedial action or by collection by a local government of hazardous waste from households shall not be subject to a tonnage fee under subsections (g) and (l) of this section.

(j) A person who transports hazardous waste shall pay an annual fee of eight hundred forty dollars ($840.00).

(k) A storage, treatment, or disposal facility shall pay an annual activity fee of one thousand six hundred eighty dollars ($1,680) for each activity.

(l) A commercial hazardous waste storage, treatment, or disposal facility shall pay annually, in addition to the fees applicable to all hazardous waste storage, treatment, or disposal facilities, a single tonnage charge of two dollars and forty-five cents ($2.45) per ton or any part thereof of hazardous waste stored, treated, or disposed of at the facility. A manufacturing facility that receives hazardous waste generated from the use of a product typical of its manufacturing process for the purpose of recycling is exempt from this tonnage charge. A facility must have a permit issued under this Article which includes the recycling activity and specifies the type and amount of waste allowed to be received from off-site for recycling.

(m) An applicant for a permit for a hazardous waste storage, treatment, or disposal facility that proposes to operate as a commercial facility shall pay an application fee for each proposed activity as follows:

(1) Storage facility $14,000.

(2) Treatment facility $21,000.

(3) Disposal facility $35,000.

(n) The Commission may adopt rules setting fees for modifications to permits. Such fees shall not exceed fifty percent (50%) of the application fee.

(o) Annual fees established under this section are due no later than 31 July for the fiscal year beginning 1 July in the same year. Tonnage fees established under this section are due no later than 31 July for the previous calendar year.

(p) Repealed by Session Laws 2012-200, s. 21(c), effective August 1, 2012. (1987, c. 773, ss. 2, 4-8; 1987 (Reg. Sess., 1988), c. 1020, s. 2; 1989, c. 168, s. 23; c. 724, s. 4; 1991, c. 286, s. 1; 1991 (Reg. Sess., 1992), c. 890, s. 10; c. 1039, s. 9; 2003-284, s. 35.2(a), (b); 2007-495, s. 24; 2010-31, s. 13.8(a); 2010-123, s. 5.1; 2011-145, s. 31.15; 2012-200, s. 21(c).)

§ 130A-295. Additional requirements for hazardous waste facilities.

(a) An applicant for a permit for a hazardous waste facility shall satisfy the Department that:

(1) Any hazardous waste facility constructed or operated by the applicant, or any parent or subsidiary corporation if the applicant is a corporation, has

been operated in accordance, with sound waste management practices and in substantial compliance with federal and state laws, regulations and rules; and

(2) The applicant, or any parent or subsidiary corporation if the applicant is a corporation, is financially qualified to operate the proposed hazardous waste facility.

(b) An applicant for a permit for a hazardous waste facility shall satisfy the Department that he has met the requirements of subsection (a) of this section before the Department is required to otherwise review the application. In order to continue to hold a permit under this Chapter, a permittee must remain financially qualified and must provide any information requested by the Department to demonstrate that he continues to be financially qualified.

(c) No permit for any new commercial hazardous waste treatment, storage, or disposal facility shall be issued or become effective, and no permit for a commercial hazardous waste treatment, storage, or disposal facility shall be modified until the applicant has satisfied the Department that such facility is needed to meet the current or projected hazardous waste management needs of this State or to comply with the terms of any interstate agreement for the management of hazardous waste to which the State is a party. The Commission shall adopt rules to implement this subsection.

(d) At least 120 days prior to submitting an application, an applicant for a permit for a hazardous waste facility shall provide to the county in which the facility is located, to any municipality with planning jurisdiction over the site of the facility, and to all emergency response agencies that have a role under the contingency plan for the facility all of the following information:

(1) Information on the nature and type of operations to occur at the facility.

(2) Identification of the properties of the hazardous waste to be managed at the facility.

(3) A copy of the draft contingency plan for the facility that includes the proposed role for each local government and each emergency response agency that received information under this subsection.

(4) Information on the hazardous waste locations within the facility.

(e) Within 60 days of receiving the information, each local government and emergency response agency that receives information under subsection (d) of this section shall respond to the applicant in writing as to the adequacy of the contingency plan and the availability and adequacy of its resources and equipment to respond to an emergency at the facility that results in a release of hazardous waste or hazardous waste constituents into the environment according to the role set forth for the local government or emergency response agency under the contingency plan.

(f) An applicant for a permit for a hazardous waste facility shall include documentation that each local government and emergency response agency received the information required under subsection (d) of this section, the written responses the applicant received under subsection (e) of this section, and verification by each that its resources and equipment are available and adequate to respond to an emergency at the facility in accordance with its role as set forth in the contingency plan. If the applicant does not receive a timely verification from a local government or emergency response agency notified under subsection (d) of this section, the Department shall verify the adequacy of resources and equipment for emergency response during the course of review of the permit application, taking into account any contracts entered into by the applicant for such emergency response resources.

(g) At each two-year interval after a permit for a hazardous waste facility is issued, the permit holder shall verify that the resources and equipment of each local government and emergency response agency are available and adequate to respond to an emergency at the facility in accordance with its role as set forth in the contingency plan and shall submit this verification to the Department. (1981, c. 704, s. 7; 1983, c. 891, s. 2; 1983 (Reg. Sess., 1984), c. 973, s. 8; 1987, § 461, s. 3; 1989, c. 168, s. 24; 2007-107, s. 1.2(a).)

§ 130A-295.01. Additional requirement for commercial hazardous waste facilities.

(a) As used in this section:

(1) "Commercial hazardous waste facility" means any hazardous waste facility that accepts hazardous waste from the general public or from another person for a fee, but does not include any facility owned or operated by a generator of hazardous waste solely for his own use, and does not include any

facility owned by the State or by any agency or subdivision thereof solely for the management of hazardous waste generated by agencies or subdivisions of the State.

(2) "New", when used in connection with "facility", refers to a planned or proposed facility, or a facility that has not been placed in operation, but does not include facilities that have commenced operations as of 22 June 1987, including facilities operated under interim status.

(3) "Modified", when used in connection with "permit", means any change in any permit in force on or after 22 June 1987 that would either expand the scope of permitted operations, or extend the expiration date of the permit, or otherwise constitute a Class 2 or Class 3 modification of the permit as defined in 40 Code of Federal Regulations § 270.41 (1 July 2006).

(4) "7Q10 conditions", when used in connection with "surface water," refers to the minimum average flow for a period of seven consecutive days that has an average occurrence of once in 10 years as referenced in 15 NCAC 2B.0206(a)(3) as adopted 1 February 1976.

(b) No permit for any new commercial hazardous waste facility shall be issued or become effective, and no permit for a commercial hazardous waste facility shall be modified, until the applicant has satisfied the Department that such facility meets, in addition to all other applicable requirements, the following requirements:

(1) The facility shall not discharge directly a hazardous or toxic substance into a surface water that is upstream from a public drinking water supply intake in North Carolina, unless there is a dilution factor of 1000 or greater at the point of discharge into the surface water under 7Q10 conditions.

(2) The facility shall not discharge indirectly through a publicly owned treatment works (POTW) a hazardous or toxic substance into a surface water that is upstream from a public drinking water supply intake in North Carolina, unless there is a dilution factor of 1000 or greater, irrespective of any dilution occurring in a wastewater treatment plant, at the point of discharge into the surface water under 7Q10 conditions.

(c) The Department shall not issue a permit for a commercial hazardous waste facility for a period of more than five years. A permit holder for a commercial hazardous waste facility who intends to apply for renewal of the permit shall submit an application for the renewal of the permit at least one year before the permit expires unless the Department approves a shorter period of time.

(d) The owner or operator of a commercial hazardous waste facility shall maintain a record of information at an off-site location that identifies the generators of the waste and the quantity, type, location, and hazards of the waste at the facility and shall make this information available in a form and manner to be determined by the Department, accessible to the Department, to the county in which the facility is located, to any municipality with planning jurisdiction over the site of the facility, and to emergency response agencies that have a role under the contingency plan for the facility.

(e) (1) Within 10 days of filing an application for a permit for a commercial hazardous waste facility, the applicant shall notify every person who resides or owns property located within one-fourth mile of any property boundary of the facility that the application has been filed. The notice shall be by mail to residents and by certified mail to property owners, or by any other means approved by the Department, shall be in a form approved by the Department, and shall include all of the following:

a. The location of the facility.

b. A description of the facility.

c. The hazardous and nonhazardous wastes that are to be received and processed at the facility.

d. A description of the emergency response plan for the facility.

(2) The permit holder for a commercial hazardous waste facility shall publish a notice that includes the information set out in subdivision (1) of this subsection annually beginning one year after the permit is issued. The notice shall be published in a form and manner approved by the Department in a newspaper of general circulation in the community where the facility is located.

(3) The permit holder for a commercial hazardous waste facility shall provide the information set out in subdivision (1) of this subsection by mail to the persons described in subdivision (1) of this subsection at the midpoint of the period for which the permit is issued.

(4) Each commercial hazardous waste facility applicant and permit holder shall provide documentation to demonstrate to the Department that the requirements set out in subdivisions (1), (2), and (3) of this subsection have been met.

(f) No later than 31 January of each year, the owner or operator of a commercial hazardous waste facility shall report to the Department any increase or decrease in the number of sensitive land uses and any increase or decrease in estimated population density based on information provided by the local government that has planning jurisdiction over the site on which the facility is located that occurred during the previous calendar year in the area located within one-fourth mile of any property boundary of the facility. Changes shall be recorded in the operating record of the facility. As used in this subsection, "sensitive land use" includes residential housing, places of assembly, places of worship, schools, day care providers, and hospitals. Sensitive land use does not include retail businesses.

(g) The owner or operator of a commercial hazardous waste facility shall provide a security and surveillance system at the facility 24 hours a day, seven days a week in order to continuously monitor site conditions and to control entry. The security and surveillance system shall be capable of promptly detecting unauthorized access to the facility; monitoring conditions; identifying operator errors; and detecting any discharge that could directly or indirectly cause a fire, explosion, or release of hazardous waste or hazardous waste constituents into the environment or threaten human health. The requirements of this subsection may be satisfied either by employing trained facility personnel or by providing an electronic security and surveillance system which may include television, motion detectors, heat-sensing equipment, combustible gas monitors, or any combination of these, as approved by the Department.

(h) The operator of a commercial hazardous waste facility shall install an on-site wind monitor approved by the Department. The wind monitor required shall be located so that the real-time wind direction can be determined from a remote location in the event of a release of hazardous waste or hazardous waste constituents into the environment. (1987, c. 437, s. 1; 2007-107, ss. 1.3(a), 1.4(a), 1.5(a), 1.6(a), 1.7(a), 1.9(a), 2.1(b); 2007-495, s. 15(a)-(e).)

§ 130A-295.02. Resident inspectors required at commercial hazardous waste facilities; recovery of costs for same.

(a)   The Division shall employ full-time resident inspectors for each commercial hazardous waste facility located within the State. Such inspectors shall be employed and assigned so that at least one inspector is on duty at all times during which any component of the facility is in operation, is undergoing any maintenance or repair, or is undergoing any test or calibration. Resident inspectors shall be assigned to commercial hazardous waste management facilities so as to protect the public health and the environment, to monitor all aspects of the operation of such facilities, and to assure compliance with all laws and rules administered by the Division and by any other division of the Department. Such inspectors may also enforce laws or rules administered by any other agency of the State pursuant to an appropriate memorandum of agreement entered into by the Secretary and the chief administrative officer of such agency. The Division may assign additional resident inspectors to a facility depending upon the quantity and toxicity of waste managed at a facility, diversity of types of waste managed at the facility, complexity of management technologies utilized at the facility, the range of components which are included at the facility, operating history of the facility, and other factors relative to the need for on-site inspection and enforcement capabilities. The Division, in consultation with other divisions of the Department, shall define the duties of each resident inspector and shall determine whether additional resident inspectors are needed at a particular facility to meet the purposes of this section.

(b)   The Division shall establish requirements pertaining to education, experience, and training for resident inspectors so as to assure that such inspectors are fully qualified to serve the purposes of this section. The Division shall provide its resident inspectors with such training, equipment, facilities, and supplies as may be necessary to fulfill the purposes of this section.

(c)   As a condition of its permit, the owner or operator of each commercial hazardous waste facility located within the State shall provide and maintain such appropriate and secure offices and laboratory facilities as the Department may require for the use of the resident inspectors required by this section.

(d)   Resident inspectors assigned to a commercial hazardous waste facility shall have unrestricted access to all operational areas of such facility at all times. For the protection of resident inspectors and the public, the provisions of G.S. 143-215.107(f) shall not apply to commercial hazardous waste facilities to which a resident inspector is assigned.

(e) No commercial hazardous waste facility shall be operated, undergo any maintenance or repair, or undergo any testing or calibration unless an inspector employed by the Division is present at the facility.

(f) The requirements of this section are intended to enhance the ability of the Department to protect the public health and the environment by providing the Department with the authority and resources necessary to maintain a rigorous inspection and enforcement program at commercial hazardous waste management facilities. The requirements of this section are intended to be supplementary to other requirements imposed on hazardous waste facilities. This section shall not be construed to relieve either the owner or the operator of any such facility or the Department from any other requirement of law or to require any unnecessary duplication of reporting or monitoring requirements.

(g) For the purpose of enforcing the laws and rules enacted or adopted for the protection of the public health and the environment, resident inspectors employed pursuant to this section may be commissioned as special peace officers as provided in G.S. 113-28.1. The provisions of Article 1A of Chapter 113 of the General Statutes shall apply to resident inspectors commissioned as special peace officers pursuant to this subsection.

(h) The Department shall determine the full cost of the employment and assignment of resident inspectors at each commercial hazardous waste facility located within the State. Such costs shall include, but are not limited to, costs incurred for salaries, benefits, travel, training, equipment, supplies, telecommunication and data transmission, offices and other facilities other than those provided by the owner or operator, and administrative expenses. The Department shall establish and revise as necessary a schedule of fees to be assessed on the users of each such facility to recover the actual cost of the resident inspector program at that facility. The operator of each such facility shall serve as the collection agent for such fees, shall account to the Department on a monthly basis for all fees collected, and shall deposit with the Department all funds collected pursuant to this section within 15 days following the last day of the month in which such fees are collected. Fees collected under this section shall be credited to the General Fund as nontax revenue.

(i) The Division shall establish and revise as necessary a program for assigning resident inspectors to commercial hazardous waste facilities so that scheduled rotation or equivalent oversight procedures ensure that each resident inspector will maintain objectivity.

(j)   For purposes of this subsection, special purpose commercial hazardous waste facilities include: a facility that manages limited quantities of hazardous waste; a facility that limits its hazardous waste management activities to reclamation or recycling, including energy or materials recovery or a facility that stores hazardous waste primarily for use at such facilities; or a facility that is determined to be low risk under rules adopted by the Commission pursuant to this subsection. The Commission shall adopt rules to determine whether a commercial hazardous waste facility is a special purpose commercial hazardous waste facility and to establish classifications of special purpose commercial hazardous waste facilities. The rules to determine whether a commercial hazardous waste facility is a special purpose commercial hazardous waste facility and to establish classifications of special purpose commercial hazardous waste facilities shall be based on factors including, but not limited to, the size of the facility, the type of treatment or storage being performed, the nature and volume of waste being treated or stored, the uniformity, similarity, or lack of diversity of the waste streams, the predictability of the nature of the waste streams and their treatability, whether the facility utilizes automated monitoring or safety devices that adequately perform functions that would otherwise be performed by a resident inspector, the fact that reclamation or recycling is being performed at the facility, and the compliance history of the facility and its operator. Based on the foregoing factors and any increase or decrease in the number of sensitive land uses over time or in estimated population density over time reported pursuant to G.S. 130A-295.01(f), rules adopted pursuant to this subsection shall establish times and frequencies for the presence of a resident inspector on less than a full-time basis at special purpose commercial hazardous waste facilities and specify a minimum number of additional inspections at special purpose hazardous waste facilities.

Special purpose commercial hazardous waste facilities that utilize hazardous waste as a fuel source shall be inspected a minimum of 40 hours per week, unless compliance data for these facilities can be electronically monitored and recorded off-site by the Department. The Department, considering the benefits provided by electronic monitoring, shall determine the number of hours of on-site inspection required at these facilities. The Department shall maintain records of all inspections at special purpose commercial hazardous waste facilities. Such records shall contain sufficient detail and shall be arranged in a readily understandable format so as to facilitate determination at any time as to whether the special purpose commercial hazardous waste facility is in compliance with the requirements of this subsection and of rules adopted pursuant to this subsection. Notwithstanding any other provision of this section, special purpose commercial hazardous waste facilities shall be subject to inspection at all times during which the facility is in operation, undergoing any maintenance or repair, or undergoing any test or calibration.

(k) For purposes of this section, a facility that utilizes hazardous waste as a fuel or that has used hazardous waste as a fuel within the preceding calendar year, and that is an affiliate of and adjacent or contiguous to a commercial hazardous waste facility, shall be subject to inspection as a special purpose commercial hazardous waste facility under subsection (j) of this section as if the facility that utilizes hazardous waste as a fuel were a part of the commercial hazardous waste facility.

(l) As used in this section, the words "affiliate", "parent", and "subsidiary" have the same meaning as in 17 Code of Federal Regulations § 240.12b-2 (1 April 1990 Edition).

(m) Repealed by Session Laws 2012-200, s. 21(d), effective August 1, 2012. (1989 (Reg. Sess., 1990), c. 1082, s. 1; 1991, c. 20, s. 2; c. 403, s. 4; c. 450, s. 2; 1993, c. 511, s. 1; c. 513, s. 2(b); c. 553, s. 41; 1995, c. 327, s. 1; 2006-79, s. 16; 2007-107, s. 1.5(b); 2009-570, s. 16; 2012-200, s. 21(d).)

§ 130A-295.03. Additional requirement for hazardous waste disposal facilities; hazardous waste to be placed in containers.

(a) For purposes of this section, the term "container" means any portable device into which waste is placed for storage, transportation, treatment, disposal, or other handling, and includes the first enclosure which encompasses the waste.

(b) All hazardous waste shall be placed in containers for disposal, except as the Commission shall provide for by rule. The Commission shall adopt standards for the design and construction of containers for disposal. Standards for containers may vary for different types of waste. The standards for disposal containers may supplement or duplicate any of the performance or engineering standards for hazardous waste disposal facilities required under State or federal law; however, the performance or engineering standards for hazardous waste disposal facilities are separate and cumulative, and the performance or engineering standards for hazardous waste disposal facilities and containers may not substitute for or replace one another. (1991, c. 450, s. 1; c. 761, s. 22.)

§ 130A-295.04. Financial responsibility requirements for applicants for a permit and permit holders for hazardous waste facilities.

(a) In addition to any other financial responsibility requirements for solid waste management facilities under this Part, the applicant for a permit or a permit holder for a hazardous waste facility shall establish financial assurance that will ensure that sufficient funds are available for facility closure, post-closure maintenance and monitoring, any corrective action that the Department may require, and to satisfy any potential liability for sudden and nonsudden accidental occurrences, and subsequent costs incurred by the Department in response to an incident at a facility, even if the applicant or permit holder becomes insolvent or ceases to reside, be incorporated, do business, or maintain assets in the State.

(b) To establish sufficient availability of funds under this section, the applicant for a permit or a permit holder for a hazardous waste facility may use insurance, financial tests, third-party guarantees by persons who can pass the financial test, guarantees by corporate parents who can pass the financial test, irrevocable letters of credit, trusts, surety bonds, or any other financial device, or any combination of the foregoing, shown to provide protection equivalent to the financial protection that would be provided by insurance if insurance were the only mechanism used.

(c) The applicant for a permit or a permit holder for a hazardous waste facility, and any parent, subsidiary, or other affiliate of the applicant, permit holder, or parent, including any joint venturer with a direct or indirect interest in the applicant, permit holder, or parent, shall be a guarantor of payment for closure, post-closure maintenance and monitoring, any corrective action that the Department may require, and to satisfy any potential liability for sudden and nonsudden accidental occurrences arising from the operation of the hazardous waste facility.

(d), (e) Repealed by Session Laws 2011-394, s. 23(a), effective July 1, 2011.

(f) Assets used to meet the financial assurance requirements of this section shall be in a form that will allow the Department to readily access funds for the purposes set out in this section. Assets used to meet financial assurance requirements of this section shall not be accessible to the permit holder except as approved by the Department. Compliance with the financial assurance requirements set forth in Subpart H of Part 264 of 40 Code of Federal

Regulations (July 1, 2010 edition) shall be sufficient to meet the requirements of this subsection.

(g)   The Department may provide a copy of any filing that an applicant for a permit or a permit holder for a hazardous waste facility submits to the Department to meet the financial responsibility requirements under this section to the State Treasurer. The State Treasurer shall review the filing and provide the Department with a written opinion as to the adequacy of the filing to meet the purposes of this section, including any recommended changes.

(h)   In order to continue to hold a permit for a hazardous waste facility, a permit holder must maintain financial responsibility as required by this Part and must provide any information requested by the Department to establish that the permit holder continues to maintain financial responsibility.

(i)   An applicant for a permit or a permit holder for a hazardous waste facility shall satisfy the Department that the applicant or permit holder has met the financial responsibility requirements of this Part before the Department is required to otherwise review the application.

(j)   Repealed by Session Laws 2011-394, s. 23(a), effective July 1, 2011. (2007-107, s. 1.1(a); 2011-394, s. 23(a).)

§ 130A-295.05. Hazardous waste transfer facilities.

(a)   The owner or operator of a hazardous waste transfer facility in North Carolina shall register the facility with the Department and shall obtain a hazardous waste transfer facility identification number for the facility. In order to obtain a hazardous waste transfer facility identification number for the facility, the owner or operator of the facility shall provide all of the following information to the Department at the time of registration:

(1)   The location of the hazardous waste transfer facility.

(2)   The name of the owner of the property on which the hazardous waste transfer facility is located.

(b)   Except during transportation emergencies as determined by the Department, the temporary storage, consolidation, or commingling of hazardous waste may occur only at a hazardous waste transfer facility that has been issued a facility identification number by the Department.

(c) A hazardous waste transporter and the owner or operator of a hazardous waste transfer facility shall conduct all operations at any hazardous waste transfer facility in compliance with the requirements of 40 Code of Federal Regulations Part 263 (1 July 2006), 49 U.S.C. § 5101, et seq., and any laws, regulations, or rules enacted or adopted pursuant to these federal laws. Except as preempted under 49 U.S.C. § 5125, a hazardous waste transporter and the owner or operator of a hazardous waste transfer facility shall also conduct all operations at any hazardous waste transfer facility in compliance with all applicable State laws or rules.

(d) A hazardous waste transporter shall notify the Department, on a form prescribed by the Department, of every hazardous waste transfer facility in North Carolina that the transporter uses. A hazardous waste transporter shall retain all records that are required to be maintained for at least three years.

(e) The owner or operator of a hazardous waste transfer facility shall notify the Department, on a form prescribed by the Department, of every hazardous waste transporter that makes use of the facility. The owner or operator of a hazardous waste transfer facility shall retain all records that are required to be maintained for at least three years. (2007-107, s. 1.8(c).)

§ 130A-295.1. (See Editor's note) Limitations on permits for sanitary landfills.

§ 130A-295.2. Financial responsibility requirements for applicants and permit holders for solid waste management facilities.

(a) As used in this section:

(1) "Financial assurance" refers to the ability of an applicant or permit holder to pay the costs of assessment and remediation in the event of a release of pollutants from a facility, closure of the facility in accordance with all applicable requirements, and post-closure monitoring and maintenance of the facility.

(2) "Financial qualification" refers to the ability of an applicant or permit holder to pay the costs of proper design, construction, operation, and maintenance of the facility.

(3) "Financial responsibility" encompasses both financial assurance and financial qualification.

(b) The Commission may adopt rules governing financial responsibility requirements for applicants for permits and for permit holders to ensure the availability of sufficient funds for the proper design, construction, operation, maintenance, closure, and post-closure monitoring and maintenance of solid waste management facilities and for any corrective action the Department may require during the active life of a facility or during the closure and post-closure periods.

(c) The Department may provide a copy of any filing that an applicant for a permit or a permit holder submits to the Department to meet the financial responsibility requirements under this section to the State Treasurer. The State Treasurer shall review the filing and provide the Department with a written opinion as to the adequacy of the filing to meet the purposes of this section, including any recommended changes.

(d) The Department may, in its sole discretion, require an applicant for a permit to construct a facility to demonstrate its financial qualification for the design, construction, operation, and maintenance of a facility. The Department may require an applicant for a permit for a solid waste management facility to provide cost estimates for site investigation; land acquisition, including financing terms and land ownership; design; construction of each five-year phase, if applicable; operation; maintenance; closure; and post-closure monitoring and maintenance of the facility to the Department. The Department may allow an applicant to demonstrate its financial qualifications for only the first five-year phase of the facility. If the Department allows an applicant for a permit to demonstrate its financial qualification for only the first five-year phase of the facility, the Department shall require the applicant or permit holder to demonstrate its financial qualification for each successive five-year phase of the facility when applying for a permit to construct each successive phase of the facility.

(e) If the Department requires an applicant for a permit or a permit holder for a solid waste management facility to demonstrate its financial qualification, the applicant or permit holder shall provide an audited, certified financial statement. An applicant who is required to demonstrate its financial qualification may do so through a combination of cash deposits, insurance, and binding loan commitments from a financial institution licensed to do business in the State and rated AAA by Standard & Poor's, Moody's Investor Service, or Fitch, Inc. If assets of a parent, subsidiary, or other affiliate of the applicant or a permit holder, or a joint venturer with a direct or indirect interest in the applicant or permit holder, are proposed to be used to demonstrate financial qualification, then the party whose assets are to be used must be designated as a joint permittee with the applicant on the permit for the facility.

(f)   The applicant and permit holder for a solid waste management facility shall establish financial assurance by a method or combination of methods that will ensure that sufficient funds for closure, post-closure maintenance and monitoring, and any corrective action that the Department may require will be available during the active life of the facility, at closure, and for any post-closure period of time that the Department may require even if the applicant or permit holder becomes insolvent or ceases to reside, be incorporated, do business, or maintain assets in the State. Rules adopted by the Commission shall allow a business entity that is an applicant for a permit or a permit holder to establish financial assurance through insurance, irrevocable letters of credit, trusts, surety bonds, corporate financial tests, or any other financial device as allowed pursuant to 40 Code of Federal Regulations § 258.74 (July 1, 2010 Edition), or any combination of the foregoing shown to provide protection equivalent to the financial protection that would be provided by insurance if insurance were the only mechanism used. Assets used to meet the financial assurance requirements of this section shall be in a form that will allow the Department to readily access funds for the purposes set out in this section. Assets used to meet financial assurance requirements of this section shall not be accessible to the permit holder except as approved by the Department. Where a corporate financial test is used that is substantially similar to that allowed under 40 Code of Federal Regulations § 258.74 (July 1, 2010 Edition), the assets shall be presumed both to be readily accessible by the Department and not otherwise accessible to the permit holder.

(g)   In order to continue to hold a permit under this Article, a permit holder must maintain financial responsibility and must provide any information requested by the Department to establish that the permit holder continues to maintain financial responsibility. A permit holder shall notify the Department of any significant change in the: (i) identity of any person or structure of the business entity that holds the permit for the facility; (ii) identity of any person or structure of the business entity that owns or operates the facility; or (iii) assets of the permit holder, owner, or operator of the facility. The permit holder shall notify the Department within 30 days of a significant change. A change shall be considered significant if it has the potential to affect the financial responsibility of the permit holder, owner, or operator, or if it would result in a change in the identity of the permit holder, owner, or operator for purposes of either financial responsibility or environmental compliance review. Based on its review of the changes, the Department may require the permit holder to reestablish financial responsibility and may modify or revoke a permit, or require issuance of a new permit.

(h)   To meet the financial assurance requirements of this section, the owner or operator of a sanitary landfill shall establish financial assurance sufficient to cover a minimum of two million dollars ($2,000,000) in costs for potential assessment and corrective action at the facility. The Department may require financial assurance in a higher amount and may increase the amount of financial assurance required of a permit holder at any time based upon the types of waste disposed in the landfill, the projected amount of waste to be disposed in the landfill, the location of the landfill, potential receptors of releases from the landfill, and inflation. The financial assurance requirements of this subsection are in addition to the other financial responsibility requirements set out in this section.

(i)   The Commission may adopt rules under which a unit of local government and a solid waste management authority created pursuant to Article 22 of Chapter 153A of the General Statutes may meet the financial responsibility requirements of this section by either a local government financial test or a capital reserve fund requirement.

(j)   In addition to the other methods by which financial assurance may be established as set forth in subsection (f) of this section, the Department may allow the owner or operator of a sanitary landfill permitted on or before August 1, 2009, to meet the financial assurance requirement set forth in subsection (h) of this section by establishing a trust fund which conforms to the following minimum requirements:

(1)   The trustee shall be an entity which has the authority to act as a trustee and whose trust operations are regulated and examined by a State or federal agency.

(2)   A copy of the trust agreement shall be placed in the facility's operating record.

(3) Payments into the trust fund shall be made annually by the owner or operator over a period not to exceed five years. This period is referred to as the pay-in period.

(4) Payments into the fund shall be made in equal annual installments in amounts calculated by dividing the current cost estimate for potential assessment and corrective action at the facility, which shall not be less than two million dollars ($2,000,000) in accordance with subsection (h) of this section, by the number of years in the pay-in period.

(5) The trust fund may be terminated by the owner or operator only if the owner or operator establishes financial assurance by another method or combination of methods allowed under subsection (f) of this section.

(6) The trust agreement shall be accompanied by a formal certification of acknowledgement. (2007-550, s. 5(a); 2011-262, s. 1.)

§ 130A-295.3. Environmental compliance review requirements for applicants and permit holders.

(a) For purposes of this section, "applicant" means an applicant for a permit and a permit holder and includes the owner or operator of the facility, and, if the owner or operator is a business entity, applicant also includes: (i) the parent, subsidiary, or other affiliate of the applicant; (ii) a partner, officer, director, member, or manager of the business entity, parent, subsidiary, or other affiliate of the applicant; and (iii) any person with a direct or indirect interest in the applicant, other than a minority shareholder of a publicly traded corporation who has no involvement in management or control of the corporation or any of its parents, subsidiaries, or affiliates.

(b) The Department shall conduct an environmental compliance review of each applicant for a new permit, permit renewal, and permit amendment under this Article. The environmental compliance review shall evaluate the environmental compliance history of the applicant for a period of five years prior to the date of the application and may cover a longer period at the discretion of the Department. The environmental compliance review of an applicant may include consideration of the environmental compliance history of the parents, subsidiaries, or other affiliates of an applicant or parent that is a business entity, including any business entity or joint venturer with a direct or indirect interest in the applicant, and other facilities owned or operated by any of them. The Department shall determine the scope of the review of the environmental compliance history of the applicant, parents, subsidiaries, or other affiliates of the applicant or parent, including any business entity or joint venturer with a direct or indirect interest in the applicant, and of other facilities owned or operated by any of them. An applicant for a permit shall provide environmental compliance history information for each facility, business entity, joint venture, or other undertaking in which any of the persons listed in this subsection is or has been an owner, operator, officer, director, manager, member, or partner, or in which any of the persons listed in this subsection has had a direct or indirect interest as requested by the Department.

(c) The Department shall determine the extent to which the applicant, or a parent, subsidiary, or other affiliate of the applicant or parent, or a joint venturer with a direct or indirect interest in the applicant, has substantially complied with the requirements applicable to any activity in which any of these entities previously engaged, and has substantially complied with federal and State laws, regulations, and rules for the protection of the environment. The Department may deny an application for a permit if the applicant has a history of significant or repeated violations of statutes, rules, orders, or permit terms or conditions for the protection of the environment or for the conservation of natural resources as evidenced by civil penalty assessments, administrative or judicial compliance orders, or criminal penalties.

(d) A permit holder shall notify the Department of any significant change in its environmental compliance history or other information required by G.S. 130-295.2(g). The Department may reevaluate the environmental compliance history of a permit holder and may modify or revoke a permit or require issuance of a new permit. (2007-550, s. 6(a).)

§ 130A-295.4. Combustion products landfills.

(a) The definitions set out in G.S. 130A-290(a) apply to this section.

(b) The Department may permit a combustion products landfill to be constructed partially or entirely within areas that have been formerly used for the storage or disposal of combustion products at the same facility as the coal-fired generating unit that generates the combustion products, provided the landfill is constructed with a bottom liner system consisting of three components in accordance with this section. Of the required three components, the upper two components shall consist of two separate flexible membrane liners, with a leak detection system between the two liners. The third component shall consist of a minimum of two feet of soil underneath the bottom of those liners, with the soil having a maximum permeability of 1×10^{-7} centimeters per second. The flexible membrane liners shall have a minimum thickness of thirty one-thousandths of an inch (0.030"), except that liners consisting of high-density polyethylene shall be at least sixty one-thousandths of an inch (0.060") thick. The lower flexible membrane liner shall be installed in direct and uniform contact with the compacted soil layer. The Department may approve an alternative to the soil component of the composite liner system if the Department finds, based on modeling, that the alternative liner system will provide an equivalent or greater degree of impermeability.

(c) An applicant for a permit for a combustion products landfill shall develop and provide to the Department a response plan, which shall describe the circumstances under which corrective measures are to be taken at the landfill in the event of the detection of leaks in the leak detection system between the upper two liner components at amounts exceeding an amount specified in the response plan (as expressed in average gallons per day per acre of landfill, defined as an Action Leakage Rate). The response plan shall also describe the remedial actions that the landfill is required to undertake in response to detection of leakage in amounts in excess of the Action Leakage Rate. The Department shall review the response plan as a part of the permit application for the landfill. Compliance with performance of the landfill to prevent releases of waste to the environment may be determined based on leakage rate rather than monitoring well data. (2007-550, s. 7(b).)

§ 130A-295.5. Traffic study required for certain solid waste management facilities.

(a) An applicant for a permit for a sanitary landfill or for a transfer station shall conduct a traffic study of the impacts of the proposed facility. The Department shall include as a condition of a permit for a sanitary landfill or for a transfer station a requirement that the permit holder mitigate adverse impacts identified by the traffic study. The study shall include all of the following at a minimum:

(1)   Identification of routes from the nearest limited access highway used to access the proposed facility.

(2)   Daily and hourly traffic volumes that will result along each approach route between the nearest limited access highway and the proposed facility.

(3)   A map identifying land uses located along the identified approach routes, including, but not limited to, residential, commercial, industrial development, and agricultural operations. The map shall identify residences, schools, hospitals, nursing homes, and other significant buildings that front the approach routes.

(4)   Identification of locations on approach routes where road conditions are inadequate to handle the increased traffic associated with the proposed facility and a description of the mitigation measures proposed by the applicant to address the conditions.

(5)   A description of the potential adverse impacts of increased traffic associated with the proposed facility and the mitigation measures proposed by the applicant to address these impacts.

(6)   An analysis of the impact of any increase in freight traffic on railroads and waterways.

(b)   An applicant for a permit for a sanitary landfill or for a transfer station may satisfy the requirements of subsection (a) of this section by obtaining a certification from the Division Engineer of the Department of Transportation that the proposed facility will not have a substantial impact on highway traffic. (2007-550, s. 8(a).)

§ 130A-295.6. Additional requirements for sanitary landfills.

(a)   The applicant for a proposed sanitary landfill shall contract with a qualified third party, approved by the Department, to conduct a study of the environmental impacts of any proposed sanitary landfill, in conjunction with its application for a new permit as defined in sub-subdivisions a. through d. of subdivision (1a) of subsection (b) of G.S. 130A-295.8. The study shall meet all of the requirements set forth in G.S. 113A-4 and rules adopted pursuant to G.S. 113A-4. If an environmental impact statement is required, the Department shall publish notice of the draft environmental impact statement and shall hold a public hearing in the county where the landfill will be located no sooner than 30 days following the public notice. The Department shall consider the study of environmental impacts and any mitigation measures proposed by the applicant in deciding whether to issue or deny a permit. An applicant for a permit for a sanitary landfill shall pay all costs incurred by the Department to comply with the public notice and public hearing requirements of this subsection.

(b)   The Department shall require a buffer between any perennial stream or wetland and the nearest waste disposal unit of a sanitary landfill of at least 200 feet. The Department may approve a buffer of less than 200 feet, but in no case less than 100 feet, if it finds all of the following:

(1)   The proposed sanitary landfill or expansion of the sanitary landfill will serve a critical need in the community.

(2)   There is no feasible alternative location that would allow siting or expansion of the sanitary landfill with 200-foot buffers.

(c)   A waste disposal unit of a sanitary landfill shall not be constructed within:

(1)   A 100-year floodplain or land removed from a 100-year floodplain designation pursuant to 44 Code of Federal Regulations Part 72 (1 October 2006 Edition) as a result of man-made alterations within the floodplain such as the placement of fill, except as authorized by variance granted under G.S. 143-215.54A(b). This subdivision does not apply to land removed from a 100-year floodplain designation (i) as a result of floodplain map corrections or updates not resulting from man-made alterations of the affected areas within the floodplain, or (ii) pursuant to 44 Code of Federal Regulations Part 70 (1 October 2006 Edition) by a letter of map amendment.

(2)   A wetland, unless the applicant or permit holder can show all of the following, as to the waste disposal unit:

a.   Where applicable under section 404 of the federal Clean Water Act or applicable State wetlands laws, the presumption that a practicable alternative to the proposed waste disposal unit is available which does not involve wetlands is clearly rebutted;

b.   Construction of the waste disposal unit will not do any of the following:

1. Cause or contribute to violations of any applicable State water quality standard.

2. Violate any applicable toxic effluent standard or prohibition under section 307 of the federal Clean Water Act.

3. Jeopardize the continued existence of endangered or threatened species or result in the destruction or adverse modification of a critical habitat, protected under the federal Endangered Species Act of 1973.

4. Violate any requirement under the federal Marine Protection, Research, and Sanctuaries Act of 1972.

c. Construction of the waste disposal unit will not cause or contribute to significant degradation of wetlands.

d. To the extent required under section 404 of the federal Clean Water Act or applicable State wetlands laws, any unavoidable wetlands impacts will be mitigated.

(d) The Department shall not issue a permit to construct any disposal unit of a sanitary landfill if, at the earlier of (i) the acquisition by the applicant or permit holder of the land or of an option to purchase the land on which the waste disposal unit will be located, (ii) the application by the applicant or permit holder for a franchise agreement, or (iii) at the time of the application for a permit, any portion of the proposed waste disposal unit would be located within:

(1) Five miles of the outermost boundary of a National Wildlife Refuge.

(2) One mile of the outermost boundary of a State gameland owned, leased, or managed by the Wildlife Resources Commission pursuant to G.S. 113-306, prior to July 1, 2013, except as provided in subdivision (2a) of this subsection.

(2a) Five hundred feet of the outermost boundary of a State gameland owned, leased, or managed by the Wildlife Resources Commission pursuant to G.S. 113-306, prior to July 1, 2013, when all of the following conditions apply:

a. The waste disposal unit will only be permitted to accept construction and demolition debris waste.

b. The disposal unit is located within the primary corporate limits of a municipality located in a county with a population of less than 15,000.

c. All portions of the gameland within one mile of the disposal unit are separated from the disposal unit by a primary highway designated by the Federal Highway Administration as a U.S. Highway.

(3) Two miles of the outermost boundary of a component of the State Parks System.

(e) A sanitary landfill for the disposal of construction and demolition debris waste shall be constructed with a liner system that consists of a flexible membrane liner over two feet of soil with a maximum permeability of 1×10^{-5} centimeters per second. The flexible membrane liner shall have a minimum thickness of thirty one-thousandths of an inch (0.030"), except that a liner that consists of high-density polyethylene shall be at least sixty one-thousandths of an inch (0.060") thick. The flexible membrane liner shall be installed in direct and uniform contact with the soil layer. The Department may approve an alternative to the soil component of the liner system if the Department finds, based on modeling, that the alternative liner system will provide an equivalent or greater degree of impermeability.

(f) A sanitary landfill, other than a sanitary landfill for the disposal of construction and demolition debris waste, shall be constructed so that the post-settlement bottom elevation of the liner system, or the post-settlement bottom elevation of the waste if no liner system is required, is a minimum of four feet above both the seasonal high groundwater table and the bedrock datum plane contours. A sanitary landfill for the disposal of construction and demolition debris waste shall be constructed so that the post-settlement bottom elevation of the flexible membrane liner component of the liner system is a minimum of four feet above both the seasonal high groundwater table and the bedrock datum plane contours.

(g) A permit holder for a sanitary landfill shall develop and implement a waste screening plan. The plan shall identify measures adequate to ensure compliance with State laws and rules and any applicable local ordinances that prohibit the disposal of certain items in landfills. The plan shall address all sources of waste generation. The plan is subject to approval by the Department.

(h) The following requirements apply to any sanitary landfill for which a liner is required:

(1) A geomembrane base liner system shall be tested for leaks and damage by methods approved by the Department that ensure that the entire liner is evaluated.

(2) A leachate collection system shall be designed to return the head of the liner to 30 centimeters or less within 72 hours. The design shall be based on the precipitation that would fall on an empty cell of the sanitary landfill as a result of a 25-year-24-hour storm event. The leachate collection system shall maintain a head of less than 30 centimeters at all times during leachate recirculation. The Department may require the operator to monitor the head of the liner to demonstrate that the head is being maintained in accordance with this subdivision and any applicable rules.

(3) All leachate collection lines shall be designed and constructed to permanently allow cleaning and remote camera inspection. Remote camera inspections of the leachate collection lines shall occur upon completion of the construction and at least once every five years. Cleaning of leachate collection lines found necessary for proper functioning and to address buildup of leachate over the liner shall occur.

(4) Any pipes used to transmit leachate shall provide dual containment outside of the disposal unit. The bottom liner of a sanitary landfill shall be constructed without pipe penetrations.

(h1) With respect to requirements for daily cover at sanitary landfills, o nce the Department has approved use of an alternative method of daily cover for use at any sanitary landfill, that alternative method of daily cover shall be approved for use at all sanitary landfills located within the State.

(h2) Studies and research and development pertaining to alternative disposal techniques and waste-to-energy matters shall be conducted by certain sanitary landfills as follows:

(1) The owner or operator of any sanitary landfill permitted to receive more than 240,000 tons of waste per year shall research the development of alternative disposal technologies. In addition, the owner or operator shall allow access to nonproprietary information and provide site resources for individual research and development projects related to alternative disposal techniques for the purpose of studies that may be conducted by local community or State colleges and universities or other third-party developers or consultants. The

owner or operator shall report on research and development activities conducted pursuant to this subdivision, and any results of these activities, to the Department annually on or before July 1.

(2) The owner or operator of any sanitary landfill permitted to receive more than 240,000 tons of waste per year shall perform a feasibility study of landfill gas-to-energy, or other waste-to-energy technology, to determine opportunities for production of renewable energy from landfills in order to promote economic development and job creation in the State. The owner or operator shall initiate the study when sufficient waste is in place at the landfill to produce gas, as determined by the United States Environmental Protection Agency's Landfill Gas Emissions Model (LandGEM), and may consult and coordinate with other entities to facilitate conduct of the study, including local and State government agencies, economic development organizations, consultants, and third-party developers. The study shall specifically examine opportunities for returning a portion of the benefits derived from energy produced from the landfill to the jurisdiction within which the landfill is located in the form of direct supply of energy to the local government and its citizens, or through revenue sharing with the local government from sale of the energy, with revenues owing to the local government credited to a fund specifically designated for economic development within the jurisdiction. The owner or operator shall report on its activities associated with the study, and any results of the study, to the Department annually on or before July 1.

(i) The Department shall not issue a permit for a sanitary landfill that authorizes:

(1) A capacity of more than 55 million cubic yards of waste.

(2) A disposal area of more than 350 acres.

(3) A maximum height, including the cap and cover vegetation, of more than 250 feet above the mean natural elevation of the disposal area.

(j) This section does not apply to landfills for the disposal of land clearing and inert debris or to Type I or Type II compost facilities. (2007-543, s. 1(a)-(c); 2007-550, s. 9(a), (c); 2013-25, s. 1; 2013-410, s. 47.6; 2013-413, s. 59.1.)

§ 130A-295.7: Reserved for future codification purposes.

§ 130A-295.8. Fees applicable to permits for solid waste management facilities.

(a) The Solid Waste Management Account is established as a nonreverting account within the Department. All fees collected under this section shall be credited to the Account and shall be used to support the solid waste management program established pursuant to G.S. 130A-294.

(b) As used in this section:

(1) "Major permit modification" means an application for any change to the approved engineering plans for a sanitary landfill or transfer station permitted for a 10-year design capacity that does not constitute a "permit amendment," "new permit," or "permit modification."

(1a) "New permit" means any of the following:

a. An application for a permit for a solid waste management facility that has not been previously permitted by the Department. The term includes one site suitability review, the initial permit to construct, and one permit to operate the constructed portion of a phase included in the permit to construct.

b. An application that proposes to expand the boundary of a permitted waste management facility for the purpose of expanding the permitted activity.

c. An application that includes a proposed expansion to the boundary of a waste disposal unit within a permitted solid waste management facility.

d. An application for a substantial amendment to a solid waste permit, as defined in G.S. 130A-294.

(2) "Permit amendment" means any of the following:

a. An application for a permit to construct and one permit to operate for the second and subsequent phases of landfill development described in the approved facility plan for a permitted solid waste management facility.

b. An application for the five-year renewal of a permit for a permitted solid waste management facility or for a permit review of a permitted solid waste management facility.

c. Any application that proposes a change in ownership or corporate structure of a permitted solid waste management facility.

(3) "Permit modification" means any of the following:

a. An application for any change to the plans approved in a permit for a solid waste management facility that does not constitute a "permit amendment" or a "new permit".

b. A second or subsequent permit to operate for a constructed portion of a phase included in the permit to construct.

c. An application for a five-year limited review of a 10-year permit, as required by G.S. 130A-294(a2), including review of the operations plan, closure plan, post-closure plan, financial assurance cost estimates, environmental monitoring plans, and any other applicable plans for the facility.

(c) An applicant for a permit shall pay an application fee upon submission of an application according to the following schedule:

(1) Municipal Solid Waste Landfill accepting less than 100,000 tons/year of solid waste, New Permit (Five-Year) - $25,000.

(1a) Municipal Solid Waste Landfill accepting less than 100,000 tons/year of solid waste, New Permit (Ten-Year) - $38,500.

(2) Municipal Solid Waste Landfill accepting less than 100,000 tons/year of solid waste, Amendment (Five-Year) - $15,000.

(2a) Municipal Solid Waste Landfill accepting less than 100,000 tons/year of solid waste, Amendment (Ten-Year) - $28,500.

(3) Municipal Solid Waste Landfill accepting less than 100,000 tons/year of solid waste, Modification (Five-Year) - $1,500.

(3a) Municipal Solid Waste Landfill accepting less than 100,000 tons/year of solid waste, Major Modification (Ten-Year) - $7,500.

(4) Municipal Solid Waste Landfill accepting 100,000 tons/year or more of solid waste, New Permit (Five-Year) - $50,000.

(4a)   Municipal Solid Waste Landfill accepting 100,000 tons/year or more of solid waste, New Permit (Ten-Year) - $77,000.

(5)   Municipal Solid Waste Landfill accepting 100,000 tons/year or more of solid waste, Amendment (Five-Year) - $30,000.

(5a)   Municipal Solid Waste Landfill accepting 100,000 tons/year or more of solid waste, Amendment (Ten-Year) - $57,000.

(6)   Municipal Solid Waste Landfill accepting 100,000 tons/year or more of solid waste, Modification (Five-Year) - $3,000.

(6a)   Municipal Solid Waste Landfill accepting 100,000 tons/year or more of solid waste, Major Modification (Ten-Year) - $15,000.

(7)   Construction and Demolition Landfill accepting less than 100,000 tons/year of solid waste, New Permit (Five-Year) - $15,000.

(7a)   Construction and Demolition Landfill accepting less than 100,000 tons/year of solid waste, New Permit (Ten-Year) - $22,500.

(8)   Construction and Demolition Landfill accepting less than 100,000 tons/year of solid waste, Amendment (Five-Year) - $9,000.

(8a)   Construction and Demolition Landfill accepting less than 100,000 tons/year of solid waste, Amendment (Ten-Year) - $16,500.

(9)   Construction and Demolition Landfill accepting less than 100,000 tons/year of solid waste, Modification (Five-Year) - $1,500.

(9a)   Construction and Demolition Landfill accepting less than 100,000 tons/year of solid waste, Major Modification (Ten-Year) - $4,500.

(10)   Construction and Demolition Landfill accepting 100,000 tons/year or more of solid waste, New Permit (Five-Year) - $30,000.

(10a)   Construction and Demolition Landfill accepting 100,000 tons/year or more of solid waste, New Permit (Ten-Year) - $46,000.

(11)   Construction and Demolition Landfill accepting 100,000 tons/year or more of solid waste, Amendment (Five-Year) - $18,500.

(11a) Construction and Demolition Landfill accepting 100,000 tons/year or more of solid waste, Amendment (Ten-Year) - $34,500.

(12) Construction and Demolition Landfill accepting 100,000 tons/year or more of solid waste, Modification (Five-Year) - $2,500.

(12a) Construction and Demolition Landfill accepting 100,000 tons/year or more of solid waste, Major Modification (Ten-Year) - $9,250.

(13) Industrial Landfill accepting less than 100,000 tons/year of solid waste, New Permit (Five-Year) - $15,000.

(13a) Industrial Landfill accepting less than 100,000 tons/year of solid waste, New Permit (Ten-Year) - $22,500.

(14) Industrial Landfill accepting less than 100,000 tons/year of solid waste, Amendment (Five-Year) - $9,000.

(14a) Industrial Landfill accepting less than 100,000 tons/year of solid waste, Amendment (Ten-Year) - $16,500.

(15) Industrial Landfill accepting less than 100,000 tons/year of solid waste, Modification (Five-Year) - $1,500.

(15a) Industrial Landfill accepting less than 100,000 tons/year of solid waste, Major Modification (Ten-Year) - $4,500.

(16) Industrial Landfill accepting 100,000 tons/year or more of solid waste, New Permit (Five-Year) - $30,000.

(16a) Industrial Landfill accepting 100,000 tons/year or more of solid waste, New Permit (Ten-Year) - $46,000.

(17) Industrial Landfill accepting 100,000 tons/year or more of solid waste, Amendment (Five-Year) - $18,500.

(17a) Industrial Landfill accepting 100,000 tons/year or more of solid waste, Amendment (Ten-Year) - $34,500.

(18)　Industrial Landfill accepting 100,000 tons/year or more of solid waste, Modification (Five-Year) - $2,500.

(18a)　Industrial Landfill accepting 100,000 tons/year or more of solid waste, Major Modification (Ten-Year) - $9,250.

(19)　Tire Monofill, New Permit - $1,750.

(19a)　Tire Monofill, New Permit (Ten-Year) - $2,500.

(20)　Tire Monofill, Amendment - $1,250.

(20A)　Tire Monofill, Amendment (Ten-Year) - $2,000.

(21)　Tire Monofill, Modification - $500.

(21A)　Tire Monofill, Major Modification - $625.

(22)　Treatment and Processing, New Permit - $1,750.

(23)　Treatment and Processing, Amendment - $1,250.

(24)　Treatment and Processing, Modification - $500.

(25)　Transfer Station, New Permit (Five-Year) - $5,000.

(25a)　Transfer Station, New Permit (Ten-Year) - $7,500.

(26)　Transfer Station, Amendment (Five-Year) - $3,000.

(26a)　Transfer Station, Amendment (Ten-Year) - $5,500.

(27)　Transfer Station, Modification (Five-Year) - $500.

(27a)　Transfer Station, Major Modification (Ten-Year) - $1,500.

(28)　Incinerator, New Permit - $1,750.

(29)　Incinerator, Amendment - $1,250.

(30)　Incinerator, Modification - $500.

(31) Large Compost Facility, New Permit - $1,750.

(32) Large Compost Facility, Amendment - $1,250.

(33) Large Compost Facility, Modification - $500.

(34) Land Clearing and Inert, New Permit - $1,000.

(35) Land Clearing and Inert, Amendment - $500.

(36) Land Clearing and Inert, Modification - $250.

(d) A permitted solid waste management facility shall pay an annual permit fee on or before 1 August of each year according to the following schedule:

(1) Municipal Solid Waste Landfill - $3,500.

(2) Post-Closure Municipal Solid Waste Landfill - $1,000.

(3) Construction and Demolition Landfill - $2,750.

(4) Post-Closure Construction and Demolition Landfill - $500.

(5) Industrial Landfill - $2,750.

(6) Post-Closure Industrial Landfill - $500.

(7) Transfer Station - $750.

(8) Treatment and Processing Facility - $500.

(9) Tire Monofill - $500.

(10) Incinerator - $500.

(11) Large Compost Facility - $500.

(12) Land Clearing and Inert Debris Landfill - $500.

(e) The Department shall determine whether an application for a permit for a solid waste management facility that is subject to a fee under this section is complete within 90 days after the Department receives the application for the permit. A determination of completeness means that the application includes all required components but does not mean that the required components provide all of the information that is required for the Department to make a decision on the application. If the Department determines that an application is not complete, the Department shall notify the applicant of the components needed to complete the application. An applicant may submit additional information to the Department to cure the deficiencies in the application. The Department shall make a final determination as to whether the application is complete within the later of: (i) 90 days after the Department receives the application for the permit less the number of days that the applicant uses to provide the additional information; or (ii) 30 days after the Department receives the additional information from the applicant. The Department shall issue a draft permit decision on an application for a permit within one year after the Department determines that the application is complete. The Department shall hold a public hearing and accept written comment on the draft permit decision for a period of not less than 30 or more than 60 days after the Department issues a draft permit decision. The Department shall issue a final permit decision on an application for a permit within 90 days after the comment period on the draft permit decision closes. The Department and the applicant may mutually agree to extend any time period under this subsection. If the Department fails to act within any time period set out in this subsection, the applicant may treat the failure to act as a denial of the permit and may challenge the denial as provided in Chapter 150B of the General Statutes. (2007-550, s. 13(a); 2013-408, s. 2.)

§ 130A-295.9. Solid waste disposal tax; use of proceeds.

It is the intent that the proceeds of the solid waste disposal tax imposed by Article 5G of Chapter 105 of the General Statutes shall be used only for the following purposes:

(1) Funds credited pursuant to G.S. 105-187.63(1) to the Inactive Hazardous Sites Cleanup Fund shall be used by the Department of Environment and Natural Resources to fund the assessment and remediation of pre-1983 landfills, except up to thirteen percent (13%) of the funds credited under this subdivision may be used to fund administrative expenses related to

the assessment and remediation of pre-1983 landfills and other inactive hazardous waste sites.

(2) Funds credited pursuant to G.S. 105-187.63(3) to the Solid Waste Management Trust Fund shall be used by the Department of Environment and Natural Resources to fund grants to State agencies and units of local government to initiate or enhance local recycling programs and to provide for the management of difficult to manage solid waste, including abandoned mobile homes and household hazardous waste. Up to seven percent (7%) of the funds credited under this subdivision may be used by the Department to administer this Part. (2007-550, s. 14(b); 2009-451, s. 13.3E; 2010-31, s. 13.9(a).)

§ 130A-296: Repealed by Session Laws 1993, c. 501, s. 15.

§ 130A-297. Receipt and distribution of funds.

The Department may accept loans and grants from the federal government and other sources for carrying out the purposes of this Article, and shall adopt reasonable policies governing the administration and distribution of funds to units of local government, other State agencies, and private agencies, institutions or individuals for studies, investigations, demonstrations, surveys, planning, training, and construction or establishment of solid waste management facilities. (1969, c. 899; 1973, c. 476, s. 128; 1977, 2nd Sess., c. 1216; 1983, c. 1891, s. 2.)

§ 130A-298. Hazardous waste fund.

A nonreverting hazardous waste fund is established within the Department which shall be available to defray the cost to the State for monitoring and care of hazardous waste disposal facilities after the termination of the period during which the facility operator is required by applicable State and federal statutes, rules or regulations to remain responsible for post-closure monitoring and care. The establishment of this fund shall in no way be construed to relieve or reduce the liability of facility operators or any persons for damages caused by the facility. The fund shall be maintained by fees collected pursuant to the provisions of G.S. 130A-294(a)(6). (1981, c. 704, s. 7; 1983, c. 891, s. 2; 1989, c. 168, s. 25.)

§ 130A-299. Single agency designation.

The Department is designated as the single State agency for purposes of RCRA or any State or federal legislation enacted to promote the proper management of solid waste. (1969, c. 899; 1973, c. 476, s. 128; 1977, 2nd Sess., c. 1216; 1983, c. 891, s. 2; 1989, c. 168, s. 26.)

§ 130A-300. Effect on laws applicable to water pollution control.

This Article shall not be construed as amending, repealing or in any manner abridging or interfering with those sections of the General Statutes of North Carolina relative to the control of water pollution as now administered by the Environmental Management Commission nor shall the provisions of this Article be construed as being applicable to or in any way affecting the authority of the Environmental Management Commission to control the discharges of wastes to the waters of the State as provided in Articles 21 and 21A, Chapter 143 of the General Statutes. (1977, 2nd Sess., c. 1216; 1983, c. 891, s. 2.)

§ 130A-301. Recordation of permits for disposal of waste on land and Notice of Open Dump.

(a)   Whenever the Department approves a permit for a sanitary landfill or a facility for the disposal of hazardous waste on land, the owner of the facility shall be granted both an original permit and a copy certified by the Secretary. The permit shall include a legal description of the site that would be sufficient as a description in an instrument of conveyance.

(b)   The owner of a facility granted a permit for a sanitary landfill or a facility for the disposal of hazardous waste on land shall file the certified copy of the permit in the office of the register of deeds in the county or counties in which the land is located.

(c)   Repealed by Session Laws 2012-18, s. 1.17, effective July 1, 2012.

(d)   The permit shall not be effective unless the certified copy is filed as required under subsection (b) of this section.

(e)   When a sanitary landfill or a facility for the disposal of hazardous waste on land is sold, leased, conveyed or transferred, the deed or other instrument of transfer shall contain in the description section in no smaller type than that used in the body of the deed or instrument a statement that the property has been used as a sanitary landfill or a disposal site for hazardous waste and a reference by book and page to the recordation of the permit.

(f)   When the Department determines that an open dump exists, the Department shall notify the owner or operator of the open dump of applicable requirements to take remedial action at the site of the open dump to protect public health and the environment. If the owner or operator fails to take remedial action, the Department may record a Notice of Open Dump in the office of the register of deeds in the county or counties where the open dump is located. Not less than 30 days before recording the Notice of Open Dump, the Department shall notify the owner or operator of its intention to file a Notice of Open Dump. The Department may notify the owner or operator of its intention to file a Notice of Open Dump at the time it notifies the owner or operator of applicable requirements to take remedial action. An owner or operator may challenge a decision of the Department to file a Notice of Open Dump by filing a contested case under Article 3 of Chapter 150B of the General Statutes. If an owner or operator challenges a decision of the Department to file a Notice of Open Dump, the Department shall not file the Notice of Open Dump until the contested case is resolved, but may file a notice of pending litigation under Article 11 of Chapter 1 of the General Statutes. This power is additional and supplemental to any other power granted to the Department. This subsection does not repeal or supersede any statute or rule requiring or authorizing record notice by the owner.

(1)   The Department shall file the Notice of Open Dump in the Office of the Register of Deeds in substantially the following form:

"NOTICE OF OPEN DUMP

The Division of Waste Management of the North Carolina Department of Environment and Natural Resources has determined that an open dump exists on the property described below. The Department provides the following information regarding this open dump as a public service. This Notice is filed pursuant to G.S. 130A-301(f).

Name(s) of the record owner(s): _____

Description of the real property: _____

Description of the particular area where the open dump is located: ____

Any person who has questions regarding this Notice should contact the Division of Waste Management of the North Carolina Department of Environment and Natural Resources. The contact person for this Notice is: _____ who may be reached by telephone at _____ or by mail at _____. Requests for inspection and copying of public records regarding this open dump may be directed to _____ who may be reached by telephone at _____ or by mail at _____.

_____

Secretary of Environment and Natural Resources by _____

Date: _____."

(2)   The description of the particular area where the open dump is located shall be based on the best information available to the Department but need not be a survey plat that meets the requirements of G.S. 47-30 unless a survey plat that meets those requirements and that is approved by the Department is furnished by the owner or operator.

(3)   Repealed by Session Laws 2012-18, s. 1.17, effective July 1, 2012.

(4)   When the owner removes all solid waste from the open dump site to the satisfaction of the Department, the Department shall file a Cancellation of the Notice of Open Dump. The Cancellation shall be in a form similar to the original Notice of Open Dump and shall state that all the solid waste that constituted the open dump has been removed to the satisfaction of the Department. (1973, c. 444; c. 476, s. 128; 1977, 2nd Sess., c. 1216; 1981, c. 480, s. 3; 1983, c. 891, s. 2; 1997-330, s. 2; 1997-443, s. 11A.119(b); 2012-18, s. 1.17.)

§ 130A-301.1. Land clearing and inert debris landfills with a disposal area of 1/2 acre or less; recordation.

(a)   No landfill for the on-site disposal of land clearing and inert debris shall, at the time the landfill is sited, be sited 50 feet or less from a boundary of an adjacent property.

(b)   The owner of a landfill for the on-site disposal of land clearing and inert debris shall file a certified copy of a survey of the property on which the landfill is located in the register of deeds' office in the county in which the property is located, which survey shall accurately show the location of the landfill and the record owner of the land on which the landfill is situated.

(c)   Prior to the lease or conveyance of any lot or tract of land which directly abuts or is contiguous to the disposal area used for land clearing and inert debris, the owner of the lot or tract shall prepare a document disclosing that a portion of the property has been used as a disposal area for land clearing and inert debris or has been used to meet applicable minimum buffer requirements. The disclosure shall include a legal description of the property that would be sufficient in an instrument of conveyance and shall be filed in the register of deeds office prior to any lease or conveyance.

(d)   No public, commercial, or residential building shall be located or constructed on the property, or any portion of the property on which the landfill for the on-site disposal of land clearing and inert debris is located, 50 feet or less from the landfill. Construction of such buildings, with the exception of site preparation and foundation work, shall not commence until after closure of the on-site land clearing and inert debris landfill.

(e)   Source reduction methods including, but not limited to, chipping and mulching of land clearing and inert debris shall be utilized to the maximum degree technically and economically feasible.

(f)   The Department of Transportation is exempt from subsections (b) and (c) of this section for the on-site disposal of land clearing and inert debris on highway rights-of-way. (1993 (Reg. Sess., 1994), c. 580, s. 2.)

§ 130A-301.2: Expired September 30, 2003, pursuant to Session Laws 1995, c. 502, s. 4, as amended by Session Laws 2001-357.

§ 130A-301.3. Disposal of demolition debris generated from the decommissioning of manufacturing buildings, including electric generating stations, on-site.

(a)   A person may dispose of demolition debris from the decommissioning of manufacturing buildings, including electric generating stations, on the same site as the decommissioned buildings if the demolition debris meets all of the following requirements:

(1)   It is composed only of inert debris such as brick or other masonry materials, dirt, sand, gravel, rock, and concrete if the material, when characterized using the toxicity characteristic leaching procedure developed by the United States Environmental Protection Agency, is not a hazardous waste. The debris may contain small amounts of wood, paint, sealants, and metal associated with the inert debris.

(2)   It does not extend beyond the footprint of the decommissioned buildings and shall be at least 50 feet from the property boundary or enclosed by the walls of the building that are left in place below grade. Walls left in place below grade are not subject to the requirements of subdivision (4) of this subsection.

(3)   It is placed at least 500 feet from the nearest drinking water well.

(4)   It is placed to assure at least two feet of clean soil between any coated inert debris and the seasonal high groundwater table. Uncoated inert debris may be used as fill anywhere within the footprint of the decommissioned building or as beneficial fill on the site.

(5)   It complies with all other applicable federal, State, and local laws, regulations, rules, and ordinances.

(b)   After the decommissioning is completed or terminated, the owner or operator shall compact the demolition debris and cover it with at least two feet of compacted earth finer than a sandy texture soil. The cover of the demolition debris shall be graded so as to minimize water infiltration, promote proper drainage, and control erosion. Erosion of the cover shall be controlled by establishing suitable vegetative cover. All site stabilization should be completed within 90 days of the completed demolition.

(c)   Within 30 days of completing the final site stabilization or at least 30 days before the land, or any interest in the land, on which the demolition debris is located is transferred, whichever is earlier, the owner or owners of record of the land on which the demolition debris is located shall file each of the following with the register of deeds of the county in which the demolition debris is located:

(1) A survey plat of the property that meets the requirements of G.S. 47-30. The plat shall accurately show the location of the demolition debris in a manner that will allow the demolition debris disposal site to be accurately delineated and shall reference this section.

(2) A notice that disposal of demolition debris has been located on the land. The notice shall include a description of the land that would be sufficient as a description in an instrument of conveyance. The notice shall list the owners of record of the land at the time the notice is filed and shall reference the book and page number where the deed or other instrument by which the owners of record acquired title is located. The notice shall reference the book and page number where the survey plat required by subdivision (1) of this subsection is recorded. The notice shall reference this section, shall describe with particularity the type and size of the building or other structure that was demolished, and shall state the dates on which the demolition began and ended. The notice shall be executed by the owner or owners of record as provided in Chapter 47 of the General Statutes. The register of deeds shall record the notice and index it in the grantor index under the names of all owners of record of the land.

(d) A certified copy of both the plat and notice required by subsection (c) of this section shall also be filed with the Department. The plat and the notice shall indicate on the face of the document the book and page number where recorded.

(e) When the land, or any portion of the land, on which the demolition debris is located is sold, leased, conveyed, or transferred, the deed or other instrument of transfer shall contain a statement that the property has been used for the disposal of demolition debris. The statement shall include a reference to this section and to the book and page number where the notice required by subdivision (2) of subsection (c) of this section is recorded. (2013-55, s. 2.)

§ 130A-302. Sludge deposits at sanitary landfills.

Sludges generated by the treatment of wastewater discharges which are point sources subject to permits granted under Section 402 of the Federal Water

Pollution Control Act, as amended (P.L. 92-500), or permits generated under G.S. 143-215.1 by the Environmental Management Commission shall not be deposited in or on a sanitary landfill permitted under this Article unless in a compliance with the rules concerning solid waste adopted under this Article. (1977, 2nd Sess., c. 1216; 1983, c. 891, s. 2.)

§ 130A-303. Imminent hazard.

(a) The judgment of the Secretary that an imminent hazard exists concerning solid waste shall be supported by findings of fact made by the Secretary.

(b) In order to eliminate an imminent hazard, the Secretary may, without notice or hearing, issue an order requiring that immediate action be taken to protect the public health or the environment. This order may be directed to a generator or transporter of solid waste or to the owner or operator of a solid waste management facility. Where the imminent hazard is caused by an inactive hazardous substance or waste disposal site, the Secretary shall follow the procedures set forth in G.S. 130A-310.5. (1977, 2nd Sess., c. 1216; 1981, c. 704, s. 7; 1983, c. 891, s. 2; 1987, c. 574, s. 3; 2009-570, s. 27.)

§ 130A-304. Confidential information protected.

(a) The following information received or prepared by the Department in the course of carrying out its duties and responsibilities under this Article is confidential information and shall not be subject to disclosure under G.S. 132-6:

(1) Information which the Secretary determines is entitled to confidential treatment pursuant to G.S. 132-1.2. If the Secretary determines that information received by the Department is not entitled to confidential treatment, the Secretary shall inform the person who provided the information of that determination at the time such determination is made. The Secretary may refuse to accept or may return any information that is claimed to be confidential that the Secretary determines is not entitled to confidential treatment.

(2) Information that is confidential under any provision of federal or state law.

(3)   Information compiled in anticipation of enforcement or criminal proceedings, but only to the extent disclosure could reasonably be expected to interfere with the institution of such proceedings.

(b)   Confidential information may be disclosed to officers, employees, or authorized representatives of federal or state agencies if such disclosure is necessary to carry out a proper function of the Department or the requesting agency or when relevant in any proceeding under this Article.

(c)   Except as provided in subsection (b) of this section or as otherwise provided by law, any officer or employee of the State who knowingly discloses information designated as confidential under this section shall be guilty of a Class 1 misdemeanor and shall be removed from office or discharged from employment. (1977, 2nd Sess., c. 1216; 1983, c. 891, s. 2; 1985, c. 738, s. 5; 1987, c. 282, s. 20; 1991, c. 745, s. 2; 1993, c. 539, s. 951; 1994, Ex. Sess., c. 24, s. 14(c).)

§ 130A-305. Construction.

This Article shall be interpreted as enabling the State to obtain federal financial assistance in carrying out its solid waste management program and to obtain the authority needed to assume primary enforcement responsibility for that portion of the solid waste management program concerning the management of hazardous waste. (1983, c. 891, s. 2.)

§ 130A-306. Emergency Response Fund.

There is established under the control and direction of the Department, an Emergency Response Fund which shall be a nonreverting fund consisting of any money appropriated for such purpose by the General Assembly or available to it from grants, fees, charges, and other money paid to or recovered by or on behalf of the Department pursuant to this Article, except fees and penalties specifically designated by this Article for some other use or purpose. The Emergency Response Fund shall be treated as a special trust fund and shall be credited with interest by the State Treasurer pursuant to G.S. 147-69.2 and G.S. 147-69.3. The Fund shall be used to defray expenses incurred by the Department in developing and implementing an emergency hazardous waste remedial plan and to reimburse any federal, State or local agency and any agent or contractor for expenses incurred in developing and implementing such a plan that has been approved by the Department. These funds shall be used upon a determination that sufficient funds or corrective action cannot be obtained from other sources without incurring a delay that would significantly increase the threat to life or risk of damage to the environment. This Fund may not exceed five hundred thousand dollars ($500,000); money in excess of five hundred thousand dollars ($500,000) shall be deposited in the Inactive Hazardous Sites Cleanup Fund. The Secretary is authorized to take the necessary action to recover all costs incurred by the State for site investigation and the development and implementation of an emergency hazardous waste remedial plan, including attorney's fees and other expenses of bringing the cost recovery action from the responsible party or parties. The provisions of G.S. 130A-310.7 shall apply to actions to recover costs under this section except that: (i) reimbursement shall be to the Emergency Response Fund and (ii) the State need not show that it has complied with the provisions of Part 3 of this Article. (1983 (Reg. Sess., 1984), c. 1034, s. 74; 1989, c. 286, s. 1; 1998-215, s. 54(b).)

§ 130A-307. Reserved for future codification purposes.

§ 130A-308. Continuing releases at permitted facilities; notification of completed corrective action.

(a)   Standards adopted under G.S. 130A-294(c) and a permit issued under G.S. 130A-294(c) shall require corrective action for all releases of hazardous waste or constituents from any solid waste management unit at a treatment, storage, or disposal facility seeking a permit under G.S. 130A-294(c), regardless of the time at which waste was placed in such unit. Permits issued under G.S. 130A-294(c) which implement Section 3005 of RCRA (42 U.S.C. § 6925) shall contain schedules of compliance for corrective action if corrective action cannot be completed prior to issuance of the permit and establishment of financial assurance for completing corrective action. Notwithstanding any other provision of this section, this section shall apply only to units, facilities, and permits that are covered by Section 3004(u) of RCRA (42 U.S.C. § 6924(u)). Notwithstanding the foregoing, corrective action authorized elsewhere in this Chapter shall not be limited by this section.

(b) The definitions set out in G.S. 130A-310.31(b) apply to this subsection. Any person may submit a written request to the Department for a determination that a corrective action for a release of a hazardous waste or constituents from a solid waste management unit that is a treatment, storage, or disposal facility permitted under G.S 130A-294(c) has been completed to unrestricted use standards. A request for a determination that a corrective action at a facility has been completed to unrestricted use standards shall be accompanied by the fee required by G.S. 130A-310.39(a)(2). If the Department determines that the corrective action at a facility has been completed to unrestricted use standards, the Department shall issue a written notification that no further corrective action will be required at the facility. The notification shall state that no further corrective action will be required at the facility unless the Department later determines, based on new information or information not previously provided to the Department, that the corrective action at the facility has not been completed to unrestricted use standards or that the Department was provided with false or incomplete information. Under any of those circumstances, the Department may withdraw the notification and require responsible parties to take corrective action at a facility to bring the facility into compliance with unrestricted use standards. (1985, c. 738, s. 4; 1989, c. 168, s. 27; 1997-357, s. 4; 2001-384, s. 11; 2007-107, s. 1.1(f).)

§ 130A-309. Corrective actions beyond facility boundary.

Standards adopted under G.S. 130A-294(c) shall require that corrective action be taken beyond the facility boundary where necessary to protect human health and the environment unless the owner or operator of the facility concerned demonstrates to the satisfaction of the Department that, despite the owner or operator's best efforts, the owner or operator was unable to obtain the necessary permission to undertake such action. Such standards shall take effect upon adoption and shall apply to:

(1) All facilities operating under permits issued under G.S. 130A-294(c); and

(2) All disposal facilities, surface impoundments, and waste pile units (including any new units, replacements of existing units or lateral expansions of existing units) which receive hazardous waste after July 26, 1982.

Pending adoption of such rules, the Department shall issue corrective action orders for facilities referred to in (1) and (2), on a case-by-case basis, consistent with the purposes of this section. Notwithstanding any other provision of this section, this section shall apply only to units, facilities, and permits that are covered by Section 3004(v) of RCRA (42 U.S.C. § 6924(v)). Notwithstanding the foregoing, corrective action authorized elsewhere in this Chapter shall not be limited by this section. (1985, c. 738, s. 4; 1989, c. 168, s. 28.)

Part 2A. Nonhazardous Solid Waste Management.

§ 130A-309.01. Title.

This Part may be cited as the Solid Waste Management Act of 1989. (1989, c. 784, s. 2.)

§ 130A-309.02. Applicability.

This Part shall apply to solid waste other than hazardous waste and sludges. (1989, c. 784, s. 2.)

§ 130A-309.03. Findings, purposes.

(a)   The General Assembly finds that:

(1)   Inefficient and improper methods of managing solid waste create hazards to public health, cause pollution of air and water resources, constitute a waste of natural resources, have an adverse effect on land values, and create public nuisances.

(2)   Problems of solid waste management have become a matter statewide in scope and necessitate State action to assist local governments in improving methods and processes to promote more efficient methods of solid waste collection and disposal.

(3)   The continuing technological progress and improvements in methods of manufacture, packaging, and marketing of consumer products have resulted in an ever-mounting increase of the mass of material discarded by the purchasers

of the products, thereby necessitating a statewide approach to assisting local governments around the State with their solid waste management programs.

(4) The economic growth and population growth of our State have required increased industrial production together with related commercial and agricultural operations to meet our needs, which have resulted in a rising tide of unwanted and discarded materials.

(5) The failure or inability to economically recover material and energy resources from solid waste results in the unnecessary waste and depletion of our natural resources; such that, maximum resource recovery from solid waste and maximum recycling and reuse of the resources must be considered goals of the State.

(6) Certain solid waste, due to its quantity; concentration; or physical, chemical, biological, or infectious characteristics; is exceptionally hazardous to human health, safety, and to the environment; such that exceptional attention to the transportation, disposal, storage, and treatment of the waste is necessary to protect human health, safety, and welfare; and to protect the environment.

(7) This Part should be integrated with other State laws and rules and applicable federal law.

(b) It is the purpose of this Part to:

(1) Regulate in the most economically feasible, cost-effective, and environmentally safe manner the storage, collection, transport, separation, processing, recycling, and disposal of solid waste in order to protect the public health, safety, and welfare; enhance the environment for the people of this State; and recover resources which have the potential for further usefulness.

(2) Establish and maintain a cooperative State program of planning, technical assistance, and financial assistance for solid waste management.

(3) Require counties and municipalities to adequately plan and provide efficient, environmentally acceptable solid waste management programs; and require counties to plan for proper hazardous waste management.

(4) Require review of the design, and issue permits for the construction, operation, and closure of solid waste management facilities.

(5) Promote the application of resource recovery systems that preserve and enhance the quality of air, water, and land resources.

(6) Ensure that exceptionally hazardous solid waste is transported, disposed of, stored, and treated in a manner adequate to protect human health, safety, and welfare; and the environment.

(7) Promote the reduction, recycling, reuse, or treatment of solid waste, specifically including hazardous waste, in lieu of disposal of the waste.

(8) Promote methods and technology for the treatment, disposal, and transportation of hazardous waste which are practical, cost-effective, and economically feasible.

(9) Encourage counties and municipalities to utilize all means reasonably available to promote efficient and proper methods of managing solid waste and to promote the economical recovery of material and energy resources from solid waste, including contracting with persons to provide or operate resource recovery services or facilities on behalf of the county or municipality.

(10) Promote the education of the general public and the training of solid waste professionals to reduce the production of solid waste, to ensure proper disposal of solid waste, and to encourage recycling.

(11) Encourage the development of waste reduction and recycling as a means of managing solid waste, conserving resources, and supplying energy through planning, grants, technical assistance, and other incentives.

(12) Encourage the development of the State's recycling industry by promoting the successful development of markets for recycled items and by promoting the acceleration and advancement of the technology used in manufacturing processes that use recycled items.

(13) Give the State a leadership role in recycling efforts by granting a preference in State purchasing to products with recycled content.

(14) Require counties to develop and implement recycling programs so that valuable materials may be returned to productive use, energy and natural resources conserved, and the useful life of solid waste management facilities extended.

(15) Ensure that medical waste is transported, stored, treated, and disposed of in a manner sufficient to protect human health, safety, and welfare; and the environment.

(16) Require counties, municipalities, and State agencies to determine the full cost of providing storage, collection, transport, separation, processing, recycling, and disposal of solid waste in an environmentally safe manner; and encourage counties, municipalities, and State agencies to contract with private persons for any or all the services in order to assure that the services are provided in the most cost-effective manner. (1989, c. 784, s. 2.)

§ 130A-309.04. State solid waste management policy and goals.

(a) It is the policy of the State to promote methods of solid waste management that are alternatives to disposal in landfills and to assist units of local government with solid waste management. In furtherance of this State policy, there is established a hierarchy of methods of managing solid waste, in descending order of preference:

(1) Waste reduction at the source;

(2) Recycling and reuse;

(3) Composting;

(4) Incineration with energy recovery;

(5) Incineration without energy recovery;

(6) Disposal in landfills.

(b) It is the policy of the State to encourage research into innovative solid waste management methods and products and to encourage regional solid waste management projects.

(c) It is the goal of this State to reduce the municipal solid waste stream, primarily through source reduction, reuse, recycling, and composting, by forty percent (40%) on a per capita basis by 30 June 2001.

(1), (2) Repealed by Session Laws 1995 (Regular Session, 1996), c. 594, s. 8.

(c1)　To measure progress toward the municipal solid waste reduction goal in a given year, comparison shall be made between the amount by weight of the municipal solid waste that, during the baseline year and the given year, is received at municipal solid waste management facilities and is:

(1)　Disposed of in a landfill;

(2)　Incinerated;

(3)　Converted to tire-derived fuel; or

(4)　Converted to refuse-derived fuel.

(c2)　Comparison shall be between baseline and given years beginning on 1 July and ending on 30 June of the following year. The baseline year shall be the year beginning 1 July 1991 and ending 30 June 1992. However, a unit of local government may use an earlier baseline year if it demonstrates to the satisfaction of the Department that it has sufficient data to support the use of the earlier baseline year.

(c3)　Repealed by Session Laws 1995 (Regular Session, 1996), c. 594, s. 8.

(d)　In furtherance of the State's solid waste management policy, each State agency shall develop a solid waste management plan that is consistent with the solid waste management policy of the State.

(d1)　It is the policy of the State to obtain, to the extent practicable, economic benefits from the recovery from solid waste and reuse of material and energy resources. In furtherance of this policy, it is the goal of the State to foster partnerships between the public and private sectors that strengthen the supply of, and demand for, recyclable and reusable materials and that foster opportunities for economic development from the recovery and reuse of materials.

(e), (f) Repealed by Session Laws 1995 (Regular Session, 1996), c. 594, s. 8. (1989, c. 784, s. 2; 1991, c. 621, s. 2; 1991 (Reg. Sess., 1992), c. 1013, s. 6; 1995 (Reg. Sess., 1996), c. 594, s. 8.)

§ 130A-309.05. Regulated wastes; certain exclusions.

(a) Notwithstanding other provisions of this Article, the following waste shall be regulated pursuant to this Part:

(1) Medical waste; and

(2) Ash generated by a solid waste management facility from the burning of solid waste.

(b) Ash generated by a solid waste management facility from the burning of solid waste shall be disposed of in a properly designed solid waste disposal area that complies with standards developed by the Department for the disposal of the ash. The Department shall work with solid waste management facilities that burn solid waste to identify and develop methods for recycling and reusing incinerator ash or treated ash.

(c) Recovered material is not subject to regulation as solid waste under this Article. In order for a material that would otherwise be regulated as solid waste to qualify as a recovered material, the Department may require any person who owns or has control over the material to demonstrate that the material meets the requirements of this subsection. In order to protect public health and the environment, the Commission may adopt rules to implement this subsection. In order to qualify as a recovered material:

(1) A majority of the recovered material at a facility shall be sold, used, or reused within one year;

(2) The recovered material or the products or by-products of operations that process recovered material shall not be discharged, deposited, injected, dumped, spilled, leaked, or placed into or upon any land or water so that the products or by-products or any constituent thereof may enter other lands or be emitted into the air or discharged into any waters including groundwaters, or otherwise enter the environment or pose a threat to public health and safety; and

(3) The recovered material shall not be a hazardous waste or have been recovered from a hazardous waste. (1989, c. 784, s. 2; 1995 (Reg. Sess., 1996), c. 594, s. 9.)

§ 130A-309.06. Additional powers and duties of the Department.

(a) In addition to other powers and duties set forth in this Part, the Department shall:

(1) Develop a comprehensive solid waste management plan consistent with this Part. The plan shall be developed in consultation with units of local government and shall be updated at least every three years. In developing the State solid waste management plan, the Department shall hold public hearings around the State and shall give notice of these public hearings to all units of local government and regional planning agencies.

(2) Provide guidance for the orderly collection, transportation, storage, separation, processing, recovery, recycling, and disposal of solid waste throughout the State.

(3) Encourage coordinated local activity for solid waste management within a common geographical area.

(4) Provide planning, technical, and financial assistance to units of local government and State agencies for reduction, recycling, reuse, and processing of solid waste and for safe and environmentally sound solid waste management and disposal.

(5) Cooperate with appropriate federal agencies, local governments, and private organizations in carrying out the provisions of this Part.

(6) Promote and assist the development of solid waste reduction, recycling, and resource recovery programs that preserve and enhance the quality of the air, water, and other natural resources of the State.

(7) Maintain a directory of recycling and resource recovery systems in the State and provide assistance with matching recovered materials with markets.

(8) Manage a program of grants for programs for recycling and special waste management, and for programs that provide for the safe and proper management of solid waste.

(9) Provide for the education of the general public and the training of solid waste management professionals to reduce the production of solid waste, to

ensure proper processing and disposal of solid waste, and to encourage recycling and solid waste reduction.

(10) Develop descriptive literature to inform units of local government of their solid waste management responsibilities and opportunities.

(11) Repealed by Session Laws 1995 (Regular Session, 1996), c. 594, s. 10.

(12) Provide and maintain recycling bins for the collection and recycling of newspaper, aluminum cans, glass containers, and recyclable plastic beverage containers at the North Carolina Zoological Park.

(13) Identify, based on reports required under G.S. 130A-309.14 and any other relevant information, those materials in the municipal solid waste stream that are marketable in the State or any portion thereof and that should be recovered from the waste stream prior to treatment or disposal.

(14) Identify and analyze, with assistance from the Department of Commerce pursuant to G.S. 130A-309.14, components of the State's recycling industry and present and potential markets for recyclable materials in this State, other states, and foreign countries.

(b) Repealed by Session Laws 2007-550, s. 6(b), effective August 1, 2007, and applicable to any application for a permit for a solid waste management facility that is pending on that date.

(c) The Department shall report to the Environmental Review Commission on or before 15 January of each year on the status of solid waste management efforts in the State. The report shall include:

(1) A comprehensive analysis, to be updated in each report, of solid waste generation and disposal in the State projected for the 20-year period beginning on 1 July 1991.

(2) The total amounts of solid waste recycled and disposed of and the methods of solid waste recycling and disposal used during the calendar year prior to the year in which the report is published.

(3) An evaluation of the development and implementation of local solid waste management programs and county and municipal recycling programs.

(4) An evaluation of the success of each county or group of counties in meeting the municipal solid waste reduction goal established in G.S. 130A-309.04.

(5) Recommendations concerning existing and potential programs for solid waste reduction and recycling that would be appropriate for units of local government and State agencies to implement to meet the requirements of this Part.

(6) An evaluation of the recycling industry, the markets for recycled materials, the recycling of polystyrene, and the success of State, local, and private industry efforts to enhance the markets for these materials.

(7) Recommendations to the Governor and the Environmental Review Commission to improve the management and recycling of solid waste in the State, including any proposed legislation to implement the recommendations.

(8) A description of the condition of the Solid Waste Management Trust Fund and the use of all funds allocated from the Solid Waste Management Trust Fund, as required by G.S. 130A-309.12(c).

(9) A description of the review and revision of bid procedures and the purchase and use of reusable, refillable, repairable, more durable, and less toxic supplies and products by both the Department of Administration and the Department of Transportation, as required by G.S. 130A-309.14(a1)(3).

(10) A description of the implementation of the North Carolina Scrap Tire Disposal Act that includes the amount of revenue used for grants and to clean up nuisance tire collection under the provisions of G.S 130A-309.64.

(11) A description of the management of white goods in the State, as required by G.S. 130A-309.85.

(12) A summary of the report by the Department of Transportation on the amounts and types of recycled materials that were specified or used in contracts that were entered into by the Department of Transportation during the previous fiscal year, as required by G.S. 136-28.8(g).

(13) Repealed by Session Laws 2010-142, s. 1, effective July 22, 2010.

(14)   (Expiring October 1, 2023) A description of the activities related to the management of abandoned manufactured homes in the State in accordance with G.S. 130A-117, the beginning and ending balances in the Solid Waste Management Trust Fund for the reporting period and the amount of funds used, itemized by county, for grants made under Part 2F of Article 9 of Chapter 130A of the General Statutes.

(d)   Repealed by Session Laws 2001-452, s. 3.1, effective October 28, 2001. (1989, c. 784, s. 2; 1991, c. 336, s. 4; c. 621, ss. 3, 4; 1993, c. 250, s. 3; 1995 (Reg. Sess., 1996), c. 594, s. 10; 2001-452, s. 3.1; 2007-550, s. 6(b); 2008-136, s. 2; 2010-142, s. 1; 2013-360, s. 14.16(d).)

§ 130A-309.07.   State solid waste management plan.

The State solid waste management plan shall include, at a minimum:

(1)   Procedures to encourage cooperative efforts in solid waste management by counties and municipalities and groups of counties and municipalities where appropriate, including the establishment of joint agencies pursuant to G.S. 160A-462.

(2)   Provisions for the continuation of existing effective regional resource recovery, recycling, and solid waste management facilities and programs.

(3)   Planning guidance and technical assistance to counties and municipalities to aid in meeting the municipal solid waste reduction goals established in G.S. 130A-309.04.

(4)   Planning guidance and technical assistance to counties and municipalities to assist the development and implementation of solid waste reduction programs.

(5)   Technical assistance to counties and municipalities in determining the full cost for solid waste management as required in G.S. 130A-309.08.

(6)   Planning guidance and technical assistance to counties and municipalities to assist the development and implementation of programs for alternative disposal, processing, or recycling of the solid wastes prohibited from disposal in landfills pursuant to G.S. 130A-309.10 and for special wastes.

(7) A public education program, to be developed in cooperation with the Department of Public Instruction, units of local government, other State agencies, and business and industry organizations, to inform the public of the need for and the benefits of recycling solid waste and reducing the amounts of solid and hazardous waste generated and disposed of in the State. The public education program shall be implemented through public workshops and through the use of brochures, reports, public service announcements, and other materials.

(8) Provisions to encourage partnerships between the public and private sectors that strengthen the supply of, and demand for, recyclable materials and that foster opportunities for economic development from the recovery and reuse of materials. (1989, c. 784, s. 2; 1991, c. 621, s. 5; 1995 (Reg. Sess., 1996), c. 594, s. 11.)

§ 130A-309.08. Determination of cost for solid waste management; local solid waste management fees.

(a) Each county and each municipality shall annually determine the full cost for solid waste management within the service area of the county or municipality for the preceding year. The Commission shall establish by rule the method for units of local government to use in calculating full cost.

(b) Each municipality shall establish a system to inform, no less than once a year, residential and nonresidential users of solid waste management services within the municipality's service area of the user's share, on an average or individual basis, of the full cost for solid waste management as determined pursuant to subsection (a) of this section. Counties shall provide the information required of municipalities only to residential and nonresidential users of solid waste management services within the county's service area that are not served by a municipality. Municipalities shall include costs charged to them or to persons contracting with them for disposal of solid waste in the full cost information provided to residential and nonresidential users of solid waste management services. Counties and municipalities are encouraged to operate their solid waste management systems through use of an enterprise fund.

(c) For purposes of this section, "service area" means the area in which the county or municipality provides, directly or by contract, solid waste management services. The provisions of this section shall not be construed to require a person operating under a franchise contract or other agreement to collect or dispose of solid waste within the service area of a county or municipality to make the calculations or to establish a system to provide the information required under this section, unless such person agrees to do so as part of such franchise contract or other agreement.

(d) A county may charge fees for the collection, processing, or disposal of solid waste as provided in Article 15 of Chapter 153A of the General Statutes. A city may charge fees for the collection, processing, or disposal of solid waste as provided in Article 16 of Chapter 160A of the General Statutes.

(e), (f) Repealed by Session Laws 1995 (Regular Session, 1996), c. 594, s. 12. (1989, c. 784, s. 2; 1991, c. 621, s. 6; 1995 (Reg. Sess., 1996), c. 594, s. 12.)

§ 130A-309.09: Recodified as §§ 130A-309.09A to 130A-309.09C by Session Laws 1991, c. 621, ss. 7 to 10.

§ 130A-309.09A. Local government solid waste responsibilities.

(a) The governing board of each unit of local government shall assess local solid waste collection services and disposal capacity and shall determine the adequacy of collection services and disposal capacity to meet local needs and to protect human health and the environment. Each unit of local government shall implement programs and take other actions that it determines are necessary to address deficiencies in service or capacity required to meet local needs and to protect human health and the environment. A unit of local government may adopt ordinances governing the disposal, in facilities that it operates, of solid waste generated outside of the area designated to be served by the facility. Such ordinances shall not be construed to apply to privately operated disposal facilities located within the boundaries of the unit of local government.

(b) Units of local government shall make a good-faith effort to achieve the State's forty percent (40%) municipal solid waste reduction goal and to comply with the State's comprehensive solid waste management plan.

(c) Repealed by Session Laws 1995 (Regular Session, 1996), c. 594, s. 12.

(d) In order to assess the progress in meeting the goal set out in G.S. 130A-309.04, each unit of local government shall report to the Department on the solid waste management programs and waste reduction activities within the unit of local government by 1 September of each year. At a minimum, the report shall include:

(1) A description of public education programs on recycling.

(2) The amount of solid waste received at municipal solid waste management facilities, by type of solid waste.

(3) The amount and type of materials from the solid waste stream that were recycled.

(4) The percentage of the population participating in various types of recycling activities instituted.

(5) The annual reduction in municipal solid waste, measured as provided in G.S. 130A-309.04.

(6) Repealed by Session Laws 2013-409, s. 1, effective August 23, 2013.

(7) A statement of the costs of solid waste management programs implemented by the unit of local government and the methods of financing those costs.

(8) Information regarding permanent recycling programs for discarded computer equipment and televisions for which funds are received pursuant to G.S. 130A-309.137, and information on operative interlocal agreements executed in conjunction with funds received, if any.

(9) A description of the disaster debris management program.

(10) A description of scrap tire disposal procedures.

(11) A description of white goods management procedures.

(12) Information regarding the prevention of illegal disposal and management of litter.

(e) Repealed by Session Laws 1995 (Regular Session, 1996), c. 594, s. 13.

(f) Each operator of a municipal solid waste management facility shall weigh all solid waste when it is received.

(g) A unit of local government that is a collector of municipal solid waste shall not knowingly collect for disposal, and the owner or operator of a municipal solid waste management facility that is owned or operated by a unit of local government shall not knowingly dispose of, any type or form of municipal solid waste that is generated within the boundaries of a unit of local government that by ordinance:

(1) Prohibits generators or collectors of municipal solid waste from disposing of that type or form of municipal solid waste.

(2) Requires generators or collectors of municipal solid waste to recycle that type or form of municipal solid waste.

(h) The storage, retention, and use of nonhazardous recyclable materials, including asphalt pavement, rap, or roofing shingles, shall be encouraged by units of local government. A unit of local government shall not impede the storage, retention, or use of nonhazardous recyclable materials in properly zoned storage facilities through the regulation of the height or setback of recyclable material stockpiles, except when such facilities are located on lots within 200 yards of residential districts. (1989, c. 784, s. 2; 1989 (Reg. Sess., 1990), c. 1009, s. 4; 1991, c. 621, s. 7; 1995 (Reg. Sess., 1996), c. 594, s. 13; 2007-550, s. 16.2; 2008-136, s. 3; 2008-198, s. 11.4; 2008-208, ss. 2, 7; 2009-484, s. 16(a), (b); 2009-550, s. 10(a), (b); 2010-67, ss. 1(a)-(d), 3(a), (b); 2013-409, s. 1; 2013-413, s. 50.)

§ 130A-309.09B. Local government waste reduction programs.

(a) Each unit of local government shall establish and maintain a solid waste reduction program. The following requirements shall apply:

(1) Demolition debris consisting of used asphalt or used asphalt mixed with dirt, sand, gravel, rock, concrete, or similar nonhazardous material may be used as fill and need not be disposed of in a permitted landfill or solid waste disposal

facility, provided that demolition debris may not be placed in the waters of the State or at or below the seasonal high water table.

(2) Repealed by Session Laws 1991, c. 621, s. 8.

(3) Units of local government are encouraged to separate marketable plastics, glass, metal, and all grades of paper for recycling prior to final disposal and are further encouraged to recycle yard trash and other organic solid waste into compost available for agricultural and other acceptable uses.

(b) To the maximum extent practicable, units of local government should participate in the preparation and implementation of joint waste reduction and solid waste management programs, whether through joint agencies established pursuant to G.S. 153A-421, G.S. 160A-462, or any other means provided by law. Nothing in a county's solid waste management or waste reduction program shall affect the authority of a municipality to franchise or otherwise provide for the collection of solid waste generated within the boundaries of the municipality.

(c) through (e) Repealed by Session Laws 1995 (Regular Session, 1996), c. 594, s. 14.

(f) A county or counties and its or their municipalities may jointly determine, through a joint agency established pursuant to G.S. 153A-421 or G.S. 160A-462, which local governmental agency shall administer a solid waste management or waste reduction program.

(g) Repealed by Session Laws 1995 (Regular Session, 1996), c. 594, s. 14. (1989, c. 784, s. 2; 1989 (Reg. Sess., 1990), c. 1009, s. 4; 1991, c. 537, s. 2; c. 621, s. 8; 1993, c. 86, s. 1; 1995 (Reg. Sess., 1996), c. 594, s. 14; 2013-409, s. 2.)

§ 130A-309.09C. Additional powers of local governments; construction of this Part; effect of noncompliance.

(a) To effect the purposes of this Part, counties and municipalities are authorized, in addition to other powers granted pursuant to this Part:

(1) To contract with persons to provide resource recovery services or operate resource recovery facilities on behalf of the county or municipality.

(2) To indemnify persons providing resource recovery services or operating resource recovery facilities for liabilities or claims arising out of the provision or operation of such services or facilities that are not the result of the sole negligence of the persons providing the services or operating the facilities.

(3) To contract with persons to provide solid waste disposal services or operate solid waste disposal facilities on behalf of the county or municipality.

(b) A county or municipality may enter into a written agreement with other persons, including persons transporting solid waste, to undertake to fulfill some or all of the county's or municipality's responsibilities under this Part.

(c) Nothing in this Part shall be construed to prevent the governing board of any county or municipality from providing by ordinance or regulation for solid waste management standards which are stricter or more extensive than those imposed by the State solid waste management program and rules and orders issued to implement the State program.

(d) Nothing in this Part or in any rule adopted by any agency shall be construed to require any county or municipality to participate in any regional solid waste management until the governing board of the county or municipality has determined that participation in such a program is economically feasible for that county or municipality. Nothing in this Part or in any special or local act or in any rule adopted by any agency shall be construed to limit the authority of a municipality to regulate the disposal of solid waste located within its boundaries or generated within its boundaries so long as a facility for any such disposal has been approved by the Department, unless the municipality is included within a solid waste management program created under a joint agency or special or local act. If bonds had been issued to finance a solid waste management program in reliance on State law granting to a unit of local government, a region, or a special district the responsibility for the solid waste management program, nothing herein shall permit any governmental agency to withdraw from the program if the agency's participation is necessary for the financial feasibility of the project, so long as the bonds are outstanding.

(e) Nothing in this Part or in any rule adopted by any State agency pursuant to this Part shall require any person to subscribe to any private solid waste collection service.

(f) In the event a region, special district, or other entity by special act or joint agency, has been established to manage solid waste, any duty or responsibility or penalty imposed under this Part on a unit of local government shall apply to such region, special district, or other entity to the extent of the grant of the duty or responsibility or imposition of such penalty. To the same extent, such region, special district, or other entity shall be eligible for grants or other benefits provided pursuant to this Part.

(g)   In addition to any other penalties provided by law, a unit of local government that does not comply with the requirements of G.S. 130A-309.09A(b), G.S. 130A-309.09A(d), and G.S. 130A-309.09B(a) shall not be eligible for grants from the Solid Waste Management Trust Fund or the White Goods Management Account and shall not receive the proceeds of the scrap tire disposal tax imposed by Article 5B of Chapter 105 of the General Statutes or the proceeds of the white goods disposal tax imposed by Article 5C of Chapter 105 of the General Statutes to which the unit of local government would otherwise be entitled. The Secretary shall notify the Secretary of Revenue to withhold payment of these funds to any unit of local government that fails to comply with the requirements of G.S. 130A-309.09A(b), G.S. 130A-309.09A(d), and G.S. 130A-309.09B(a). Proceeds of the scrap tire disposal tax that are withheld pursuant to this subsection shall be credited to the General Fund and may be used as provided in G.S. 130A-309.64. Proceeds of the white goods disposal tax that are withheld pursuant to this subsection shall be credited to the General Fund and may be used as provided in G.S. 130A-309.83. (1989, c. 784, s. 2; 1989 (Reg. Sess., 1990), c. 1009, s. 4; 1991, c. 621, s. 9; 1995 (Reg. Sess., 1996), c. 594, s. 15; 2013-360, ss. 14.16(e), 14.17(d); 2013-409, s. 3.)

§ 130A-309.09D.   Responsibilities of generators of municipal solid waste owners and operators of privately owned solid waste management facilities and collectors of municipal solid waste.

(a)   A generator of municipal solid waste shall not knowingly dispose of, a collector of municipal solid waste shall not knowingly collect for disposal, and the owner or operator of a privately owned or operated municipal solid waste management facility shall not knowingly dispose of, any type or form of municipal solid waste that is generated within the boundaries of a unit of local government that by ordinance:

(1)   Prohibits generators or collectors of municipal solid waste from disposing of that type or form of municipal solid waste.

(2) Requires generators or collectors of municipal solid waste to recycle that type or form of municipal solid waste.

(b) On or before 1 August, the owner or operator of a privately owned solid waste management facility shall report to the Department, for the previous year beginning 1 July and ending 30 June, the amount by weight of the solid waste that was received at the facility and disposed of in a landfill, incinerated, or converted to fuel. To the maximum extent practicable, the reports shall indicate by weight the county of origin of all solid waste. The owner or operator shall transmit a copy of the report to the county in which the facility is located and to each county from which solid waste originated.

(c) A generator of industrial solid waste that owns and operates an industrial solid waste facility for the management of industrial solid waste generated by that generator shall develop a 10-year waste management plan. The plan shall be updated at least every three years. In order to assure compliance with this subsection, each generator to which this subsection applies shall provide the Department with a copy of its current plan upon request by the Department. Each generator to which this subsection applies shall file a report on its implementation of the plan required by this subsection with the Department by 1 August of each year. A generator to which this subsection applies may provide the Department with a copy of a current plan prepared pursuant to an ordinance adopted by a unit of local government or prepared for any other purpose if the plan meets the requirements of this subsection. The plan shall have the following components:

(1) A waste reduction goal established by the generator.

(2) Options for the management and reduction of wastes evaluated by the generator.

(3) A waste management strategy, including plans for waste reduction and waste disposal, for the 10-year period covered by the plan. (1991, c. 621, s. 11; 1995 (Reg. Sess., 1996), c. 594, s. 16.)

§ 130A-309.10. Prohibited acts relating to packaging; coded labeling of plastic containers required; disposal of certain solid wastes in landfills or by incineration prohibited.

(a) No beverage shall be sold or offered for sale within the State in a beverage container designed and constructed so that the container is opened by detaching a metal ring or tab.

(b) No person shall distribute, sell, or offer for sale in this State, any product packaged in a container or packing material manufactured with fully halogenated chlorofluorocarbons (CFC). Producers of containers or packing material manufactured with chlorofluorocarbons (CFC) are urged to introduce alternative packaging materials that are environmentally compatible.

(c) (1) No plastic bag shall be provided at any retail outlet to any retail customer to use for the purpose of carrying items purchased by that customer unless the bag is composed of material that is recyclable.

(2) It is the goal of the State that at least twenty-five percent (25%) of the plastic bags provided at retail outlets in the State to retail customers for carrying items purchased by the customer be recycled.

(d) (1) No person shall distribute, sell, or offer for sale in this State any polystyrene foam product that is to be used in conjunction with food for human consumption unless the product is composed of material that is recyclable.

(2) Repealed by Session Laws 1995, c. 321, s. 1.

(e) No person shall distribute, sell, or offer for sale in this State any rigid plastic container, including a plastic beverage container, unless the container has a molded label indicating the plastic resin used to produce the container. The code shall consist of a number placed within three triangulated arrows and letters placed below the triangulated arrows. The three arrows shall form an equilateral triangle with the common point of each line forming each angle of the triangle at the midpoint of each arrow and rounded with a short radius. The arrowhead of each arrow shall be at the midpoint of each side of the triangle with a short gap separating the arrowhead from the base of the adjacent arrow. The triangle formed by the three arrows curved at their midpoints shall depict a clockwise path around the code number. The label shall appear on or near the bottom of the container and be clearly visible. A container having a capacity of less than eight fluid ounces or more than five gallons is exempt from the requirements of this subsection. The numbers and letters shall be as follows:

(1) For polyethylene terephthalate, the letters "PETE" and the number 1.

(2) For high density polyethylene, the letters "HDPE" and the number 2.

(3) For vinyl, the letter "V" and the number 3.

(4) For low density polyethylene, the letters "LDPE" and the number 4.

(5) For polypropylene, the letters "PP" and the number 5.

(6) For polystyrene, the letters "PS" and the number 6.

(7) For any other, the letters "OTHER" and the number 7.

(e1) (See Editor's note for applicability) No person shall distribute, sell, or offer for sale in this State any rigid plastic container, including a plastic beverage container labeled "degradable," "biodegradable," "compostable," or other words suggesting the container will biodegrade unless (i) the container complies with the requirements of subsection (e) of this section and (ii) the container includes a label with the statement "Not Recyclable, Do Not Recycle" in print of the same color, contrast, font, and size as the language suggesting the container will biodegrade.

(f) No person shall knowingly dispose of the following solid wastes in landfills:

(1) Repealed by Session Laws 1991, c. 375, s. 1.

(2) Used oil.

(3) Yard trash, except in landfills approved for the disposal of yard trash under rules adopted by the Commission. Yard trash that is source separated from solid waste may be accepted at a solid waste disposal area where the area provides and maintains separate yard trash composting facilities.

(4) White goods.

(5) Antifreeze (ethylene glycol).

(6) Aluminum cans.

(7) Whole scrap tires, as provided in G.S. 130A-309.58(b). The prohibition on disposal of whole scrap tires in landfills applies to all whole pneumatic rubber coverings, but does not apply to whole solid rubber coverings.

(8) Lead-acid batteries, as provided in G.S. 130A-309.70.

(9) Repealed by Session Laws 2011-394, s. 4, effective July 1, 2011.

(10) Motor vehicle oil filters.

(11) Recyclable rigid plastic containers that are required to be labeled as provided in subsection (e) of this section, that have a neck smaller than the body of the container, and that accept a screw top, snap cap, or other closure. The prohibition on disposal of recyclable rigid plastic containers in landfills does not apply to rigid plastic containers that are intended for use in the sale or distribution of motor oil or pesticides.

(12) Wooden pallets, except that wooden pallets may be disposed of in a landfill that is permitted to only accept construction and demolition debris.

(13) Oyster shells.

(14) Discarded computer equipment, as defined in G.S. 130A-309.131.

(15) Discarded televisions, as defined in G.S. 130A-309.131.

(f1) No person shall knowingly dispose of the following solid wastes by incineration in an incinerator for which a permit is required under this Article:

(1) Antifreeze (ethylene glycol) used solely in motor vehicles.

(2) Aluminum cans.

(3) Repealed by Session Laws 1995 (Regular Session, 1996), c. 594, s. 17.

(4) White goods.

(5) Lead-acid batteries, as provided in G.S. 130A-309.70.

(6) Repealed by Session Laws 2011-394, s. 4, effective July 1, 2011.

(7) Discarded computer equipment, as defined in G.S. 130A-309.131.

(8) Discarded televisions, as defined in G.S. 130A-309.131.

(f2) Subsections (f1) and (f3) of this section shall not apply to solid waste incinerated in an incinerator solely owned and operated by the generator of the solid waste. Subsection (f1) of this section shall not apply to antifreeze (ethylene glycol) that cannot be recycled or reclaimed to make it usable as antifreeze in a motor vehicle.

(f3) Holders of on-premises malt beverage permits, on-premises unfortified wine permits, on-premises fortified wine permits, and mixed beverages permits shall not knowingly dispose of beverage containers that are required to be recycled under G.S. 18B-1006.1 in landfills or by incineration in an incinerator for which a permit is required under this Article.

(g) Repealed by Session Laws 1995 (Regular Session, 1996), c. 594, s. 17.

(h) The accidental or occasional disposal of small amounts of prohibited solid waste by landfill shall not be construed as a violation of subsection (f) or (f3) of this section.

(i) The accidental or occasional disposal of small amounts of prohibited solid waste by incineration shall not be construed as a violation of subsection (f1) or (f3) of this section if the Department has approved a plan for the incinerator as provided in subsection (j) of this section or if the incinerator is exempt from subsection (j) of this section.

(j) The Department may issue a permit pursuant to this Article for an incinerator that is subject to subsection (f1) of this section only if the applicant for the permit has a plan approved by the Department pursuant to this subsection. The applicant shall file the plan at the time of the application for the permit. The Department shall approve a plan only if it complies with the requirements of this subsection. The plan shall provide for the implementation of a program to prevent the incineration of the solid waste listed in subsections (f1) and (f3) of this section. The program shall include the random visual inspection prior to incineration of at least ten percent (10%) of the solid waste to be incinerated. The program shall also provide for the retention of the records of the random visual inspections and the training of personnel to recognize the solid waste listed in subsections (f1) and (f3) of this section. If a random visual inspection discovers solid waste that may not be incinerated pursuant to subsections (f1) and (f3) of this section, the program shall provide that the operator of the incinerator shall dispose of the solid waste in accordance with applicable federal and State laws, regulations, and rules. This subsection does not apply to an incinerator that disposes only of medical waste.

(k)   A county or city may petition the Department for a waiver from the prohibition on disposal of a material described in subdivisions (9), (10), (11), (12), and (13) of subsection (f) of this section and subsection (f3) of this section in a landfill based on a showing that prohibiting the disposal of the material would constitute an economic hardship.

(l)   Oyster shells that are delivered to a landfill shall be stored at the landfill for at least 90 days or until they are removed for recycling. If oyster shells that are stored at a landfill are not removed for recycling within 90 days of delivery to the landfill, then, notwithstanding subdivision (13) of subsection (f) of this section, the oyster shells may be disposed of in the landfill.

(m)   No person shall knowingly dispose of fluorescent lights and thermostats that contain mercury in a sanitary landfill for the disposal of construction and demolition debris waste that is unlined or in any other landfill that is unlined. (1989, c. 784, s. 2; 1991, c. 23, s. 1; c. 375, s. 1; 1991 (Reg. Sess., 1992), c. 932, ss. 1, 2; 1993, c. 290, s. 1; 1995, c. 321, s. 1; c. 504, s. 9; 1995 (Reg. Sess., 1996), c. 594, s. 17; 2001-440, ss. 3.1, 3.2; 2005-348, s. 3; 2005-362, ss. 2, 3; 2006-226, s. 24(a); 2006-264, ss. 98.5(a), (c); 2007-550, ss. 16.3, 16.4; 2008-198, s. 11.4; 2008-208, ss. 3, 4, 7; 2009-499, s. 1; 2009-484, s. 16(a), (b); 2009-550, s. 10(a), (b); 2010-67, ss. 1(a)-(d), 4(a), (b); 2010-142, s. 10; 2010-180, s. 14(b); 2011-394, s. 4; 2012-194, s. 28; 2012-201, s. 3; 2013-74, s. 1.)

§ 130A-309.11. Compost standards and applications.

(a)   In order to protect the State's land and water resources, compost produced, utilized, or disposed of by the composting process at solid waste management facilities in the State must meet criteria established by the Department.

(b)   The Commission shall adopt rules to establish standards for the production of compost. Rules shall be adopted not later than 24 months after the initiation of rule making. Such rules shall include:

(1) Requirements necessary to produce hygienically safe compost products for varying applications.

(2) A classification scheme for compost based on:

a. The types of waste composted, including at least one type containing only yard trash;

b. The maturity of the compost, including at least three degrees of decomposition for fresh, semi-mature, and mature; and

c. The levels of organic and inorganic constituents in the compost.

(c) The compost classification scheme shall address:

(1) Methods for measurement of the compost maturity.

(2) Particle sizes.

(3) Moisture content.

(4) Average levels of organic and inorganic constituents, including heavy metals, for such classes of compost as the Department establishes, and the analytical methods to determine those levels.

(d) The Commission shall adopt rules to prescribe the allowable uses and application rates of compost. Rules shall be adopted not later than 24 months after the initiation of rule making. Such rules shall be based on the following criteria:

(1) The total quantity of organic and inorganic constituents, including heavy metals, allowed to be applied through the addition of compost to the soil per acre per year.

(2) The allowable uses of compost based on maturity and type of compost.

(e) If compost is produced which does not meet the criteria prescribed by the Department for agricultural and other use, the compost must be reprocessed or disposed of in a manner approved by the Department, unless a different application is specifically permitted by the Department. (1989, c. 784, s. 2; 1995 (Reg. Sess., 1996), c. 594, s. 18.)

§ 130A-309.12: Repealed by Session Laws 2013-360, s. 14.18(b), effective July 1, 2013.

§ 130A-309.13. Solid Waste Management Outreach Program.

(a) The Department shall develop an outreach program to promote waste reduction and recycling. From funds available to the Department for this program, the Department may engage in any of the following outreach activities:

(1) Provide public education regarding waste reduction and recycling.

(2) Provide technical assistance regarding waste reduction and recycling to units of local government.

(3) Conduct research on the solid waste stream in North Carolina.

(4) Develop secondary materials markets by providing technical and financial support, including providing technical and financial support to private recycling businesses, including use of processed scrap tire materials.

(5) Provide funding for the activities of the Division of Environmental Assistance and Outreach.

(b) It is the intent of the General Assembly to allow the Department to satisfy grant obligations that extend beyond the end of the fiscal year.

(c) The Department shall include in the report required by G.S. 130A-309.06(c) a description of the outreach program under this section. This report shall specify the type of outreach activity under each of subdivisions (1) through (5) under subsection (a) of this section and the amount of program funds the Department expended for each activity during the previous year. (2013-360, s. 14.18(c).)

§ 130A-309.14. Duties of State agencies.

(a) Each State agency, including the General Assembly, the General Court of Justice, and The University of North Carolina shall:

(1) Establish a program in cooperation with the Department and the Department of Administration for the collection of all recyclable materials generated in State offices throughout the State. The program shall provide that recycling containers are readily accessible on each floor where State employees are located in a building occupied by a State agency. Recycling containers required pursuant to this subdivision shall be clearly labeled to identify the types of recyclable materials to be deposited in each container and, to the extent practicable, recycling containers for glass, plastic, and aluminum shall be located near trash receptacles. The program shall provide for the collection of all of the following recyclable materials.

a. Aluminum.

b. Newspaper.

c. Sorted office paper.

d. Recyclable glass.

e. Plastic bottles.

As used in this subdivision, the term "sorted office paper" means paper used in offices that is of a high quality for purposes of recycling and includes copier paper, computer paper, letterhead, ledger, white envelopes, and bond paper.

(2) Provide procedures for collecting and storing recyclable materials, containers for storing materials, and contractual or other arrangements with buyers of the recyclable materials.

(3) The Department of Administration and the Department of Transportation shall each provide by 1 October of each year to the Department of Environment and Natural Resources a detailed description of the respective Agency's review and revision of bid procedures and purchase and use of reusable, refillable, repairable, more durable, and less toxic supplies and products. The information provided by the Department of Administration and the Department of Transportation to the Department of Environment and Natural Resources shall also be included in the report required by G.S. 130A-309.06(c).

(4) Establish and implement, in cooperation with the Department and the Department of Administration, a solid waste reduction program for materials used in the course of agency operations. The program shall be designed and

implemented to achieve maximum feasible reduction of solid waste generated as a result of agency operations.

(5) Prepare any written report in compliance with the model report under subsection (j) of this section. The State agency shall, in lieu of distributing the report in mass:

a. Notify persons to whom each agency is required to report, and any other persons it deems appropriate, that a report has been published, its subject and title, and the locations, including State libraries, at which the report is available;

b. Deliver any report to only those State libraries that each agency determines is likely to receive requests for a particular report; and

c. Distribute a report to only those who request the report.

A State library that has received a report shall distribute a report only upon request. Any State agency required by law to report to an entity shall be in compliance with that law by notifying that entity under sub-subdivision a. of this subdivision.

(a1) The Department of Administration shall review and revise its bid procedures and specifications set forth in Article 3 of Chapter 143 of the General Statutes and the Department of Transportation shall review and revise its bid procedures and specifications set forth in Article 2 of Chapter 136 of the General Statutes to encourage the purchase or use of reusable, refillable, repairable, more durable, and less toxic supplies and products.

(1) The Department of Administration shall require the procurement of such supplies and products to the extent that the purchase or use is practicable and cost-effective. The Department of Administration shall require the purchase or use of remanufactured toner cartridges for laser printers to the extent practicable.

(2) The Department of Transportation shall require the purchase or use of such supplies and products in the construction and maintenance of highways and bridges to the extent that the purchase or use is practicable and cost-effective.

(3) The Department of Administration and the Department of Transportation shall each provide by 1 October of each year to the Department of Environment

and Natural Resources a detailed description of the respective Agency's review and revision of bid procedures and purchase and use of reusable, refillable, repairable, more durable, and less toxic supplies and products. The information provided by the Department of Administration and the Department of Transportation to the Department of Environment and Natural Resources shall also be included in the report required by G.S. 130A-309.06(c).

(b)   The Department of Commerce shall assist and encourage the recycling industry in the State. Assistance and encouragement of the recycling industry shall include:

(1)   Assisting the Department in the identification and analysis, by the Department pursuant to G.S. 130A-309.06, of components of the State's recycling industry and present and potential markets for recyclable materials in this State, other states, and foreign countries;

(2)   Providing information on the availability and benefits of using recycled materials to businesses and industries in the State; and

(3)   Distributing any material prepared in implementing this section to the public, businesses, industries, units of local government, or other organizations upon request.

(c)   Repealed by Session Laws 1993, c. 250, s. 2.

(d)   The Department of Commerce shall investigate the potential markets for composted materials and shall submit its findings to the Department for the waste registry informational program administered by the Department in order to stimulate absorption of available composted materials into such markets.

(e)   On or before 1 March 1991, the Department of Commerce shall report to the General Assembly its findings relative to:

(1)   Potential markets for composted materials, including private and public sector markets;

(2)   The types of materials which may legally and effectively be used in a successful composting operation; and

(3)   The manner in which the composted materials should be marketed for optimum use.

(f) (1) All State agencies, including the Department of Transportation and the Department of Administration, and units of local government are required to procure compost products when they can be substituted for, and cost no more than, regular soil amendment products, provided the compost products meet all applicable engineering and environmental quality standards, specifications, and rules. This product preference shall apply to, but not be limited to, highway construction and maintenance projects, highway planting and beautification projects, recultivation and erosion control programs, and other projects.

(2) The Department of Transportation shall, consistent with economic feasibility and applicable engineering and environmental quality standards, use scrap tires, demolition debris, and untreated, stabilized, or encapsulated ash from boilers and incinerators in highway construction and maintenance projects.

(g) The Department of Public Instruction, with the assistance of the Department and The University of North Carolina, shall develop, distribute, and encourage the use of guidelines for the collection of recyclable materials and for solid waste reduction in the State system of education. At a minimum, the guidelines shall address solid waste generated in administrative offices, classrooms, dormitories, and cafeterias. The guidelines shall be developed by 1 January 1991.

(h) In order to orient students and their families to the recycling of waste and to encourage the participation of schools, communities, and families in recycling programs, the school board of each school district in the State shall make available an awareness program in the recycling of waste materials. The program shall be provided at both the elementary and secondary levels of education.

(i) The Department of Public Instruction is directed to develop, from funds appropriated for environmental education, curriculum materials and resource guides for a recycling awareness program for instruction at the elementary, middle, and high school levels.

(j) The Department of Administration shall develop a model report for reports published by any State agency, the General Assembly, the General Court of Justice, or The University of North Carolina. This model report shall satisfy the following:

(1) The paper in the report shall, to the extent economically practicable, be made from recycled paper and shall be capable of being recycled.

(2) The other constituent elements of the report shall, to the extent economically practicable, be made from recycled products and shall be capable of being recycled or reused.

(3) The report shall be printed on both sides of the paper if no additional time, staff, equipment, or expense would be required to fulfill this requirement.

(4) State publications that are of historical and enduring value and importance to the citizens of North Carolina shall be printed on alkaline (acid-free) paper according to G.S. 125-11.13.

(k) The Department of Transportation shall provide and maintain recycling containers at each rest area located in this State on a highway in the Interstate Highway System or in the State highway system for the collection of each of the following recyclable materials for which recycling is feasible:

(1) Aluminum.

(2) Newspaper.

(3) Recyclable glass.

(4) Plastic bottles.

For each rest area that has recycling containers, the Department of Transportation shall install signs, or modify existing signs, that are proximately located to the rest area to notify motorists that the rest area has recycling containers.

(l) Any State agency or agency of a political subdivision of the State that is using State funds, or any person contracting with any agency with respect to work performed under contract, shall procure products of recycled steel if all of the following conditions are satisfied:

(1) The product must be acquired competitively within a reasonable time frame.

(2) The product must meet appropriate performance standards.

(3) The product must be acquired at a reasonable price.

(m) The Alcoholic Beverage Control Commission, with the assistance of the Department, shall develop a model recycling program for holders of on-premises malt beverage permits, on-premises unfortified wine permits, on-premises fortified wine permits, and mixed beverages permits under G.S. 18B-1001 that are required to recycle beverage containers under G.S. 18B-1006.1. The model program shall provide for the separation, storage, and collection for recycling of all beverage containers that are required to be recycled under G.S. 18B-1006.1 and shall provide alternatives that reflect variations in local circumstances across the State. The Alcoholic Beverage Control Commission may adopt rules to comply with this section. (1989, c. 784, s. 2; 1991, c. 522, s. 1; 1991 (Reg. Sess., 1992), c. 959, s. 32; 1993, c. 197, s. 1; c. 250, ss. 1, 2; c. 448, ss. 1, 2; c. 553, s. 74; 2001-144, s. 1; 2001-452, s. 3.3; 2001-512, ss. 13, 14; 2003-284, s. 6.10(a); 2003-340, s. 1.6; 2005-348, s. 2.)

§ 130A-309.14A. Reports by certain State-assisted entities.

Any community college, as defined in G.S. 115D-2(2), and any nonprofit corporation that receives State funds are encouraged to prepare any written reports in compliance with G.S. 130A-309.14(j). (1993, c. 448, s. 3.)

§ 130A-309.15. Prohibited acts regarding used oil.

(a) No person may knowingly:

(1) Collect, transport, store, recycle, use, or dispose of used oil in any manner which endangers the public health or welfare.

(2) Discharge used oil into sewers, drainage systems, septic tanks, surface waters, groundwaters, watercourses, or marine waters.

(3) Dispose of used oil in landfills in the State unless such disposal has been approved by the Department.

(4) Mix used oil with solid waste that is to be disposed of in landfills.

(5) Mix used oil with hazardous substances that make it unsuitable for recycling or beneficial use.

(b) A person who violates subsection (a) of this section shall be guilty of a misdemeanor and upon conviction shall be punished as provided by G.S. 130A-25(a) and G.S. 14-3.

(c) A person who disposes of used oil in a landfill where such used oil has been mixed with other solid waste which may be lawfully disposed of in such landfill, and who is without knowledge that such solid waste has been mixed with used oil, is not guilty of a violation under this section.

(d) Used oil shall not be used for road oiling, dust control, weed abatement, or other similar purposes that have the potential to release used oil into the environment. (1989, c. 784, s. 2.)

§ 130A-309.16. Public education program regarding used oil collection and recycling.

The Department shall conduct a public education program to inform the public of the needs for and benefits of collecting and recycling used oil and shall:

(1) Encourage persons who annually sell at retail, in containers for use off the premises, more than 500 gallons of oil to provide the purchasers with information on the locations of collection facilities and information on proper disposal practices.

(2) Establish, maintain, and publicize a used oil information center that disperses materials or information explaining local, State, and federal laws and rules governing used oil and informing the public of places and methods for proper disposal of used oil.

(3) Encourage the voluntary establishment of used oil collection and recycling programs and provide technical assistance to persons who organize such programs.

(4) Encourage the procurement of recycled automotive, industrial, and fuel oils and oils blended with recycled oils for all State and local government uses.

Recycled oils procured under this section shall meet equipment manufacturer's specifications. (1989, c. 784, s. 2.)

§ 130A-309.17. Registration of persons transporting, collecting, or recycling used oil; fees; reports and records.

(a) The following persons shall register annually with the Department pursuant to rules of the Department on forms prescribed by it:

(1) Any person who transports over public highways more than 500 gallons of used oil per week.

(2) Any person who maintains a collection facility that receives more than 6,000 gallons of used oil annually. For purposes of registration, the amount received does not include used oil delivered to collection centers by individuals that change their own personal motor oil.

(3) Any facility that recycles more than 10,000 gallons of used oil annually.

(b) An electric utility which generates during its operation used oil that is then reclaimed, recycled, or rerefined by the electric utility for use in its operations is not required to register or report pursuant to this section.

(c) An on-site burner which only burns a specification used oil generated by the burner is not required to register or report pursuant to this section, provided that the burning is done in compliance with any air permits issued by the Department.

(d) The Department may prescribe a fee for the registration required by this section in an amount which is sufficient to cover the cost of processing applications but which does not exceed twenty-five dollars ($25.00).

(e) The Department shall require each registered person to submit, no later than 1 July of each year, a report which specifies the type and quantity of used oil transported, collected, and recycled during the preceding calendar year.

(f) Each registered person who transports or recycles used oil shall maintain records which identify:

(1) The source of the materials transported or recycled;

(2) The quantity of materials received;

(3) The date of receipt; and

(4) The destination or end use of the materials.

(g) The Department shall perform technical studies to sample used oil at facilities of representative used oil transporters and at representative recycling facilities to determine the incidence of contamination of used oil with hazardous, toxic, or other harmful substances.

(h) Any person who fails to register with the Department as required by this section shall be guilty of a misdemeanor and upon conviction shall be punished as provided by G.S. 130A-25(a) and G.S. 14-3.

(i) The proceeds from the registration fees imposed by this section shall be deposited into the Solid Waste Management Trust Fund. (1989, c. 784, s. 2.)

§ 130A-309.18. Regulation of used oil as hazardous waste.

Nothing in this Part shall prohibit the Department from regulating used oil as a hazardous waste in a manner consistent with applicable federal law and this Article. (1989, c. 784, s. 2.)

§ 130A-309.19. Coordination with other State agencies.

The Department of Transportation shall study the feasibility of using recycled oil products in road construction activities and shall report to the President Pro Tempore of the Senate and the Speaker of the House of Representatives annually, beginning 1 January 1991, on the results of its study. (1989, c. 784, s. 2.)

§ 130A-309.20. Public used oil collection centers.

(a) The Department shall encourage the voluntary establishment of public used oil collection centers and recycling programs and provide technical assistance to persons who organize such programs.

(b) All State agencies and businesses that change motor oil for the public are encouraged to serve as public used oil collection centers.

(c) A public used oil collection center must:

(1) Notify the Department annually that it is accepting used oil from the public; and

(2) Annually report quantities of used oil collected from the public.

(d) No person may recover from the owner or operator of a used oil collection center any costs of response actions resulting from a release of either used oil or a hazardous substance against the owner or operator of a used oil collection center if such used oil is:

(1) Not mixed with any hazardous substance by the owner or operator of the used oil collection center;

(2) Not knowingly accepted with any hazardous substances contained therein;

(3) Transported from the used oil collection center by a certified transporter pursuant to G.S. 130A-309.23; and

(4) Stored in a used oil collection center that is in compliance with this section.

(e) Subsection (d) of this section applies only to that portion of the public used oil collection center used for the collection of used oil and does not apply if the owner or operator is grossly negligent in the operation of the public used oil collection center. Nothing in this section shall affect or modify in any way the obligations or liability of any person under any other provisions of State or federal law, including common law, for injury or damage resulting from a release of used oil or hazardous substances. For purposes of this section, the owner or operator of a used oil collection center may presume that a quantity of no more than five gallons of used oil accepted from any member of the public is not mixed with a hazardous substance, provided that the owner or operator acts in good faith. (1989, c. 784, s. 2)

§ 130A-309.21. Incentives program.

(a)   The Department is authorized to establish an incentives program for individuals who change their own oil to encourage them to return their used oil to a used oil collection center.

(b)   The incentives used by the Department may involve the use of discount or prize coupons, prize drawings, promotional giveaways, or other activities the Department determines will promote collection, reuse, or proper disposal of used oil.

(c)   The Department may contract with a promotion company to administer the incentives program. (1989, c. 784, s. 2.)

§ 130A-309.22. Grants to local governments.

(a)   The Department shall develop a grants program for units of local government to encourage the collection, reuse, and proper disposal of used oil. No grant may be made for any project unless the project is approved by the Department.

(b)   The Department shall consider for grant assistance any unit of local government project that uses one or more of the following programs or any activity that the Department feels will reduce the improper disposal and reuse of used oil:

(1)   Curbside pickup of used oil containers by a unit of local government or its designee.

(2)   Retrofitting of solid waste equipment to promote curbside pickup or disposal of used oil at used oil collection centers designated by the unit of local government.

(3) Establishment of publicly operated used oil collection centers at landfills or other public places.

(4) Providing containers and other materials and supplies that the public can utilize in an environmentally sound manner to store used oil for pickup or return to a used oil collection center.

(5) Providing incentives for the establishment of privately operated public used oil collection centers.

(c) Eligible projects shall be funded according to provisions established by the Department; however, no grant may exceed twenty-five thousand dollars ($25,000).

(d) The Department shall initiate rule making on or before 1 January 1991, necessary to carry out the purposes of this section. (1989, c. 784, s. 2.)

§ 130A-309.23. Certification of used oil transporters.

(a) Any person who transports over public highways after 1 January 1992, more than 500 gallons of used oil in any week must be a certified transporter or must be employed by a person who is a certified transporter.

(b) The Department of Transportation shall develop a certification program for transporters of used oil, and shall issue, deny, or revoke certifications authorizing the holder to transport used oil. Certification requirements shall help assure that a used oil transporter is familiar with appropriate rules and used oil management procedures.

(c) The Department of Transportation shall adopt rules governing certification, which shall include requirements for the following:

(1) Registration and annual reporting pursuant to G.S. 130A-309.17.

(2) Evidence of familiarity with applicable State laws and rules governing used oil transportation.

(3) Proof of liability insurance or other means of financial responsibility for any liability which may be incurred in the transport of used oil.

(4) Marking, by the certified transporter of used oil, of all vehicles which transport used oil or all containers of used oil when it is not feasible to mark the vehicle. The mark must clearly identify the certified used oil transporter and clearly indicate that the vehicle is used to transport used oil. The marking must be visible to others travelling on the highway. (1989, c. 784, s. 2; 1991, c. 488.)

§ 130A-309.24. Permits for used oil recycling facilities.

(a) Each person who intends to operate, modify, or close a used oil recycling facility shall obtain an operation or closure permit from the Department prior to operating, modifying, or closing the facility.

(b) By 1 January 1992, the Department shall develop a permitting system for used oil recycling facilities after reviewing and considering the applicability of the permit system for hazardous waste treatment, storage, or disposal facilities.

(c) Permits shall not be required under this section for the burning of used oil as a fuel, provided:

(1) A valid air permit issued by the Department is in effect for the facility; and

(2) The facility burns used oil in accordance with applicable United States Environmental Protection Agency regulations, local government regulations, and the requirements and conditions of its air permit.

(d) No permit is required under this section for the use of used oil for the beneficiation or flotation of phosphate rock. (1989, c. 784, s. 2.)

§ 130A-309.25. Training of operators of solid waste management facilities.

(a) The Department shall establish qualifications for, and encourage the development of training programs for, operators of incinerators, operators of landfills, coordinators of local recycling programs, and other solid waste management facilities.

(b) The Department shall work with accredited community colleges, vocational technical centers, State universities, and private institutions in developing educational materials, courses of study, and other such information to be made available for persons seeking to be trained as operators of solid waste management facilities.

(c) A person may not perform the duties of an operator of a solid waste management facility after 1 January 1998, unless he has completed an operator training course approved by the Department. An owner of a solid waste management facility may not employ any person to perform the duties of an operator unless the person has completed an approved solid waste management facility operator training course.

(d) The Commission may adopt rules and minimum standards to effectuate the provisions of this section and to ensure the safe, healthy, and lawful operation of solid waste management facilities. The Commission may establish, by rule, various classifications for operators to address the need for differing levels of training required to operate various types of solid waste management facilities due to different operating requirements at the facilities.

(e) In developing training programs for incinerator operators under this section, the Department shall establish and consult with ad hoc advisory groups to help coordinate the requirements under this section with other training programs for incinerator operators.

(f) This section does not apply to any operator of a solid waste management facility who has five years continuous experience as an operator of a solid waste management facility immediately preceding January 1, 1998, provided that the operator attends a course and completes the continuing education requirements approved by the Department. (1989, c. 784, s. 2; 1993, c. 29, s. 1; 1995 (Reg. Sess., 1996), c. 594, s. 19; 1997-443, s. 15.49(a).)

§ 130A-309.26. Regulation of medical waste.

(a) As used in this section:

(1) "Sharps" means needles, syringes, and scalpel blades.

(2) "Treatment" means any process, including steam sterilization, chemical treatment, incineration, and other methods approved by the Commission which changes the character or composition of medical waste so as to render it noninfectious.

(b) It is the intent of the General Assembly to protect the public health by establishing standards for the safe packaging, storage, treatment, and disposal of medical waste. The Commission shall adopt and the Department shall enforce rules for the packaging, storage, treatment, and disposal of:

(1) Medical waste at facilities where medical waste is generated;

(2) Medical waste from the point at which the waste is transported from the facility where it was generated;

(3) On-site and off-site treatment of medical waste; and

(4) The off-site transport, storage, treatment or disposal of medical waste.

(c) No later than 1 August 1990, the Commission shall adopt rules necessary to protect the health, safety, and welfare of the public and to carry out the purpose of this section. Such rules shall address, but need not be limited to, the packaging of medical waste, including specific requirements for the safe packaging of sharps and the segregation, storage, treatment, and disposal of medical wastes at the facilities in which such waste is generated. (1989, c. 784, s. 2; 1995 (Reg. Sess., 1996), c. 594, s. 20.)

§ 130A-309.27. Joint and several liability.

(a) As used in this section:

(1) "Owner or operator" means, in addition to the usual meanings of the term, any owner of record of any interest in land on which a landfill is or has been sited, any person or business entity that owns a majority interest in any other business entity which is the owner or operator of a landfill, and any person designated as a joint permittee pursuant to G.S. 130A-295.2(e).

(2) "Proceeds" means all funds collected and received by the Department, including interest and penalties on delinquent fees.

(b) Every owner or operator of a landfill is jointly and severally liable for the improper operation and closure of the landfill, as provided by law.

(c) through (f) Repealed by Session Laws 2007-550, s. 5(b), effective August 1, 2007. (1989, c. 784, s. 2; 2007-550, s. 5(b).)

§ 130A-309.28. University research.

Research, training, and service activities related to solid and hazardous waste management conducted by The University of North Carolina shall be coordinated by the Board of Governors of The University of North Carolina through the Office of the President. Proposals for research contracts and grants; public service assignments; and responses to requests for information and technical assistance by the State and units of local government, business, and industry shall be addressed by a formal process involving an advisory board of university personnel appointed by the President and chaired and directed by an individual appointed by the President. The Board of Governors of The University of North Carolina shall consult with the Department in developing the research programs and provide the Department with a copy of the proposed research program for review and comment before the research is undertaken. Research contracts shall be awarded to independent nonprofit colleges and universities within the State which are accredited by the Southern Association of Colleges and Schools on the same basis as those research contracts awarded to The University of North Carolina. Research activities shall include the following areas:

(1) Methods and processes for recycling solid and hazardous waste;

(2) Methods of treatment for detoxifying hazardous waste; and

(3) Technologies for disposing of solid and hazardous waste. (1989, c. 784, s. 2.)

§ 130A-309.29. Adoption of rules.

The Commission may adopt rules to implement the provisions of this Part pursuant to Article 2A of Chapter 150B of the General Statutes. (1991, c. 621, s. 12; 2000-189, s. 12.)

§§ 130A-309.30 through 130A-309.50. Reserved for future codification purposes.

Part 2B. Scrap Tire Disposal Act.

§ 130A-309.51. Title.

This Part may be cited as the "North Carolina Scrap Tire Disposal Act." (1989, c. 784, s. 3.)

§ 130A-309.52. Findings; purpose.

(a) The General Assembly finds that:

(1) Scrap tire disposal poses a unique and troublesome solid waste management problem.

(2) Scrap tires are a usable resource that may be recycled for energy value.

(3) Uncontrolled disposal of scrap tires may create a public health and safety problem because tire piles act as breeding sites for mosquitoes and other disease-transmitting vectors, pose substantial fire hazards, and present a difficult disposal problem for landfills.

(4) A significant number of scrap tires are illegally dumped in North Carolina.

(5) It is in the State's best interest to encourage efforts to recycle or recover resources from scrap tires.

(6) It is desirable to allow units of local government to control tire disposal for themselves and to encourage multicounty, regional approaches to scrap tire disposal and collection.

(7) It is desirable to encourage reduction in the volume of scrap tires being disposed of at public sanitary landfills.

(b) The purpose of this Part is to provide statewide guidelines and structure for the environmentally safe disposal of scrap tires to be administered through units of local government. (1989, c. 784, s. 3.)

§ 130A-309.53. Definitions.

Unless a different meaning is required by the context, the following definitions shall apply throughout this Part:

(1) "Collection site" means a site used for the storage of scrap tires.

(2) "Disposal fee" is any amount charged by a tire collector, tire processor, or unit of local government in exchange for accepting scrap tires.

(3) "In-county scrap tire" means any scrap tire brought for disposal from inside the county in which the collection or processing site is located.

(4) "Out-of-county scrap tire" means any scrap tire brought for disposal from outside the county in which the collection or processing site is located.

(5) "Processing site" means a site actively used to produce or manufacture usable materials, including fuel, from scrap tires. Commercial enterprises processing scrap tires shall not be considered solid waste management facilities insofar as the provisions of G.S. 130A-294(a)(4) and G.S. 130A-294(b) are concerned.

(6) "Scrap tire" means a tire that is no longer suitable for its original, intended purpose because of wear, damage, or defect.

(7) "Tire" means a continuous solid or pneumatic rubber covering that encircles the wheel of a vehicle. Bicycle tires and other tires for vehicles propelled by human power are not subject to the provisions of this Part.

(8) "Tire collector" means a person who owns or operates a site used for the storage, collection, or deposit of more than 50 scrap tires.

(9) "Tire hauler" means a person engaged in the picking up or transporting of scrap tires for the purpose of storage, processing, or disposal.

(10) "Tire processor" means a person who engages in the processing of scrap tires or one who owns or operates a tire processing site.

(11) "Tire retailer" means a person who engages in the retail sale of a tire in any quantity for any use or purpose by the purchaser other than for resale. (1989, c. 784, s. 3; 1991, c. 221, s. 2; 1995 (Reg. Sess., 1996), c. 594, s. 21.)

§ 130A-309.54. Use of scrap tire tax proceeds.

Article 5B of Chapter 105 imposes a tax on new tires to provide funds for the disposal of scrap tires, for the cleanup of inactive hazardous waste sites under Part 3 of this Article, and for all the purposes for which the Bernard Allen Memorial Emergency Drinking Water Fund may be used under G.S. 87-98. A county may use proceeds of the tax distributed to it under that Article only for the disposal of scrap tires pursuant to the provisions of this Part or for the abatement of a nuisance pursuant to G.S. 130A-309.60. (1989, c. 784, s. 3; 1991, c. 221, s. 3; 1993, c. 364, s. 1(a); 2009-451, s. 13.3B(b).)

§§ 130A-309.55 through 130A-309.56: Repealed by Session Laws 1991, c. 221, s. 4.

§ 130A-309.57. Scrap tire disposal program.

(a) The owner or operator of any scrap tire collection site shall, within six months after October 1, 1989, provide the Department with information concerning the site's location, size, and the approximate number of scrap tires that are accumulated at the site and shall initiate steps to comply with subsection (b) of this section.

(b) On or after July 1, 1990:

(1) A person may not maintain a scrap tire collection site or a scrap tire disposal site unless the site is permitted.

(2) It is unlawful for any person to dispose of scrap tires in the State unless the scrap tires are disposed of at a scrap tire collection site or at a tire disposal site, or disposed of for processing at a scrap tire processing facility.

(c) The Commission shall adopt rules to carry out the provisions of this section. Such rules shall:

(1) Provide for the administration of scrap tire collector and collection center permits and scrap tire disposal site permits, which may not exceed two hundred fifty dollars ($250.00) annually.

(2) Set standards for scrap tire processing facilities and associated scrap tire sites, scrap tire collection centers, and scrap tire collectors.

(3) Authorize the final disposal of scrap tires at a permitted solid waste disposal facility provided the tires have been cut into sufficiently small parts to assure their proper disposal.

(4) Repealed by Session Laws 2013-413, s. 18. For effective date, see Editor's note.

(d) A permit is not required for:

(1) A tire retreading business where fewer than 1,000 scrap tires are kept on the business premises;

(2) A business that, in the ordinary course of business, removes tires from motor vehicles if fewer than 1,000 of these tires are kept on the business premises; or

(3) A retail tire-selling business which is serving as a scrap tire collection center if fewer than 1,000 scrap tires are kept on the business premises.

(e) The Department shall encourage the voluntary establishment of scrap tire collection centers at retail tire-selling businesses, scrap tire processing facilities, and solid waste disposal facilities, to be open to the public for the deposit of used and scrap tires. The Department may establish an incentives program for individuals to encourage them to return their used or scrap tires to a scrap tire collection center.

(f) Permitted scrap tire collectors may not contract with a scrap tire processing facility, unless the processing facility documents that it has access to a facility permitted to receive the scrap tires. (1989, c. 784, s. 3; 2012-200, s. 14(a); 2013-413, s. 18.)

§ 130A-309.58. Disposal of scrap tires.

(a) Each county is responsible for providing for the disposal of scrap tires located within its boundaries in accordance with the provisions of this Part and any rules issued pursuant to this Part. The following are permissible methods of scrap tire disposal:

(1) Incinerating;

(2) Retreading;

(3) Constructing crash barriers;

(4) Controlling soil erosion when whole tires are not used;

(5) Chopping or shredding;

(6) Grinding into crumbs for use in road asphalt, tire derived fuel, and as raw material for other products;

(7) Slicing vertically, resulting in each scrap tire being divided into at least two pieces;

(8) Sludge composting;

(9) Using for agriculture-related purposes;

(10) Chipping for use as an oyster cultch as approved by rules adopted by the Marine Fisheries Commission;

(11)　Cutting, stamping, or dyeing tires;

(12)　Pyrolizing and other physico-chemical processing;

(13)　Hauling to out-of-State collection or processing sites; and

(14)　Monofilling split, ground, chopped, sliced, or shredded scrap tires.

(b)　The Commission may adopt rules approving other permissible methods of scrap tire disposal. Landfilling of whole scrap tires is prohibited. The prohibition against landfilling whole tires applies to all whole pneumatic rubber coverings, but does not apply to whole solid rubber coverings.

(c)　Units of local government may enter into joint ventures or other cooperative efforts with other units of local government for the purpose of disposing of scrap tires. Units of local government may enter into leases or other contractual arrangements with units of local government or private entities in order to dispose of scrap tires.

(d)　Each county is responsible for developing a description of scrap tire disposal procedures. These procedures shall be included in the annual report required under G.S. 130A-309.09A. Further, any revisions to the initial description of the scrap tire disposal procedures shall be forwarded to the Department.

(e)　A county shall provide, directly or by contract with another unit of local government or private entity, at least one site for scrap tire disposal for that county. The unit of local government or contracting party may not charge a disposal fee for the disposal of scrap tires except as provided in this subsection. A unit of local government or contracting party may charge a disposal fee that does not exceed the cost of disposing of the scrap tires only if:

(1)　The scrap tires are new tires that are being disposed of by their manufacturer because they do not meet the manufacturer's standards for salable tires; or

(2)　The scrap tires are delivered to a local government scrap tire disposal site without an accompanying certificate required by G.S. 130A-309.58(f) that indicates that the tires originated in a county within North Carolina.

(f) Every tire retailer or other person disposing of scrap tires shall complete and sign a certification form prescribed by the Department and distributed to each county, certifying that the tires were collected in the normal course of business for disposal, the county in which the tires were collected, and the number of tires to be disposed of. This form also shall be completed and signed by the tire hauler, certifying that the load contains the same tires that were received from the tire retailer or other person disposing of scrap tires. The tire hauler shall present this certification form to the tire processor or tire collector at the time of delivery of the scrap tires for disposal, collection, or processing. Copies of these certification forms shall be retained for a minimum of three years after the date of delivery of the scrap tires.

(g) The provisions of subsection (f) of this section do not apply to tires that are brought for disposal in quantities of five or less by someone other than a tire collector, tire processor, or tire hauler. (1989, c. 784, s. 3; 1991, c. 221, s. 5; 1993, c. 548, s. 4; 1995 (Reg. Sess., 1996), c. 594, s. 22; 1997-209, s. 1; 2013-409, s. 4.)

§ 130A-309.59. Registration of tire haulers.

(a) Before engaging in the hauling of scrap tires in this State, any tire hauler must register with the Department whereupon the Department shall issue to the tire hauler a scrap tire hauling identification number. A tire retailer licensed under G.S. 105-164.29 and solely engaged in the hauling of scrap tires received by it in connection with the retail sale of replacement tires is not required to register under this section.

(b) Each tire hauler shall furnish its hauling identification number on all certification forms required under G.S. 130A-309.58(f). Any tire retailer engaged in the hauling of scrap tires and not required by subsection (a) of this section to be registered shall supply its merchant identification number on all certification forms required by G.S. 130A-309.58(f). (1989, c. 784, s. 3.)

§ 130A-309.60. Nuisance tire collection sites.

(a) On or after July 1, 1990, if the Department determines that a tire collection site is a nuisance, it shall notify the person responsible for the nuisance and request that the tires be processed or removed within 90 days. If the person fails to take the requested action within 90 days, the Department shall order the person to abate the nuisance within 90 days. If the person responsible for the nuisance is not the owner of the property on which the tire collection site is located, the Department may order the property owner to permit abatement of the nuisance. If the person responsible for the nuisance fails to comply with the order, the Department shall take any action necessary to abate the nuisance, including entering the property where the tire collection site is located and confiscating the scrap tires, or arranging to have the scrap tires processed or removed.

(b)   When the Department abates the nuisance pursuant to subsection (a) of this section, the person responsible for the nuisance shall be liable for the actual costs incurred by the Department for its nuisance abatement activities and its administrative and legal expenses related to the abatement. The Department may ask the Attorney General to initiate a civil action to recover these costs from the person responsible for the nuisance. Nonpayment of the actual costs incurred by the Department shall result in the imposition of a lien on the owner's real property on which the tire collection site is located.

(c)   This section does not apply to any of the following:

(1)   A retail business premises where tires are sold if no more than 500 scrap tires are kept on the premises at one time;

(2)   The premises of a tire retreading business if no more than 3,000 scrap tires are kept on the premises at one time;

(3)   A premises where tires are removed from motor vehicles in the ordinary course of business if no more than 500 scrap tires are kept on the premises at one time;

(4)   A solid waste disposal facility where no more than 60,000 scrap tires are stored above ground at one time if all tires received for storage are processed, buried, or removed from the facility within one year after receipt;

(5)   A site where no more than 250 scrap tires are stored for agricultural uses; and

(6)   A construction site where scrap tires are stored for use or used in road surfacing and construction of embankments.

(d) The descending order of priority for the Department's abatement activities under subsection (a) of this section is as follows:

(1) Tire collection sites determined by the Department to contain more than 1,000,000 tires;

(2) Tire collection sites which constitute a fire hazard or threat to public health;

(3) Tire collection sites in densely populated areas; and

(4) Any other tire collection sites that are determined to be a nuisance.

(e) This section does not change the existing authority of the Department to enforce any existing laws or of any person to abate a nuisance.

(f) As used in this section, "nuisance" means an unreasonable danger to public health, safety, or welfare or to the environment. (1989, c. 784, s. 3.)

§ 130A-309.61. Effect on local ordinances.

This Part preempts any local ordinance regarding the disposal of scrap tires to the extent the local ordinance is inconsistent with this Part or the rules adopted pursuant to this Part. (1989, c. 784, s. 3; 1993, c. 548, s. 5; 1997-209, s. 1.)

§ 130A-309.62. Fines and penalties.

Any person who knowingly hauls or disposes of a tire in violation of this Part or the rules adopted pursuant to this Part shall be assessed a civil penalty of fifty dollars ($50.00) per violation. Each tire hauled or disposed of in violation of this Part or rules adopted pursuant to this Part constitutes a separate violation.

The clear proceeds of civil penalties assessed pursuant to this section shall be remitted to the Civil Penalty and Forfeiture Fund in accordance with G.S. 115C-457.2. (1989, c. 784, s. 3; 1998-215, s. 55.)

§ 130A-309.63: Repealed by Session Laws 2013-360, s. 14.16(b), effective July 1, 2013.

§ 130A-309.64. Scrap Tire Disposal Program; other Department activities related to scrap tires.

(a)   The Department may make grants to units of local government to assist them in disposing of scrap tires. To administer the grants, the Department shall establish procedures for applying for a grant and the criteria for selecting among grant applicants. The criteria shall include the financial ability of a unit of local government to provide for scrap tire disposal, the severity of a unit of local government's scrap tire disposal problem, the effort made by a unit of local government to ensure that only tires generated in the normal course of business in this State are provided free disposal, and the effort made by a unit of local government to provide for scrap tire disposal within the resources available to it.

(b)   A unit of local government is not eligible for a grant under subsection (a) of this section unless its costs for disposing of scrap tires for the six-month period preceding the date the unit of local government files an application for a grant exceeded the amount the unit of local government received during that period from the proceeds of the scrap tire tax under G.S. 105-187.19. A grant to a unit of local government for scrap tire disposal may not exceed the unit of local government's unreimbursed cost for the six-month period.

(c)   The Department may support a position to provide local governments with assistance in developing and implementing scrap tire management programs designed to complete the cleanup of nuisance tire collection sites and prevent scrap tires generated from outside of the State from being presented for free disposal in the State.

(d)   The Department may clean up scrap tire collection sites that the Department has determined are a nuisance. The Department may use funds to clean up a nuisance tire collection site only if no other funds are available for that purpose.

(e)   The Department shall include in the report to be delivered to the Environmental Review Commission on or before January 15 of each year pursuant to G.S. 130A-309.06(c) a description of the implementation of the North Carolina Scrap Tire Disposal Act under this Part for the fiscal year ending the preceding June 30. The description of the implementation of the North

Carolina Scrap Tire Disposal Act shall include a list of the recipients of grants under subsection (a) of this section and the amount of each grant for the previous 12-month period. The report also shall include the amount of funds used to clean up nuisance sites under subsection (d) of this section.

(f) It is the intent of the General Assembly to allow the Department to satisfy grant obligations that extend beyond the end of the fiscal year.

(g) The Department may adopt any rules necessary to implement this section. (2013-360, s. 14.16(c).)

§ 130A-309.65: Reserved for future codification purposes.

§ 130A-309.66: Reserved for future codification purposes.

§ 130A-309.67: Reserved for future codification purposes.

§ 130A-309.68: Reserved for future codification purposes.

§ 130A-309.69: Reserved for future codification purposes.

Part 2C. Lead-Acid Batteries.

§ 130A-309.70. Landfilling and incineration of lead-acid batteries prohibited; delivery for recycling.

(a) No person shall knowingly place or dispose of a used lead-acid battery in a landfill, incinerator, or in any waste-to-energy facility. Any person may deliver a lead-acid battery to a battery retailer or wholesaler, or to a secondary lead smelter, or to a collection or recycling facility authorized under this Chapter or by the United States Environmental Protection Agency.

(b) No battery retailer shall knowingly place or dispose of a used lead-acid battery in a landfill, incinerator, or waste-to-energy facility. Any battery retailer may deliver a used lead-acid battery to the agent of a battery wholesaler or a secondary lead smelter, to a battery manufacturer for delivery to a secondary lead smelter, or to a collection or recycling facility authorized under this Chapter or by the United States Environmental Protection Agency.

(c) Any person who knowingly places or disposes of a lead-acid battery in violation of this section shall be assessed a civil penalty of not more than fifty dollars ($50.00) per violation. Each battery improperly disposed of shall constitute a separate violation.

The clear proceeds of civil penalties assessed pursuant to this section shall be remitted to the Civil Penalty and Forfeiture Fund in accordance with G.S. 115C-457.2. (1991, c. 375, s. 2; 1998-215, s. 56.)

§ 130A-309.71. Retailers required to accept lead-acid batteries for recycling; posting of notice required.

(a) A person who sells or offers for sale lead-acid batteries at retail in this State shall accept from customers, at the point of transfer or sale, used lead-acid batteries of the type and in a quantity at least equal to the number of new batteries purchased, if offered by customers.

(b) A person who sells or offers for sale lead-acid batteries at retail in this State shall post written notice which must be at least 8 1/2 inches by 11 inches in size and must contain the universal recycling symbol and the following language:

(1) "It is illegal to improperly dispose of a motor vehicle battery or other lead-acid battery."

(2) "Recycle your used batteries."

(3) "State law requires us to accept used motor vehicle batteries or other lead-acid batteries for recycling in exchange for new batteries purchased."

(c) Any person who fails to post the notice required by subsection (b) of this section after receiving a written warning from the Department to do so shall be assessed a civil penalty of not more than fifty dollars ($50.00) per day for each day the person fails to post the required notice.

The clear proceeds of civil penalties assessed pursuant to this section shall be remitted to the Civil Penalty and Forfeiture Fund in accordance with G.S. 115C-457.2. (1991, c. 375, s. 2; 1998-215, s. 57.)

§ 130A-309.72. Wholesalers required to accept lead-acid batteries.

(a) No person selling new lead-acid batteries at wholesale shall refuse to accept from customers at the point of transfer, used lead-acid batteries of the type and in a quantity at least equal to the number of new batteries purchased, if offered by customers. A person accepting batteries in transfer from a battery retailer shall be allowed a period not to exceed 90 days to remove batteries from the retail point of collection.

(b) Any person who violates this section shall be assessed a civil penalty of fifty dollars ($50.00) per violation. Each battery refused by a wholesaler or not removed from the retail point of collection within 90 days shall constitute a separate violation.

The clear proceeds of civil penalties assessed pursuant to this section shall be remitted to the Civil Penalty and Forfeiture Fund in accordance with G.S. 115C-457.2. (1991, c. 375, s. 2; 1998-215, s. 58.)

§ 130A-309.73. Inspections of battery retailers authorized; construction of this Part.

(a) The Department may inspect any place, building, or premise subject to the provisions of G.S. 130A-309.71. The Department may issue warnings to persons who fail to comply with the provisions of this Part.

(b) The provisions of this Part shall not be construed to prohibit any person who does not sell lead-acid batteries from collecting and recycling such batteries. (1991, c. 375, s. 2.)

§§ 130A-309.74 through 130A-309.79. Reserved for future codification purposes.

Part 2D. Management of Discarded White Goods.

§ 130A-309.80. Findings and purpose.

The General Assembly finds that white goods are difficult to dispose of, that white goods that contain chlorofluorocarbon refrigerants pose a danger to the environment, and that it is in the best interest of the State to require that chlorofluorocarbon refrigerants be removed from discarded white goods. This Part therefore provides for the management of discarded white goods. (1993, c. 471, s. 4.)

§ 130A-309.81. Management of discarded white goods; disposal fee prohibited.

(a)   Duty. - Each county is responsible for providing at least one site for the collection of discarded white goods. It must also provide for the disposal of discarded white goods and for the removal of chlorofluorocarbon refrigerants from white goods. A county may contract with another unit of local government or a private entity in accordance with Article 15 of Chapter 153A of the General Statutes to provide for the management of discarded white goods or for the removal of chlorofluorocarbon refrigerants from white goods.

(b)   Restrictions. - A unit of local government or a contracting party may not charge a disposal fee for the disposal of white goods. A white good may not be disposed of in a landfill, an incinerator, or a waste-to-energy facility.

(c)   Plan. - Each county shall establish written procedures for the management of white goods. These procedures shall be included in the annual report required under G.S. 130A-309.09A. (1993, c. 471, ss. 4, 6; 1993 (Reg. Sess., 1994), c. 745, ss. 36, 37; 2001-265, s. 6; 2013-409, s. 5.)

§ 130A-309.82. Use of disposal tax proceeds by counties.

Article 5C of Chapter 105 of the General Statutes imposes a tax on new white goods to provide funds for the management of discarded white goods. A county must use the proceeds of the tax distributed to it under that Article for the management of discarded white goods. The purposes for which a county may use the tax proceeds include, but are not limited to, the following:

(1)   Capital improvements for infrastructure to manage discarded white goods, such as concrete pads for loading, equipment essential for moving white

goods, storage sheds for equipment essential to white goods disposal management, and freon extraction equipment.

(2) Operating costs associated with managing discarded white goods, such as labor, transportation, and freon extraction.

(3) The cleanup of illegal white goods disposal sites, the cleanup of illegal disposal sites consisting of more than fifty percent (50%) discarded white goods, and, as to those illegal disposal sites consisting of fifty percent (50%) or less discarded white goods, the cleanup of the discarded white goods portion of the illegal disposal sites.

Except as provided in subdivision (3) of this section, a county may not use the tax proceeds for a capital improvement or operating expense that does not directly relate to the management of discarded white goods. Except as provided in subdivision (3) of this section, if a capital improvement or operating expense is partially related to the management of discarded white goods, a county may use the tax proceeds to finance a percentage of the costs equal to the percentage of the use of the improvement or expense directly related to the management of discarded white goods. (1993, c. 471, s. 4; 1998-24, ss. 4, 7; 2000-109, s. 9(a); 2001-265, s. 5.)

§ 130A-309.83. (Repealed effective June 30, 2017) White Goods Management Account.

(a) The White Goods Management Account is established within the Department.

(b) The Department shall use revenue in the Account to make grants to units of local government to assist them in managing discarded white goods. To administer the grants, the Department shall establish procedures for applying for a grant and the criteria for selecting among grant applicants. The criteria shall include the financial ability of a unit to manage white goods, the severity of a unit's white goods management problem, and the effort made by a unit to manage white goods within the resources available to it.

(c) A unit of local government is not eligible for a grant unless its costs of managing white goods for a six-month period preceding the date the unit files an application for a grant exceeded the amount the unit received during that period from the proceeds of the white goods disposal tax under G.S. 105-187.24. The Department shall determine the six-month period to be used in determining who is eligible for a grant. A grant to a unit may not exceed the unit's unreimbursed cost for the six-month period.

(d) If a unit of local government anticipates that its costs of managing white goods during a six-month period will exceed the amount the unit will receive during that period because the unit will make a capital expenditure for the management of white goods or because the unit will incur other costs resulting from improvements to that unit's white goods management program, the unit may request that the Department make an advance determination that the costs are eligible to be paid by a grant from the White Goods Management Account and that there will be sufficient funds available in the Account to cover those costs. If the Department determines that the costs are eligible for reimbursement and that funds will be available, the Department shall reserve funds for that unit of local government in the amount necessary to reimburse allowable costs. The Department shall notify the unit of its determination and fund availability within 60 days of the request from the unit of local government. This subsection applies only to capital expenditures for the management of white goods and to costs resulting from improvements to a unit's white goods management program. (1993, c. 471, s. 4; 1995 (Reg. Sess., 1996), c. 594, s. 24; 1998-24, s. 7; 2000-109, s. 9(a); 2001-265, s. 5; 2013-360, s. 14.17(b), (e).)

§ 130A-309.84. Civil penalties for improper disposal.

The Department may assess a civil penalty of not more than one hundred dollars ($100.00) against a person who, knowing it is unlawful, places or otherwise disposes of a discarded white good in a landfill, an incinerator, or a waste-to-energy facility. The Department may assess this penalty for the day the unlawful disposal occurs and each following day until the white good is disposed of properly.

The Department may assess a penalty of up to one hundred dollars ($100.00) against a person who, knowing it is required, fails to remove chlorofluorocarbon refrigerants from a discarded white good. The Department may assess this penalty for the day the failure occurs and each following day until the chlorofluorocarbon refrigerants are removed.

The clear proceeds of civil penalties assessed pursuant to this section shall be remitted to the Civil Penalty and Forfeiture Fund in accordance with G.S. 115C-457.2. (1993, c. 471, s. 4; 1998-215, s. 59.)

§ 130A-309.85. Reporting on the management of white goods.

The Department shall include in the report to be delivered to the Environmental Review Commission on or before 15 January of each year pursuant to G.S. 130A-309.06(c) a description of the management of white goods in the State for the fiscal year ending the preceding 30 June. The description of the management of white goods shall include the following information:

(1)   The amount of taxes collected and distributed under G.S. 105-187.24 during the period covered by the report.

(2)   The cost to each county of managing white goods during the period covered by the report.

(3)   (Repealed effective June 20, 2017) The beginning and ending balances of the White Goods Management Account for the period covered by the report and a list of grants made from the Account for the period.

(4)   Any other information the Department considers helpful in understanding the problem of managing white goods.

(5)   A summary of the information concerning the counties' white goods management programs contained in the counties' Annual Financial Information Report. (1993, c. 471, s. 4; 1995 (Reg. Sess., 1996), c. 594, s. 25; 1998-24, ss. 5, 7; 2000-109, s. 9(a); 2001-265, s. 5; 2001-452, s. 3.5; 2013-360, s. 14.17(f).)

§ 130A-309.86. Effect on local ordinances.

This Part preempts any local ordinance regarding the management of white goods that is inconsistent with this Part or the rules adopted pursuant to this Part. It does not preempt any local ordinance regarding the management of white goods that is consistent with this Part or rules adopted pursuant to this Part. (1993, c. 471, s. 4.)

§ 130A-309.87. Eligibility for disposal tax proceeds.

(a) Receipt of Funds. - A county may not receive a quarterly distribution of the white goods disposal tax proceeds under G.S. 105-187.24 unless the undesignated balance in the county's white goods account at the end of its fiscal year is less than the threshold amount. Based upon the information in a county's Annual Financial Information Report, the Department must notify the Department of Revenue by March 1 of each year which counties may not receive a distribution of the white goods disposal tax for the current calendar year. The Department of Revenue will credit the undistributed tax proceeds to the General Fund.

If the undesignated balance in a county's white goods account subsequently falls below the threshold amount, the county may submit a statement to the Department, certified by the county finance officer, that the undesignated balance in its white goods account is less than the threshold amount. Upon receipt of the statement, the Department will notify the Department of Revenue to distribute to the county its quarterly distribution of the white goods disposal tax proceeds. The Department must notify the Department of Revenue of the county's change of status at least 30 days prior to the next quarterly distribution.

For the purposes of this subsection, the term "threshold amount" means twenty-five percent (25%) of the amount of white goods disposal tax proceeds a county received, or would have received if it had been eligible to receive them under G.S. 130A-309.87, during the preceding fiscal year.

(b) Annual Financial Information Report. - On or before November 1 of each year, a county must submit a copy of its Annual Financial Information Report, prepared in accordance with G.S. 159-33.1, to the Department. The Secretary of the Local Government Commission must require the following information in that report:

(1) The tonnage of white goods scrap metal collected.

(2) (Effective until June 30, 2017) The amount of revenue credited to its white goods account. This revenue should include all receipts derived from the white goods disposal tax, the sale of white goods scrap metals and freon, and a grant from the White Goods Management Account.

(2) (Effective June 30, 2017) The amount of revenue credited to its white goods account. This revenue should include all receipts derived from the white goods disposal tax, and the sale of white goods scrap metals and freon.

(3) The expenditures from its white goods account. The expenditures should include operating expenses and capital improvement costs associated with its white goods management program.

(4) The designated and undesignated balance of its white goods account.

(5) A comparison of the undesignated balance of its white goods account at the end of the fiscal year and the amount of white goods disposal tax proceeds it received, or would have received if it had been eligible to receive it under G.S. 130A-309.87, during the fiscal year. (1998-24, s. 6; 2013-360, s. 14.17(c), (g).)

§ 130A-309.88: Reserved for future codification purposes.

§ 130A-309.89: Reserved for future codification purposes.

§ 130A-309.90: Repealed by Session Laws 2010-67, s. 1, effective July 1, 2010.

§ 130A-309.91: Repealed by Session Laws 2010-67, s. 1, effective July 1, 2010.

§ 130A-309.92: Repealed by Session Laws 2010-67, s. 1, effective July 1, 2010.

§ 130A-309.93: Repealed by Session Laws 2010-67, s. 1, effective July 1, 2010.

§ 130A-309.93A: Repealed by Session Laws 2010-67, s. 1, effective July 1, 2010.

§ 130A-309B.93: Repealed by Session Laws 2010-67, s. 1, effective July 1, 2010

§ 130A-309.94: Repealed by Session Laws 2010-67, s. 1, effective July 1, 2010.

§ 130A-309.95: Repealed by Session Laws 2010-67, s. 1, effective July 1, 2010.

§ 130A-309.96: Repealed by Session Laws 2010-67, s. 1, effective July 1, 2010.

§ 130A-309.97: Repealed by Session Laws 2010-67, s. 1, effective July 1, 2010.

§ 130A-309.98: Repealed by Session Laws 2010-67, s. 1, effective July 1, 2010.

§ 130A-309.99: Repealed by Session Laws 2010-67, s. 1, effective July 1, 2010.

Part 2F. Management of Abandoned Manufactured Homes.

§ 130A-309.111. (Expires October 1, 2023) Purpose.

The purpose of this Part is to provide units of local government with the authority, funding, and guidance needed to provide for the efficient and proper identification, deconstruction, recycling, and disposal of abandoned manufactured homes in this State. (2008-136, s. 1.)

§ 130A-309.112. (Expires October 1, 2023) Definitions.

The following definitions apply to this Part:

(1) "Abandoned manufactured home" means a manufactured home or mobile classroom that is both:

a. Vacant or in need of extensive repair.

b. An unreasonable danger to public health, safety, welfare, or the environment.

(2) "Intact" when used in connection with "abandoned manufactured home" means an abandoned manufactured home from which the wheels and axles, white goods, and recyclable materials have not been removed.

(3) "Manufactured home" is defined in G.S. 105-164.3.

(4) "Responsible party" means any person or entity that possesses an ownership interest in an abandoned manufactured home. (2008-136, s. 1.)

§ 130A-309.113. (Expires October 1, 2023) Management of abandoned manufactured homes.

(a) Plan. - Each county shall consider whether to implement a program for the management of abandoned manufactured homes. If at any time the county decides to implement a program, the county shall develop a written plan for the management of abandoned manufactured homes. This plan shall be included in the annual report required under G.S. 130A-309.09A. At a minimum, the plan shall include:

(1) A method by which the county proposes to identify abandoned manufactured homes in the county, including, without limitation, a process by which manufactured home owners or other responsible parties may request designation of their home as an abandoned manufactured home.

(2) A plan for the deconstruction of these abandoned manufactured homes.

(3) A plan for the removal of the deconstructed components, including mercury switches from thermostats, for reuse or recycling, as appropriate.

(4) A plan for the proper disposal of abandoned manufactured homes that are not deconstructed under subdivision (2) of this subsection.

(b) Authority to Contract. - A county may contract with another unit of local government or a private entity in accordance with Article 15 of Chapter 153A of the General Statutes to provide for the management of abandoned manufactured homes within the county and the implementation of its plan under subsection (a) of this section.

(c) Fee Authority. - A unit of local government or a party that contracted with the county under subsection (b) of this section may charge a disposal fee for the disposal of any abandoned manufactured home at a landfill pursuant to this Part.

(d) An intact abandoned manufactured home shall not be disposed of in a landfill. (2008-136, s. 1; 2013-409, s. 6.)

§ 130A-309.114. (Expires October 1, 2023) Process for the disposal of abandoned manufactured homes.

(a) If a county adopts and implements a plan for the management of abandoned manufactured homes pursuant to this Part, the county shall notify the responsible party and the owner of the property on whose land the abandoned manufactured home is located for each identified abandoned manufactured home in the county that the abandoned manufactured home must be properly disposed of by the responsible party within 90 days. The notice shall be in writing and shall be served on the person as provided by Rule 4(j) of the Rules of Civil Procedure, G.S. 1A-1. The notice shall disclose the basis for the action and advise that a hearing will be held before a designated public officer at a place within the county in which the manufactured home is located not less than 10 days nor more than 30 days after the serving of the notice; that the responsible party shall be given the right to file an answer to the order and to appear in person, or otherwise, and give testimony at the place and time fixed in the notice; and that the rules of evidence prevailing in courts of law or equity shall not be controlling in hearings before the public officer.

(b) If, after notice and hearing, the public officer determines that the manufactured home under consideration is abandoned, the officer shall state in writing the officer's findings of fact in support of that determination, and the county shall order the responsible party to dispose of the abandoned manufactured home within 90 days of the expiration of this period. If the responsible party fails to comply with this order, the county shall take any action it deems reasonably necessary to dispose of the abandoned manufactured home, including entering the property where the abandoned manufactured home is located and arranging to have the abandoned manufactured home deconstructed and disposed of in a manner consistent with the plan developed under G.S. 130A-309.113(a). If the responsible party is not the owner of the property on which the abandoned manufactured home is located, the county may order the property owner to permit entry onto the owner's property by an appropriate party to permit the removal and proper disposal of the abandoned manufactured home.

(c) When a county removes, deconstructs, and disposes of an abandoned manufactured home pursuant to this section, whether directly or through a party that contracted with the county, the responsible party shall be liable for the actual costs incurred by the county, directly or indirectly, for its abatement activities and its administrative and legal expenses incurred, less the amount of grants for reimbursement received by the county under G.S. 130A-309.115 for the disposal activities for that manufactured home. The county may initiate a civil action to recover these unpaid costs from the responsible party. Nonpayment of any portion of the actual costs incurred by the county shall result in the imposition of a lien on any real property in the county owned by the responsible party.

(d)   This section does not apply to any of the following:

(1)   A retail business premises where manufactured homes are sold.

(2)   A solid waste disposal facility where no more than 10 manufactured homes are stored at one time if all of the manufactured homes received for storage are deconstructed or removed from the facility within one year after receipt.

(e)   This section does not change the existing authority of a county or a municipality to enforce any existing laws or of any person to abate a nuisance. (2008-136, s. 1.)

§ 130A-309.115. (Expires October 1, 2023) Grants to local governments.

(a)   The Department shall use funds from the Solid Waste Trust Fund established by G.S. 130A-309.12 to:

(1)   Provide grants to counties to reimburse their expenses for activities under this Part.

(2)   Provide technical assistance and support to counties to achieve the purposes of this Part.

(3)   Implement this Part, including costs associated with staffing, training, submitting reports, and fulfilling program goals.

(b)   Each county that requests a reimbursement grant from the Department shall also submit to the Department a proposed budget specifying in detail the expenses it expects to incur in a specified time period in connection with the activities under this Part. The Department shall review each submitted budget and make modifications, if necessary, in light of the availability of funds, the county's capacity to effectively and efficiently manage the abatement of abandoned manufactured homes, and any other factors that the Department reasonably determines are relevant. When the Department and a county agree on the amount of the county's budget under this subsection, the Department and the county shall execute an agreement that reflects this amount and that specifies the time period covered by the agreement, and the Department shall reserve funds for the county in the amount necessary to reimburse allowable costs. The amount of a reimbursement grant shall be calculated in accordance with subsections (c) and (d) of this section. A county shall not receive a reimbursement grant unless it has filed all the annual reports it is required to submit under G.S. 130A-309.117.

(c) Reimbursement grants shall be made in accordance with the terms of the grant agreement developed pursuant to subsection (b) of this section, but in any event, all reimbursements shall be calculated on a per-unit basis and based on the actual cost of such activities, not to exceed one thousand dollars ($1,000) for each unit. For a county designated as a development tier one or two area pursuant to G.S. 143B-437.08 where the costs associated with the disposition of an abandoned manufactured home in a manner consistent with this Part exceed one thousand dollars ($1,000) per unit, a county may request a supplemental grant in an amount equal to fifty percent (50%) of the amount in excess of one thousand dollars ($1,000). The Department shall consider the efficiency and effectiveness of the county program in making the supplemental grant, and the county participation must be a cash match.

(d) A county shall use reimbursement grant funds only for operating expenses that are directly related to the management of abandoned manufactured homes. If an operating expense is partially related to the management of abandoned manufactured homes, a county may use the reimbursement grant funds to finance the percentage of the cost that equals the percentage of the expense that is directly related to the management of abandoned manufactured homes. (2008-136, s. 1.)

§ 130A-309.116. (Expires October 1, 2023) Authority to adopt ordinances.

A county, or a unit of local government that is delegated authority to do so by the county, may adopt ordinances it deems necessary in order to implement this Part. (2008-136, s. 1.)

§ 130A-309.117. (Expires October 1, 2023) Reporting on the management of abandoned manufactured homes.

(a) On or before 1 August of each year, any county that receives a reimbursement grant under G.S. 130A-309.115 shall submit a report to the Department that includes all of the following information:

(1) The number of units and approximate tonnage of abandoned manufactured homes removed, deconstructed, recycled, and disposed of during the previous fiscal year.

(2) A detailed statement of the county's abandoned manufactured homes account receipts and disbursements during the previous fiscal year that sets out the source of all receipts and the purpose of all disbursements.

(3) The obligated and unobligated balances in the county's abandoned manufactured homes account at the end of the fiscal year.

(4) An assessment of the county's progress in removing, deconstructing, recycling, and disposing of abandoned manufactured homes consistent with this Part.

(b) The Department shall include in its annual report to the Environmental Review Commission under G.S. 130A-309.06(c) a description of the management of abandoned manufactured homes in the State for the fiscal year ending the preceding 30 June. The description of the management of abandoned manufactured homes shall include all of the following information:

(1) The cost to each county of managing its abandoned manufactured home program during the reporting period.

(2) The beginning and ending balances of the Solid Waste Management Trust Fund for the reporting period and a list of grants made from the Fund for the period, itemized by county.

(3) A summary of the information contained in the reports submitted by counties pursuant to subsection (a) of this section.

(4) Any other information the Department considers helpful in understanding the problem of managing abandoned manufactured homes in the State. (2008-136, s. 1.)

§ 130A-309.118. (Expires October 1, 2023) Effect on local ordinances.

This Part shall not be construed to limit the authority of counties under Article 18 of Chapter 153A of the General Statutes or the authority of cities under Article 19 of Chapter 160A of the General Statutes. (2008-136, s. 1.)

§ 130A-309.119: Reserved for future codification purposes.

Part 2G. Plastic Bag Management.

§ 130A-309.120. Findings.

The General Assembly makes the following findings:

(1) Distribution of plastic bags by retailers to consumers for use in carrying, transporting, or storing purchased goods has a detrimental effect on the environment of the State.

(2) Discarded plastic bags contribute to overburdened landfills, threaten wildlife and marine life, degrade the beaches and other natural landscapes of North Carolina's coast, and, in many cases, require consumption of oil and natural gas during the manufacturing process.

(3) It is in the best interest of the citizens of this State to gradually reduce the distribution and use of plastic bags.

(4) Environmental degradation is especially burdensome in counties with barrier islands where soundside and ocean pollution are more significant, where removing refuse from such isolated places is more difficult and expensive, where such refuse deters tourism, and where the presence of a National Wildlife Refuge or National Seashore shows that the federal government places special value on protecting the natural environment in that vicinity.

(5) The barrier islands are most relevant in that they are where sea turtles come to nest. North Carolina has some of the most important sea turtle nesting areas on the East Coast, due to the proximity of the islands to the Gulf Stream. Plastic bag debris can be harmful to sea turtles and other land and marine life.

The waters adjacent to the barrier islands, because they serve as habitat for the turtles, are particularly sensitive to waterborne debris pollution.

(6) Inhabited barrier islands are visited by a high volume of tourists and therefore experience a high consumption of bags relative to their permanent population due to large numbers of purchases from restaurants, groceries, beach shops, and other retailers by the itinerant tourist population.

(7) Barrier islands are small and narrow, and therefore the comparative impact of plastic bags on the barrier islands is high. (2009-163, s. 1.)

§ 130A-309.121. Definitions.

As used in this Part, the following definitions apply:

(1) Plastic bag. - A carryout bag composed primarily of thermoplastic synthetic polymeric material, which is provided by a store to a customer at the point of sale and incidental to the purchase of other goods.

(2) Prepared foods retailer. - A retailer primarily engaged in the business of selling prepared foods, as that term is defined in G.S. 105-164.3, to consumers.

(2a) Recycled content. - Content that is either postconsumer, postindustrial, or a mix of postconsumer and postindustrial.

(3) Recycled paper bag. - A paper bag that meets all of the following requirements:

a. The bag is manufactured from at least forty percent (40%) recycled content.

b. The bag displays the words "made from recycled material" and "recyclable."

(4) Repealed by Session Laws 2010-31, s. 13.10(a), effective October 1, 2010.

(5) Retailer. - A person who offers goods for sale in this State to consumers and who provides a single-use plastic bag to the consumer to carry or transport the goods for free or for a nominal charge.

(6) Reusable bag. - A bag with handles that is specifically designed and manufactured for multiple reuse and is made of one of the following materials:

a. Nonwoven polypropylene or other plastic material with a minimum weight of 80 grams per square meter.

b. Cloth or other machine washable fabric. (2009-163, s. 1; 2010-31, s. 13.10(a).)

§ 130A-309.122. Certain plastic bags banned.

No retailer shall provide customers with plastic bags unless the bag is a reusable bag, or the bag is used solely to hold sales to an individual customer of otherwise unpackaged portions of the following items:

(1) Fresh fish or fresh fish products.

(2) Fresh meat or fresh meat products.

(3) Fresh poultry or fresh poultry products.

(4) Fresh produce. (2009-163, s. 1.)

§ 130A-309.123. Substitution of paper bags restricted.

(a) A retailer subject to G.S. 130A-309.122 may substitute paper bags for the plastic bags banned by that section, but only if all of the following conditions are met:

(1) The paper bag is a recycled paper bag.

(2) The retailer offers a cash refund to any customer who uses the customer's own reusable bags instead of the bags provided by the retailer. The

amount of the refund shall be equal to the cost to the retailer of providing a recycled paper bag, multiplied by the number of reusable bags filled with the goods purchased by the customer. For purposes of this subdivision, "cash refund" includes a credit against the cost of goods purchased.

(b)   Nothing in this Part shall prevent a retailer from providing customers with reused packaging materials originally used for goods received from the retailer's wholesalers or suppliers.

(c)   Notwithstanding subsection (a) of this section, a prepared foods retailer may package prepared foods in a recycled paper bag, regardless of the availability of a reusable bag, in order to comply with food sanitation or handling standards or best practices. (2009-163, s. 1; 2010-31, s. 13.10(b); 2010-123, s. 5.2(a).)

§ 130A-309.124. Required signage.

A retailer subject to G.S. 130A-309.122 other than a prepared foods retailer shall display a sign in a location viewable by customers containing the following notice: "[county name] County discourages the use of single-use plastic and paper bags to protect our environment from excess litter and greenhouse gases. We would appreciate our customers using reusable bags, but if you are not able to, a 100% recycled paper bag will be furnished for your use." The name of the county where the retailer displaying the sign is located should be substituted for "[county name]" in the language set forth in this section. (2009-163, s. 1.)

§ 130A-309.125. Applicability.

(a)   This Part applies only in a county which includes a barrier island or barrier peninsula, in which the barrier island or peninsula meets both of the following conditions:

(1)   It has permanent inhabitation of 200 or more residents and is separated from the North Carolina mainland by a sound.

(2)   It contains either a National Wildlife Refuge or a portion of a National Seashore.

(b) Within any county covered by subsection (a) of this section, this Part applies only to an island or peninsula that both:

(1) Is bounded on the east by the Atlantic Ocean.

(2) Is bounded on the west by a coastal sound. (2009-163, s. 1.)

Part 2H. Discarded Computer Equipment and Television Management.

§ 130A-309.130. Findings.

The General Assembly makes the following findings:

(1) The computer equipment and television waste stream is growing rapidly in volume and complexity and can introduce toxic materials into solid waste landfills.

(2) It is in the best interest of the citizens of this State to have convenient, simple, and free access to recycling services for discarded computer equipment and televisions.

(3) Collection programs operated by manufacturers and local government and nonprofit agencies are an efficient way to divert discarded computer equipment and televisions from disposal and to provide recycling services to all citizens of this State.

(4) The development of local and nonprofit collection programs is hindered by the high costs of recycling and transporting discarded computer equipment and televisions.

(5) No comprehensive system currently exists, provided either by electronics manufacturers, retailers, or others, to adequately serve all citizens of the State and to divert large quantities of discarded computer equipment and televisions from disposal.

(6) Manufacturer responsibility is an effective way to ensure that manufacturers of computer equipment and televisions take part in a solution to the electronic waste problem.

(7) The recycling of certain discarded computer equipment and televisions recovers valuable materials for reuse and will create jobs and expand the tax base of the State.

(8) While some computers and computer monitors can be refurbished and reused and other consumer electronics products contain valuable materials, some older and bulkier consumer electronic products, including some televisions, may not contain any valuable products but should nevertheless be recycled to prevent the release of toxic substances to the environment.

(9) For the products covered by this Part, differences in product life expectancy, market economics, residual value, and product portability necessitate different approaches to recycling.

(10) In order to ensure that end-of-life computer equipment and televisions are responsibly recycled, to promote conservation, and to protect public health and the environment, a comprehensive and convenient system for recycling and reuse of certain electronic equipment should be established on the basis of shared responsibility among manufacturers, retailers, consumers, and the State. (2010-67, s. 2(a).)

§ 130A-309.131. Definitions.

As used in this Part, the following definitions apply:

(1) Business entity. - Defined in G.S. 55-1-40(2a).

(2) Computer equipment. - Any desktop computer, notebook computer, monitor or video display unit for a computer system, and the keyboard, mice, other peripheral equipment, and a printing device such as a printer, a scanner, a combination print-scanner-fax machine, or other device designed to produce hard paper copies from a computer. Computer equipment does not include an automated typewriter, professional workstation, server, ICI device, ICI system, mobile telephone, portable handheld calculator, portable digital assistant (PDA), MP3 player, or other similar device; an automobile; a television; a household appliance; a large piece of commercial or industrial equipment, such as commercial medical equipment, that contains a cathode ray tube, a cathode ray tube device, a flat panel display, or similar video display device that is contained

within, and is not separate from, the larger piece of equipment, or other medical devices as that term is defined under the federal Food, Drug, and Cosmetic Act.

(3) Computer equipment manufacturer. - A person that manufactures or has manufactured computer equipment sold under its own brand or label; sells or has sold under its own brand or label computer equipment produced by other suppliers; imports or has imported into the United States computer equipment that was manufactured outside of the United States; or owns or has owned a brand that it licenses or has licensed to another person for use on computer equipment. Computer equipment manufacturer includes a business entity that acquires another business entity that manufactures or has manufactured computer equipment. Computer equipment manufacturer does not include any existing person that does not and has not manufactured computer equipment of the type that would be used by consumers.

(4) Consumer. - Any of the following:

a. An occupant of a single detached dwelling unit or a single unit contained within a multiple dwelling unit who used a covered device primarily for personal or home business use.

b. A nonprofit organization with fewer than 10 employees that used a covered device in its operations.

(5) Covered device. - Computer equipment and televisions used by consumers primarily for personal or home business use. The term does not include a device that is any of the following:

a. Part of a motor vehicle or any component of a motor vehicle assembled by, or for, a vehicle manufacturer or franchised dealer, including replacement parts for use in a motor vehicle.

b. Physically a part of or integrated within a larger piece of equipment designed and intended for use in an industrial, governmental, commercial, research and development, or medical setting.

c. Equipment used for diagnostic, monitoring, or other medical products as that term is defined under the federal Food, Drug, and Cosmetic Act.

d. Equipment used for security, sensing, monitoring, antiterrorism purposes, or emergency services purposes.

e. Contained within a household appliance, including, but not limited to, a clothes washer, clothes dryer, refrigerator, refrigerator and freezer, microwave oven, conventional oven or range, dishwasher, room air conditioner, dehumidifier, air purifier, or exercise equipment.

(6) Desktop computer. - An electronic, magnetic, optical, electrochemical, or other high-speed data processing device that has all of the following features:

a. Performs logical, arithmetic, and storage functions for general purpose needs that are met through interaction with a number of software programs contained in the computer.

b. Is not designed to exclusively perform a specific type of limited or specialized application.

c. Achieves human interface through a stand-alone keyboard, stand-alone monitor or other display unit, and a stand-alone mouse or other pointing device.

d. Is designed for a single user.

e. Has a main unit that is intended to be persistently located in a single location, often on a desk or on the floor.

(7) Discarded computer equipment. - Computer equipment that is solid waste generated by a consumer.

(8) Discarded computer equipment or television collector. - A municipal or county government, nonprofit agency, recycler, or retailer that knowingly accepts for recycling discarded computer equipment or a television from a consumer.

(9) Discarded television. - A television that is solid waste generated by a consumer.

(10) Market share. - A television manufacturer's obligation to recycle discarded televisions. A television manufacturer's market share is the television manufacturer's prior year's sales of televisions as calculated by the Department pursuant to G.S. 130A-309.138(4) divided by all manufacturers' prior year's sales for all televisions as calculated by the Department pursuant to G.S. 130A-309.138(4). Market share may be expressed as a percentage, a fraction, or a decimal fraction.

(11) Notebook computer. - An electronic, magnetic, optical, electrochemical, or other high-speed data processing device that has all of the following features:

a. Performs logical, arithmetic, or storage functions for general purpose needs that are met through interaction with a number of software programs contained in the computer.

b. Is not designed to exclusively perform a specific type of limited or specialized application.

c. Achieves human interface through a keyboard, video display greater than four inches in size, and mouse or other pointing device, all of which are contained within the construction of the unit that comprises the computer.

d. Is able to be carried as one unit by an individual.

e. Is able to use external power, internal power, or batteries for a power source.

Notebook computer includes those that have a supplemental stand-alone interface device attached to the notebook computer. Notebook computer does not include a portable handheld calculator, a PDA, or similar specialized device. A notebook computer may also be referred to as a laptop computer.

(12) Recover. - The process of reusing or recycling covered devices.

(13) Recycle. - The processing, including disassembling, dismantling, and shredding, of covered devices or their components to recover a usable product. Recycle does not include any process that results in the incineration of a covered device.

(14) Recycler. - A person that recycles covered devices.

(15) Retailer. - A person that sells computer equipment or televisions in the State to a consumer. Retailer includes a computer equipment manufacturer or a television manufacturer that sells directly to a consumer through any means, including transactions conducted through sales outlets, catalogs, the Internet, or any similar electronic means, but does not include a person that sells computer equipment or televisions to a distributor or retailer through a wholesale transaction.

(16) Television. - Any electronic device that contains a tuner that locks on to a selected carrier frequency and is capable of receiving and displaying of television or video programming via broadcast, cable, or satellite, including, without limitation, any direct view or projection television with a viewable screen of nine inches or larger whose display technology is based on cathode ray tube (CRT), plasma, liquid crystal display (LCD), digital light processing (DLP), liquid crystal on silicon (LCOS), silicon crystal reflective display (SXRD), light emitting diode (LED), or similar technology marketed and intended for use by a consumer primarily for personal purposes. The term does not include computer equipment.

(17) Television manufacturer. - A person that: (i) manufactures for sale in this State a television under a brand that it licenses or owns; (ii) manufactures for sale in this State a television without affixing a brand; (iii) resells into this State a television under a brand it owns or licenses produced by other suppliers, including retail establishments that sell a television under a brand that the retailer owns or licenses; (iv) imports into the United States or exports from the United States a television for sale in this State; (v) sells at retail a television acquired from an importer that is the manufacturer as described in sub-subdivision (iv) of this subdivision, and the retailer elects to register in lieu of the importer as the manufacturer of those products; (vi) manufactures a television for or supplies a television to any person within a distribution network that includes wholesalers or retailers in this State and that benefits from the sale in this State of the television through the distribution network; or (vii) assumes the responsibilities and obligations of a television manufacturer under this Part. In the event the television manufacturer is one that manufactures, sells, or resells under a brand it licenses, the licensor or brand owner of the brand shall not be considered to be a television manufacturer under (i) or (iii) of this subdivision. (2010-67, s. 2(a); 2010-180, s. 20.)

§ 130A-309.132. Responsibility for recycling discarded computer equipment and televisions.

In addition to the specific requirements of this Part, discarded computer equipment and television collectors and computer equipment manufacturers and television manufacturers share responsibility for the recycling of discarded computer equipment and televisions and the education of citizens of the State as to recycling opportunities for discarded computer equipment and televisions. (2010-67, s. 2(a).)

§ 130A-309.133. Data security.

Computer equipment manufacturers, television manufacturers, discarded computer equipment and television collectors, recyclers, and retailers shall not be liable in any way for data or other information left on a covered device that is collected or recovered pursuant to the provisions of this Part. (2010-67, s. 2(a).)

§ 130A-309.134. (See editor's note for first report due date) Requirements for computer equipment manufacturers.

(a) Registration Required. - Each computer equipment manufacturer, before selling or offering for sale computer equipment in North Carolina, shall register with the Department.

(b) Manufacturer Label Required. - A computer equipment manufacturer shall not sell or offer to sell computer equipment in this State unless a visible, permanent label clearly identifying the manufacturer of that equipment is affixed to the equipment.

(c) Computer Equipment Recycling Plan Required. - Each computer equipment manufacturer shall develop, submit to the Department, and implement one of the following plans to provide a free and reasonably convenient recycling program to take responsibility for computer equipment discarded by consumers:

(1) Level I recycling plan. - A computer equipment manufacturer shall submit a recycling plan for reuse or recycling of computer equipment discarded by consumers in the State produced by the manufacturer. The manufacturer shall submit a proposed plan to the Department within 90 days of registration as required by subsection (a) of this section. The plan shall:

a. Provide that the manufacturer will take responsibility for computer equipment discarded by consumers that it manufactured.

b. Describe any direct take-back program to be implemented by the manufacturer. Collection methods that are deemed to meet the requirements of this subdivision include one or more of the following:

1. A process offered by the computer equipment manufacturer or the manufacturer's designee for consumers to return discarded computer equipment by mail.

2. A physical collection site operated and maintained by the computer equipment manufacturer or the manufacturer's designee to receive discarded computer equipment from consumers, which is available to consumers during normal business hours.

3. A collection event hosted by the computer equipment manufacturer or the manufacturer's designee at which a consumer may return computer equipment.

c. Include a detailed description as to how the manufacturer will implement the plan.

d. Provide for environmentally sound management practices to transport and recycle discarded computer equipment.

e. Include a consumer recycling education program on the laws governing the recycling and reuse of discarded computer equipment under this Part and on the methods available to consumers to comply with those requirements. The manufacturer shall operate a toll-free telephone number to answer questions from consumers about computer recycling options.

(2) Level II recycling plan. - A computer equipment manufacturer shall submit a recycling plan for reuse or recycling of computer equipment discarded by consumers in the State produced by the manufacturer and by other manufacturers. The manufacturer shall submit a proposed plan to the Department within 90 days of registration as required by subsection (a) of this section. The plan may offer additional options to collect other types of electronic equipment that do not constitute discarded computer equipment, as that term is defined under G.S. 130A-309.131, and may allow for assessment of a nominal fee for collection of these other types of electronic equipment that are not discarded computer equipment. The plan shall include all of the elements set forth in subdivision (1) of subsection (c) of this section. In addition the plan shall:

a. Provide that the manufacturer will take responsibility for computer equipment discarded by consumers that was manufactured by other manufacturers, as well as computer equipment that it manufactured.

b. Provide that the manufacturer shall: (i) maintain physical collection sites to receive discarded computer equipment from consumers in the 10 most populated municipalities in the State. The physical collection sites shall be available to consumers during normal business hours, at a minimum; and (ii) host at least two collection events annually within the State.

(3) Level III recycling plan. - A computer equipment manufacturer shall submit a recycling plan for reuse or recycling of computer equipment discarded by consumers in the State produced by the manufacturer and by other manufacturers. The manufacturer shall submit a proposed plan to the Department within 90 days of registration as required by subsection (a) of this section. The plan may offer additional options to collect other types of electronic equipment that do not constitute discarded computer equipment, as that term is defined under G.S. 130A-309.131, and may allow for assessment of a nominal fee for collection of these other types of electronic equipment that are not discarded computer equipment. The plan shall include all of the elements set forth in subdivision (1) of subsection (c) of this section. In addition the plan shall:

a. Provide that the manufacturer will take responsibility for computer equipment discarded by consumers that was manufactured by other manufacturers, as well as computer equipment that it manufactured.

b. Provide that the manufacturer shall: (i) maintain physical collection sites to receive discarded computer equipment from consumers in 50 of the State's counties, of which 10 of those counties shall be the most populated counties in the State. The physical collection sites shall be available to consumers during normal business hours, at a minimum; and (ii) host at least two collection events annually within the State.

(d) Fee Required. - Within 90 days of registration as required in subsection (a) of this section, a computer equipment manufacturer shall pay an initial registration fee to the Department. A computer equipment manufacturer that has registered shall pay an annual renewal registration fee to the Department, which shall be paid each year no later than July 1. The proceeds of these fees shall be credited to the Electronics Management Fund established pursuant to G.S. 130A-309.137. A computer equipment manufacturer that sells 1,000 items of computer equipment or fewer per year is exempt from the requirement to pay the registration fee and the annual renewal fee imposed by this subsection. The amount of the fee a computer equipment manufacturer shall pay shall be determined on the basis of the plan the manufacturer develops, submits, and implements pursuant to subsection (c) of this section, as follows:

(1) A computer equipment manufacturer who develops, submits, and implements a Level I recycling plan pursuant to subdivision (1) of subsection (c) of this section shall pay an initial registration fee of fifteen thousand dollars ($15,000) and an annual renewal fee of fifteen thousand dollars ($15,000) to the Department.

(2) A computer equipment manufacturer who develops, submits, and implements a Level II recycling plan pursuant to subdivision (2) of subsection (c) of this section shall pay an initial registration fee of ten thousand dollars ($10,000) and an annual renewal fee of seven thousand five hundred dollars ($7,500) to the Department.

(3) A computer equipment manufacturer who develops, submits, and implements a Level III recycling plan pursuant to subdivision (3) of subsection (c) of this section shall pay an initial registration fee of ten thousand dollars ($10,000) and an annual renewal fee of two thousand five hundred dollars ($2,500) to the Department.

(e) Computer Equipment Recycling Plan Revision. - A computer equipment manufacturer may prepare a revised plan and submit it to the Department at any time as the manufacturer considers appropriate in response to changed circumstances or needs. The Department may require a manufacturer to revise or update a plan if the Department finds that the plan is inadequate or out of date.

(f) Payment of Costs for Plan Implementation. - Each computer equipment manufacturer is responsible for all costs associated with the development and implementation of its plan. A computer equipment manufacturer shall not collect a fee from a consumer or a local government for the management of discarded computer equipment at the time the equipment is delivered for recycling.

(g) Joint Computer Equipment Recycling Plans. - A computer equipment manufacturer may fulfill the requirements of subsection (c) of this section by participation in a joint recycling plan with other manufacturers. A joint plan shall meet the requirements of subsection (c) of this section.

(h) Annual Report. - Each computer equipment manufacturer shall submit a report to the Department by October 1 of each year stating the total weight of all computer equipment collected for recycling or reuse in the previous fiscal year. The report shall also include a summary of actions taken to comply with the requirements of subsection (c) of this section. (2010-67, s. 2(a).)

§ 130A-309.135. Requirements for television manufacturers.

(a) Registration and Fee Required. - Each television manufacturer, before selling or offering for sale televisions in the State, shall register with the Department and, at the time of registration, shall pay an initial registration fee of two thousand five hundred dollars ($2,500) to the Department. An initial registration shall be valid from the day of registration through the last day of the fiscal year in which the registration fee was paid. A television manufacturer that has registered shall pay an annual renewal registration fee of two thousand five hundred dollars ($2,500) to the Department. The annual renewal registration fee shall be paid to the Department each fiscal year no later than June 30 of the previous fiscal year. The proceeds of these fees shall be credited to the Electronics Management Fund. A television manufacturer that sells 1,000 televisions or fewer per year is exempt from the requirement to pay the registration fee and the annual renewal fee imposed by this subsection.

(b) Manufacturer Label Required. - A television manufacturer shall not sell or offer to sell any television in this State unless a visible, permanent label clearly identifying the manufacturer of that device is affixed to the equipment.

(c) Recycling of Market Share Required. - The obligation to recycle televisions shall be allocated to each television manufacturer based on the television manufacturer's market share. A television manufacturer must annually recycle or arrange for the recycling of its market share of televisions pursuant to this section.

(d) Due Diligence and Compliance Assessments. - A television manufacturer shall conduct and document due diligence assessments of the recyclers the manufacturer contracts with, including an assessment of compliance with environmentally sound recovery standards adopted by the Department.

(e) Contact Information Required. - A television manufacturer shall provide the Department with contact information for the manufacturer's designated agent or employee whom the Department may contact for information related to the manufacturer's compliance with the requirements of this section.

(f) Joint Television Recycling Plans. - A television manufacturer may fulfill the requirements of this section either individually or in participation with other television manufacturers.

(g) Annual Report. - A television manufacturer shall report to the Department by October 1 of each year the total weight of televisions the manufacturer collected and recycled in the State during the previous fiscal year. (2010-67, s. 2(a).)

§ 130A-309.136. Requirements applicable to retailers.

(a) A manufacturer must not sell or offer for sale or deliver to retailers for subsequent sale new computer equipment or televisions unless: (i) the covered device is labeled with the manufacturer's brand, which label is permanently affixed and readily visible; and (ii) the manufacturer has filed a registration with the Department and is otherwise in compliance with the requirements of this Part, as indicated on the list developed and maintained by the Department pursuant to G.S. 130A-309.138(1).

(b) A retailer that sells or offers for sale new computer equipment or televisions must: (i) determine that all new covered devices that the retailer is offering for sale are labeled with the manufacturer's brand, which label is permanently affixed and readily visible; and (ii) review the Department's Web site to confirm that the manufacturer of a new covered device is on the list developed and maintained by the Department pursuant to G.S. 130A-309.138(1).

(c) A retailer is not responsible for an unlawful sale under this section if the manufacturer's registration expired or was revoked and the retailer took possession of the covered device prior to the expiration or revocation of the manufacturer's registration and the unlawful sale occurred within six months after the expiration or revocation. (2010-67, s. 2(a).)

§ 130A-309.137. (See editor's note) Electronics Management Fund.

(a) Creation. - The Electronics Management Fund is created as a special fund within the Department. The Fund consists of revenue credited to the Fund from the proceeds of the fee imposed on computer equipment manufacturers under G.S. 130A-309.134 and television manufacturers under G.S. 130A-309.135.

(b) Use and Distribution. - Moneys in the Fund shall be used by the Department to implement the provisions of this Part concerning discarded computer equipment and televisions. The Department may use all of the proceeds of the fee imposed on television manufacturers pursuant to G.S. 130A-309.135 and may use up to ten percent (10%) of the proceeds of the fee imposed on computer equipment manufacturers under G.S. 130A-309.134 for administration of the requirements of this Part. Funds remaining shall be distributed annually by the Department to eligible local governments pursuant to this section. The Department shall distribute such funds on or before February 15 of each year. Funds shall be distributed on a pro rata basis.

(c) Eligibility. - Except as provided in subsection (d) of this section, no more than one unit of local government per county, including the county itself, may receive funding pursuant to this section for a program to manage discarded computer equipment, televisions, and other electronic devices. A unit of local government shall submit a plan to include:

(1) Information on existing programs within the jurisdiction to recycle or reuse discarded computer equipment, televisions, and other electronic devices, or information on a plan to begin such a program on a date certain. This information shall include a description of the implemented or planned practices for collection of the equipment and a description of the types of equipment to be collected and how the equipment will be marketed for recycling.

(2) Information on a public awareness and education program concerning the recycling and reuse of discarded computer equipment, televisions, and other electronic devices.

(3) Information on methods to track and report total tonnage of computer equipment, televisions, and other electronic devices collected and recycled in the jurisdiction.

(4) Information on interactions with other units of local government to provide or receive services concerning disposal of discarded computer equipment, televisions, and other electronic devices.

(5) Information on how the unit of local government will account for the expenditure of funds received pursuant to this section.

(6) Proof of contract or agreement with a recycler that is certified as adhering to Responsible Recycling ("R2") practices or that is certified as an e-

Steward recycler adhering to the e-Stewards Standard for Responsible Recycling and Reuse of Electronic Equipment/rs to process the discarded computer equipment, televisions, and other electronic devices that the unit of local government collects.

(c1) Submittal of Information for Distribution of Funding. - Documentation meeting the requirements of subdivision (6) of subsection (c) of this section, and other information required by subsection (c) of this section, including new plans or revisions to plans as necessary, must be submitted annually on or before December 31 in order to be eligible for funding during the next distribution by the Department.

(d) Local Government Designation. - If more than one unit of local government in a county, including the county itself, requests funding pursuant to this section, the units of local government in question may enter into interlocal agreements for provision of services concerning disposal of discarded computer equipment and televisions, and distribution of funds received pursuant to this section among the parties to the agreement. If the units of local government do not enter into an interlocal agreement regarding funding under this section, the Department shall distribute funds to the eligible local governments based on the percentage of the county's population to be served under each eligible local government's program.

(e) Report. - Information regarding permanent recycling programs for discarded computer equipment and televisions for which funds are received pursuant to this section, and information on operative interlocal agreements executed in conjunction with funds received, if any, shall be included in the annual report required under G.S. 130A-309.09A. (2010-67, s. 2(a); 2013-409, s. 7.)

§ 130A-309.138. Responsibilities of the Department.

In addition to its other responsibilities under this Part, the Department shall:

(1) Develop and maintain a current list of manufacturers that are in compliance with the requirements of G.S. 130A-309.134 and G.S. 130A-309.135, post the list to the Department's Web site, and provide the current list to the Office of Information Technology Services each time that the list is updated.

(2) Develop and implement a public education program on the laws governing the recycling and reuse of discarded computer equipment and televisions under this Part and on the methods available to consumers to comply with those requirements. The Department shall make this information available on the Internet and shall provide technical assistance to manufacturers to meet the requirements of G.S. 130A-309.134(c)(1)e. The Department shall also provide technical assistance to units of local government on the establishment and operation of discarded computer equipment and television collection centers and in the development and implementation of local public education programs.

(3) Maintain the confidentiality of any information that is required to be submitted by a manufacturer under this Part that is designated as a trade secret, as defined in G.S. 66-152(3) and that is designated as confidential or as a trade secret under G.S. 132-1.2.

(4) The Department shall use national televisions sales data available from commercially available analytical sources to calculate the generation of discarded televisions and to determine each television manufacturer's recovery responsibilities for televisions based on the manufacturer's market share. The Department shall extrapolate data for the State from national data on the basis of the State's share of the national population. (2010-67, s. 2(a).)

§ 130A-309.139. Enforcement.

This Part may be enforced as provided by Part 2 of Article 1 of this Chapter. (2010-67, s. 2(a).)

§ 130A-309.140. Annual report by Department of recycling under this Part; periodic report by Environmental Review Commission of electronic recycling programs in other states.

(a) No later than January 15 of each year, the Department shall submit a report on the recycling of discarded computer equipment and televisions in the State under this Part to the Environmental Review Commission. The report must include an evaluation of the recycling rates in the State for discarded computer equipment and televisions, a discussion of compliance and enforcement related to the requirements of this Part, and any recommendations for any changes to the system of collection and recycling of discarded computer equipment, televisions, or other electronic devices.

(b) The Environmental Review Commission, with the assistance of the Department of Environment and Natural Resources, shall monitor and review electronic recycling programs in other states on an ongoing basis and shall report its findings and recommendations to the General Assembly periodically. (2010-67, ss. 2(a), 7.)

§ 130A-309.141. Local government authority not preempted.

Nothing in this Part shall be construed as limiting the authority of any local government to manage computer equipment and televisions that are solid waste. (2010-67, s. 2(a).)

Part 3. Inactive Hazardous Sites.

§ 130A-310. Definitions.

Unless a different meaning is required by the context, the following definitions shall apply throughout this Part:

(1) "CERCLA/SARA" means the Comprehensive Environmental Response, Compensation, and Liability Act of 1980, Pub. L. 96-510, 94 Stat. 2767, 42 U.S.C. 9601 et seq., as amended, and the Superfund Amendments and Reauthorization Act of 1986, Pub. L. 99-499, 100 Stat. 1613, as amended.

(2) "Hazardous substance" means hazardous substance as defined in CERCLA/SARA.

(3) "Inactive hazardous substance or waste disposal site" or "site" means any facility, as defined in CERCLA/SARA. These sites do not include hazardous waste facilities permitted or in interim status under this Article.

(4) "Operator" means the person responsible for the overall operation of an inactive hazardous substance or waste disposal site.

(5) "Owner" means any person who owns an inactive hazardous substance or waste disposal site, or any part thereof.

(6) "Release" means release as defined in the CERCLA/SARA.

(7) "Remedy" or "Remedial Action" means remedy or remedial action as defined in CERCLA/SARA.

(8) "Remove" or "Removal" means remove or removal as defined in CERCLA/SARA.

(9) "Responsible party" means any person who is liable pursuant to G.S. 130A-310.7. (1987, c. 574, s. 2; 1989, c. 286, s. 2; 1999-83, s. 1.)

§ 130A-310.1. Identification, inventory, and monitoring of inactive hazardous substance or waste disposal sites; duty of owners, operators, and responsible parties to provide information and access; remedies.

(a) The Department shall develop and implement a program for locating, cataloguing, and monitoring all inactive hazardous substance or waste disposal sites in North Carolina. The Secretary shall compile and maintain an inventory of all inactive hazardous substance or waste disposal sites based on information submitted by owners, operators, and responsible parties, and on data obtained directly by the Secretary. The Secretary shall maintain records of any evidence of contamination to the air, surface water, groundwater, surface or subsurface soils, or waste streams for inventoried sites. The records shall include all available information on the extent of any actual damage or potential danger to public health or to the environment resulting from the contamination.

(b) The Commission shall develop and make available a format and checklist for submission of data relevant to inactive hazardous substance or waste disposal sites. Within 90 days of the date on which an owner, operator, or responsible party knows or should know of the existence of an inactive hazardous substance or waste disposal site, the owner, operator, or responsible party shall submit to the Secretary all site data that is known or readily available to the owner, operator, or responsible party. The owner, operator, or responsible party shall certify under oath that, to the best of his knowledge and belief, the data is complete and accurate.

(c) Whenever the Secretary determines that there is a release, or substantial threat of a release, into the environment of a hazardous substance from an inactive hazardous substance or waste disposal site, the Secretary may, in addition to any other powers he may have, order any responsible party to conduct any monitoring, testing, analysis, and reporting that the Secretary deems reasonable and necessary to ascertain the nature and extent of any hazard posed by the site. Written notice of any order issued pursuant to this section shall be given to all persons subject to the order as set out in G.S. 130A-310.3(c). The Secretary, prior to the entry of any order, shall solicit the cooperation of the responsible party.

(d) If a person fails to submit data as required in subsection (b) of this section or violates the requirements or schedules in an order issued pursuant to subsection (c) of this section, the Secretary may institute an action for injunctive relief, irrespective of all other remedies at law, in the superior court of the county where the violation occurred or where a defendant resides.

(e) Whenever a person ordered to take any action pursuant to this section is unable or fails to do so, or if the Secretary, after making a reasonable attempt, is unable to locate any responsible party, the Secretary may take the action. The cost of any action by the Secretary pursuant to this section may be paid from the Inactive Hazardous Sites Cleanup Fund, subject to a later action for reimbursement pursuant to G.S. 130A-310.7. The provisions of subdivisions (a)(1) to (a)(3) of G.S.130A-310.6 shall apply to any action taken by the Secretary pursuant to this section.

(f) Upon reasonable notice, the Secretary may require any person to furnish to the Secretary any information, document, or record in that person's possession or under that person's control that relates to:

(1) The identification, nature, and quantity of material that has been or is generated, treated, stored, or disposed of at an inactive hazardous substance or waste disposal site or that is transported to an inactive hazardous substance or waste disposal site.

(2) The nature and extent of a release or threatened release of a hazardous substance or hazardous waste at or from an inactive hazardous substance or waste disposal site.

(3) Information relating to the ability of a person to pay for or to perform a cleanup.

(g) A person who is required to furnish any information, document, or record under subsection (f) of this section shall either allow the Secretary to inspect and copy all information, documents, and records or shall copy and furnish to the Secretary all information, documents, and records at the expense of the person.

(h) To collect information to administer this Part, the Secretary may subpoena the attendance and testimony of witnesses and the production of documents, records, reports, answers to questions, and any other information that the Secretary deems necessary. Witnesses shall be paid the same fees and mileage that are paid to witnesses in proceedings in the General Court of Justice. In the event that a person fails to comply with a subpoena issued under this subsection, the Secretary may seek enforcement of the subpoena in the superior court in any county where the inactive hazardous substance or waste disposal site is located, in the county where the person resides, or in the county where the person has his or her principal place of business.

(i) A person who owns or has control over an inactive hazardous substance or waste disposal site shall grant the Secretary access to the site at reasonable times. If a person fails to grant the Secretary access to the site, the Secretary may obtain an administrative search and inspection warrant as provided by G.S. 15-27.2. (1987, c. 574, s. 2; 1989, c. 286, s. 3; 1997-53, s. 1.)

§ 130A-310.2. Inactive Hazardous Waste Sites Priority List.

(a) No later than six months after July 1, 1987, the Commission shall develop a system for the prioritization of inactive hazardous substance or waste disposal sites based on the extent to which such sites endanger the public health and the environment. The Secretary shall apply the prioritization system to the inventory of sites to create and maintain an Inactive Hazardous Waste Site Priority List, which shall rank all inactive hazardous substance or waste disposal sites in decreasing order of danger. This list shall identify the location of each site and the type and amount of hazardous substances or waste known or believed to be located on the site. The first such list shall be published within two years after July 1, 1987, with subsequent lists to be published at intervals of not more than two years thereafter. The Secretary shall notify owners, operators, and responsible parties of sites listed on the Inactive Hazardous Waste Sites Priority List of their ranking on the list. The Inactive Hazardous Sites Priority List shall be used by the Department in determining budget requests and in allocating any State appropriation which may be made for remedial action, but shall not be used so as to impede any other action by the Department, or any remedial or other action for which funds are available.

(b)   Repealed by Session Laws 2012-200, s. 21(e), effective August 1, 2012. (1987, c. 574, s. 2; 2008-107, s. 12.1A(a); 2012-200, s. 21(e).)

§ 130A-310.3. Remedial action programs for inactive hazardous substance or waste disposal sites.

(a)   The Secretary may issue a written declaration, based upon findings of fact, that an inactive hazardous substance or waste disposal site endangers the public health or the environment. After issuing such a declaration, and at any time during which the declaration is in effect, the Secretary shall be responsible for:

(1)   Monitoring the inactive hazardous substance or waste disposal site;

(2)   Developing a plan for public notice and for community and local government participation in any inactive hazardous substance or waste disposal site remedial action program to be undertaken;

(3)   Approving an inactive hazardous substance or waste disposal site remedial action program for the site;

(4)   Coordinating the inactive hazardous substance or waste disposal site remedial action program for the site; and

(5)   Ensuring that the hazardous substance or waste disposal site remedial action program is completed.

(b)   Where possible, the Secretary shall work cooperatively with any owner, operator, responsible party, or any appropriate agency of the State or federal government to develop and implement the inactive hazardous substance or waste disposal site remedial action program. The Secretary shall not take action under this section to the extent that the Environmental Management Commission, the Commissioner of Agriculture, or the Pesticide Board has assumed jurisdiction pursuant to Articles 21 or 21A of Chapter 143 of the General Statutes.

(c) Whenever the Secretary has issued such a declaration, and at any time during which the declaration is in effect, the Secretary may, in addition to any other powers he may have, order any responsible party:

(1) To develop an inactive hazardous substance or waste disposal site remedial action program for the site subject to approval by the Department, and

(2) To implement the program within reasonable time limits specified in the order.

Written notice of such an order shall be provided to all persons subject to the order personally or by certified mail. If given by certified mail, notice shall be deemed to have been given on the date appearing in the return of the receipt. If giving of notice cannot be accomplished either personally or by certified mail, notice shall be given as provided in G.S. 1A-1, Rule 4(j).

(d) In any inactive hazardous substance or waste disposal site remedial action program implemented hereunder, the Secretary shall ascertain the most nearly applicable cleanup standard as would be applied under CERCLA/SARA, and may seek federal approval of any such program to insure concurrent compliance with federal standards. State standards may exceed and be more comprehensive than such federal standards. The Secretary shall assure concurrent compliance with applicable standards set by the Environmental Management Commission.

(e) For any removal or remedial action conducted entirely on-site under this Part, to the extent that a permit would not be required under 42 U.S.C. § 9621(e) for a removal or remedial action conducted entirely on-site under CERCLA/SARA, the Secretary may grant a waiver from any State law or rule that requires that an environmental permit be obtained from the Department. The Secretary shall not waive any requirement that a permit be obtained unless either the removal or remedial action is being conducted pursuant to G.S. 130A-310.3(c), 130A-310.5, or 130A-310.6, or the owner, operator, or other responsible party has entered into an agreement with the Secretary to implement a voluntary remedial action plan under G.S. 130A-310.9(b). The Secretary shall invite public participation in the development of the remedial action plan in the manner set out in G.S. 130A-310.4 prior to granting a permit waiver, except for a removal or remedial action conducted pursuant to G.S. 130A-310.5.

(f) In order to reduce or eliminate the danger to public health or the environment posed by an inactive hazardous substance or waste disposal site, an owner, operator, or other responsible party may impose restrictions on the current or future use of the real property comprising any part of the site if the restrictions meet the requirements of this subsection. The restrictions must be agreed to by the owner of the real property, included in a remedial action plan for the site that has been approved by the Secretary, and implemented as a part of the remedial action program for the site. The Secretary may approve restrictions included in a remedial action plan in accordance with standards determined as provided in subsection (d) of this section or pursuant to rules adopted under Chapter 150B of the General Statutes. Restrictions may apply to activities on, over, or under the land, including, but not limited to, use of groundwater, building, filling, grading, excavating, and mining. Any approved restriction shall be enforced by any owner, operator, or other party responsible for the inactive hazardous substance or waste disposal site. Any land-use restriction may also be enforced by the Department through the remedies provided in Part 2 of Article 1 of this Chapter or by means of a civil action. The Department may enforce any land-use restriction without first having exhausted any available administrative remedies. A land-use restriction may also be enforced by any unit of local government having jurisdiction over any part of the site. A land-use restriction shall not be declared unenforceable due to lack of privity of estate or contract, due to lack of benefit to particular land, or due to lack of any property interest in particular land. Any person who owns or leases a property subject to a land-use restriction under this Part shall abide by the land-use restriction. (1987, c. 574, s. 2; 1989, c. 727, s. 145; 1991, c. 281, ss. 1, 2; 1997-394, s. 1; 2002-154, s. 2.)

§ 130A-310.4. Public participation in the development of the remedial action plan.

(a) Within 10 days after the Secretary issues a declaration pursuant to G.S. 130A-310.3, he shall notify in writing the local board of health and the local health director having jurisdiction in the county or counties in which an inactive hazardous substance or waste disposal site is located that the site may endanger the public health or environment and that a remedial action plan is being developed. The Secretary shall involve the local health director in the development of the remedial action plan.

(b) Before approving any remedial action plan, the Secretary shall make copies of the proposed plan available for inspection as follows:

(1) A copy of the plan shall be provided to the local health director.

(2) Repealed by Session Laws 2010-180, s. 3, effective August 2, 2010.

(3) A copy of the plan shall be provided to the public library located in closest proximity to the site in the county or counties in which the site is located.

(4) The Secretary may place copies of the plan in other locations so as to assure the availability thereof to the public.

In addition, copies of the plan shall be available for inspection and copying at cost by the public during regular business hours in the offices of the agency within the Department with responsibility for the administration of the remedial action program.

(c) Before approving any remedial action plan, the Secretary shall give notice of the proposed plan as follows:

(1) A notice and summary of the proposed plan shall be published weekly for a period of three consecutive weeks in a newspaper having general circulation in the county or counties where the site is located.

(2) Notice that a proposed remedial action plan has been developed shall be given by first class mail to persons who have requested such notice. Such notice shall state the locations where a copy of the remedial action plan is available for inspection. The Department shall maintain a mailing list of persons who request notice pursuant to this section.

(d) The Secretary may conduct a public meeting to explain the proposed plan and alternatives to the public.

(e) At least 45 days from the latest date on which notice is provided pursuant to subsection (c)(1) of this section shall be allowed for the receipt of written comment on the proposed remedial action plan prior to its approval. If a public hearing is held pursuant to subsection (f) of this section, at least 20 days will be allowed for receipt of written comment following the hearing prior to the approval of the remedial action plan.

(f) If the Secretary determines that significant public interest exists, he shall conduct a public hearing on the proposed plan and alternatives. The Department shall give notice of the hearing at least 30 days prior to the date thereof by:

(1) Publication as provided in subdivision (c)(1) of this section, with first publication to occur not less than 30 days prior to the scheduled date of the hearing; and

(2) First class mail to persons who have requested notice as provided in subdivision (c)(2) of this section.

(g) The Commission on Health Services [Commission for Public Health] shall adopt rules prescribing the form and content of the notices required by this section. The proposed remedial action plan shall include a summary of all alternatives considered in the development of the plan. A record shall be maintained of all comment received by the Department regarding the remedial action plan. (1987, c. 574, s. 2; 1997-28, s. 2; 2010-180, s. 3.)

§ 130A-310.5. Authority of the Secretary with respect to sites which pose an imminent hazard.

(a) An imminent hazard exists whenever the Secretary determines, that there exists a condition caused by an inactive hazardous substance or waste disposal site, including a release or a substantial threat of a release into the environment of a hazardous substance from the site, which is causing serious harm to the public health or environment, or which is likely to cause such harm before a remedial action plan can be developed. Whenever the Secretary determines that an imminent hazard exists he may, in addition to any other powers he may have, without notice or hearing, order any known responsible party to take immediately any action necessary to eliminate or correct the condition, or the Secretary, in his discretion, may take such action without issuing an order. Written notice of any order issued pursuant to this section shall be provided to all persons subject to the order as set out in G.S. 130A-310.3(c). Unless the time required to do so would increase the harm to the public health or the environment, the Secretary shall solicit the cooperation of responsible parties prior to the entry of any such order. The provisions of subdivisions (1) to (3) of G.S. 130A-310.6(a) shall apply to any action taken by the Secretary pursuant to this section, and any such action shall be considered part of a remedial action program, the cost of which may be recovered from any responsible party.

(b)   If a person violates the requirements or schedules in an order issued pursuant to this section, the Secretary may institute an action for injunctive relief, irrespective of all other remedies at law, in the superior court of the county where the violation occurred or where a defendant resides.

(c)   The cost of any action by the Secretary pursuant to this section may be paid from the Inactive Hazardous Sites Cleanup Fund, or the Emergency Response Fund established pursuant to G.S. 130A-306, subject to a later action for reimbursement pursuant to G.S. 130A-310.7. (1987, c. 574, s. 2; 1989, c. 286, s. 4; 1989 (Reg. Sess., 1990), c. 1004, s. 9, c. 1024, s. 30(a); 1991, c. 342, s. 8.)

§ 130A-310.6. State action upon default of responsible parties or when no responsible party can be located.

(a)   Whenever a person ordered to develop and implement an inactive hazardous substance or waste disposal site remedial action program is unable or fails to do so within the time specified in the order, the Secretary may develop and implement or cause to be developed and implemented such a program. The cost of developing and implementing a remedial action program pursuant to this section may be paid from the Inactive Hazardous Sites Cleanup Fund, subject to a later action for reimbursement pursuant to G.S. 130A-310.7.

(1)   The Department is authorized and empowered to use any staff, equipment or materials under its control or provided by other cooperating federal, State or local agencies and to contract with any agent or contractor it deems appropriate to develop and implement the remedial action program. State agencies shall provide to the maximum extent feasible such staff, equipment, and materials as may be available for developing and implementing a remedial action program.

(2)   Upon completion of any inactive hazardous substance or waste disposal remedial action program, any State or local agency that has provided personnel, equipment, or material shall deliver to the Department a record of expenses incurred by the agency. The amount of the incurred expenses shall be disbursed by the Secretary to each such agency. The Secretary shall keep a

record of all expenses incurred for the services of State personnel and for the use of the State's equipment and material.

(3)   As soon as feasible or after completion of any inactive hazardous substance or waste disposal site remedial action program, the Secretary shall prepare a statement of all expenses and costs of the program expended by the State and issue an order demanding payment from responsible parties. Written notice of such an order shall be provided to all persons subject to the order personally or by certified mail. If given by certified mail, notice shall be deemed to have been given on the date appearing on the return of the receipt. If giving of notice cannot be accomplished either personally or by certified mail, notice shall then be given as provided in G.S. 1A-1, Rule 4(j).

(b)   If the Secretary, after declaring that an inactive hazardous substance or waste disposal site may endanger the public health or the environment, is unable, after making a reasonable attempt, to locate any responsible party, the Department may develop and implement a remedial action program for the site as provided in subsection (a)(1) and (2) of this section. If responsible parties are subsequently located, the Secretary may issue an order demanding payment from such persons in the manner set forth in subdivision (a)(3) of this section for the necessary expenses incurred by the Department for developing and implementing the remedial action program. If the persons subject to such an order refuse to pay the sum expended, or fail to pay such sum within the time specified in the order, the Secretary shall bring an action in the manner set forth in G.S. 130A-310.7.

(c)   The Secretary shall use funds allocated to the Department under G.S. 130A-295.9(1) to assess pre-1983 landfills, to determine the priority for remediation of pre-1983 landfills, and to develop and implement a remedial action plan for each pre-1983 landfill that requires remediation. Environmental and human health risks posed by a pre-1983 landfill may be mitigated using a risk-based approach for assessment and remediation.

(d)   The Secretary shall not seek cost recovery from a unit of local government for assessment and remedial action performed under subsection (c) of this section at a pre-1983 landfill. The Secretary shall not seek cost recovery for assessment and remedial action performed under subsection (c) of this section at a pre-1983 landfill from any other potentially responsible party if the Secretary develops and implements a remedial action plan for that pre-1983 landfill. If any potentially responsible party fails to cooperate with assessment of a site and implementation of control and mitigation measures at any site which the potentially responsible party owns or over which the potentially responsible party exercises control through a lease or other property interest, the Secretary may seek cost recovery for assessment and remedial action. Cooperation with assessment of a site and implementation of control and mitigation measures includes, but is not limited to, granting access to the site, allowing installation of monitoring wells, allowing installation and maintenance of improvements to the landfill cap, allowing installation of security measures, agreeing to record and implement land-use restrictions, and providing access to any records regarding the pre-1983 landfill. Nothing in this section shall alter any right, duty, obligation, or liability between a unit of local government and a third party. Nothing in this section shall alter any right, duty, obligation, or liability between any other potentially responsible party and a unit of local government, a third party, or, except as provided in this subsection, to the State.

(e) The Secretary shall develop and implement remedial action plans for pre-1983 landfills in the order of their priority determined as provided in subsection (c) of this section. The Secretary shall not develop or implement a remedial action plan for a pre-1983 landfill unless the Secretary determines that sufficient funds will be available from the Inactive Hazardous Sites Cleanup Fund to pay the costs of development and implementation of a remedial action plan for that pre-1983 landfill.

(f) A unit of local government that voluntarily undertakes assessment or remediation of a pre-1983 landfill may request that the Department reimburse the costs of assessment of the pre-1983 landfill and implementation of measures necessary to remediate the site to eliminate an imminent hazard. The Department shall provide reimbursement under this subsection if the Department finds all of the following:

(1) The unit of local government undertakes assessment and remediation under a plan approved by the Department.

(2) The unit of local government provides a certified accounting of costs incurred for assessment and remediation.

(3) Each contract for assessment and remediation complies with the requirements of Articles 3D and 8 of Chapter 143 of the General Statutes.

(4) Remedial action is limited to measures necessary to abate the imminent hazard.

(g)   The Department may undertake any additional action necessary to remediate a pre-1983 landfill based on the priority ranking of the site under subsection (c) of this section. (1987, c. 574, s. 2; 1989, c. 286, s. 5; 2007-550, s. 14(c).)

§ 130A-310.7. Action for reimbursement; liability of responsible parties; notification of completed remedial action.

(a)   Notwithstanding any other provision or rule of law, and subject only to the defenses set forth in this subsection, any person who:

(1)   Discharges or deposits; or

(2)   Contracts or arranges for any discharge or deposit; or

(3)   Accepts for discharge or deposit; or

(4)   Transports or arranges for transport for the purpose of discharge or deposit

any hazardous substance, the result of which discharge or deposit is the existence of an inactive hazardous substance or waste disposal site, shall be considered a responsible party. Neither an innocent landowner who is a bona fide purchaser of the inactive hazardous substance or waste disposal site without knowledge or without a reasonable basis for knowing that hazardous substance or waste disposal had occurred nor a person whose interest or ownership in the inactive hazardous substance or waste disposal site is based on or derived from a security interest in the property shall be considered a responsible party. A responsible party shall be directly liable to the State for any or all of the reasonably necessary expenses of developing and implementing a remedial action program for such site. The Secretary shall bring an action for reimbursement of the Inactive Hazardous Sites Cleanup Fund in the name of the State in the superior court of the county in which the site is located to recover such sum and the cost of bringing the action. The State must show that a danger to the public health or the environment existed and that the State complied with the provisions of this Part.

(b) There shall be no liability under this section for a person who can establish by a preponderance of the evidence that the danger to the public health or the environment caused by the site was caused solely by:

(1) An act of God; or

(2) An act of war; or

(3) An intentional act or omission of a third party (but this defense shall not be available if the act or omission is that of an employee or agent of the defendant, or if the act or omission occurs in connection with a contractual relationship with the defendant); or

(4) Any combination of the above causes.

(c) The definitions set out in G.S. 130A-310.31(b) apply to this subsection. Any person may submit a written request to the Department for a determination that a site that is subject to this Part has been remediated to unrestricted use standards as provided in Part 5 of Article 9 of Chapter 130A of the General Statutes. A request for a determination that a site has been remediated to unrestricted use standards shall be accompanied by the fee required by G.S. 130A-310.39(a)(2). If the Department determines that the site has been remediated to unrestricted use standards, the Department shall issue a written notification that no further remediation will be required at the site. The notification shall state that no further remediation will be required at the site unless the Department later determines, based on new information or information not previously provided to the Department, that the site has not been remediated to unrestricted use standards or that the Department was provided with false or incomplete information. Under any of those circumstances, the Department may withdraw the notification and require responsible parties to remediate the site to unrestricted use standards. (1987, c. 574, s. 2; 1989, c. 286, s. 6; 1989 (Reg. Sess., 1990), c. 1004, s. 10; c. 1024, s. 30(b); 1997-357, s. 5; 2001-384, s. 11.)

§ 130A-310.8. Recordation of inactive hazardous substance or waste disposal sites.

(a) After determination by the Department of the existence and location of an inactive hazardous substance or waste disposal site, the owner of the real property on which the site is located, within 180 days after official notice to the owner to do so, shall submit to the Department a survey plat of areas designated by the Department that has been prepared and certified by a professional land surveyor, and entitled "NOTICE OF INACTIVE HAZARDOUS SUBSTANCE OR WASTE DISPOSAL SITE". Where an inactive hazardous substance or waste disposal site is located on more than one parcel or tract of land, a composite map or plat showing all parcels or tracts may be recorded. The Notice shall include a legal description of the site that would be sufficient as a description in an instrument of conveyance, shall meet the requirements of G.S. 47-30 for maps and plats, and shall identify:

(1) The location and dimensions of the disposal areas and areas of potential environmental concern with respect to permanently surveyed benchmarks.

(2) The type, location, and quantity of hazardous substances known by the owner of the site to exist on the site.

(3) Any restrictions approved by the Department on the current or future use of the site.

(b) After the Department approves and certifies the Notice, the owner of the site shall file the certified copy of the Notice in the register of deeds' office in the county or counties in which the land is located within 15 days of the date on which the owner receives approval of the Notice from the Department.

(c) Repealed by Session Laws 2012-18, s. 1.18, effective July 1, 2012.

(d) In the event that the owner of the site fails to submit and file the Notice required by this section within the time specified, the Secretary may prepare and file such Notice. The costs thereof may be recovered by the Secretary from any responsible party. In the event that an owner of a site who is not a responsible party submits and files the Notice required by this section, he may recover the reasonable costs thereof from any responsible party.

(e) When an inactive hazardous substance or waste disposal site is sold, leased, conveyed, or transferred, the deed or other instrument of transfer shall contain in the description section, in no smaller type than that used in the body of the deed or instrument, a statement that the property has been used as a hazardous substance or waste disposal site and a reference by book and page to the recordation of the Notice.

(f) A Notice of Inactive Hazardous Substance or Waste Disposal Site filed pursuant to this section may, at the request of the owner of the land, be cancelled by the Secretary after the hazards have been eliminated. If requested in writing by the owner of the land and if the Secretary concurs with the request, the Secretary shall send to the register of deeds of each county where the Notice is recorded a statement that the hazards have been eliminated and request that the Notice be cancelled of record. The Secretary's statement shall contain the names of the owners of the land as shown in the Notice and reference the plat book and page where the Notice is recorded.

(g) Recordation under this section is not required for any inactive hazardous substance or waste disposal site that is undergoing voluntary remedial action pursuant to this Part unless the Secretary determines that either:

(1) A concentration of a hazardous substance or hazardous waste that poses a danger to public health or the environment will remain following implementation of the voluntary remedial action program.

(2) The voluntary remedial action program is not being implemented in a manner satisfactory to the Secretary and in compliance with the agreement between the Secretary and the owner, operator, or other responsible party.

(h) The Secretary may waive recordation under this section with respect to any residential real property that is contaminated solely because a hazardous substance or hazardous waste migrated to the property from other property by means of groundwater flow if disclosure of the contamination is required under Chapter 47E of the General Statutes. An owner of residential real property whose recordation requirement is waived by the Secretary under this subsection and who fails to disclose contamination as required by Chapter 47E of the General Statutes is subject to both the penalties and remedies under this Chapter applicable to a person who fails to comply with the recordation requirements of this section as though those requirements had not been waived and to the remedies available under Chapter 47E of the General Statutes. (1987, c. 574, s. 2; 1989, c. 727, s. 219(34); 1989 (Reg. Sess., 1990), c. 1004, s. 19(b); 1997-394, s. 2; 1997-443, ss. 11A.119(a), (b); 1997-528, s. 1; 2012-18, s. 1.18.)

§ 130A-310.9. Voluntary remedial actions; limitation of liability; agreements; implementation and oversight by private engineering and consulting firms.

(a) No one owner, operator, or other responsible party who voluntarily participates in the implementation of a remedial action program under G.S. 130A-310.3 or G.S. 130A-310.5 may be required to pay in excess of five million dollars ($5,000,000) for the cost of implementing a remedial action program at a single inactive hazardous substance or waste disposal site. The owner, operator, or other responsible party who voluntarily participates in the implementation of a remedial action program under G.S. 130A-310.3 or G.S. 130A-310.5 shall be required to pay in addition to the cost of implementing the remedial action program a fee of one thousand dollars ($1,000) to be used for the Department's cost of monitoring and enforcing the remedial action program. The limitation of liability contained in this subsection applies to the cost of implementing the program and to the fee under this subsection. The limitation of liability contained in this subsection does not apply to the cost of developing the remedial action plan.

(b) The Secretary may enter into an agreement with an owner, operator, or other responsible party that provides for implementation of a voluntary remedial action program in accordance with a remedial action plan approved by the Department. Investigations, evaluations, and voluntary remedial actions are subject to the provisions of G.S. 130A-310.1(c), 130A-310.1(d), 130A-310.3(d), 130A-310.3(f), 130A-310.5, 130A-310.8, and any other requirement imposed by the Department. A voluntary remedial action and all documents that relate to the voluntary remedial action shall be fully subject to inspection and audit by the Department. At least 30 days prior to entering into any agreement providing for the implementation of a voluntary remedial action program, the Secretary shall mail notice of the proposed agreement as provided in G.S. 130A-310.4(c)(2). Sites undergoing voluntary remedial actions shall be so identified as a separate category in the inventory of sites maintained pursuant to G.S. 130A-310.1 but shall not be included on the Inactive Hazardous Waste Sites Priority List required by G.S. 130A-310.2.

(c) The Department may approve a private environmental consulting and engineering firm to implement and oversee a voluntary remedial action by an owner, operator, or other responsible party. An owner, operator, or other responsible party who enters into an agreement with the Secretary to implement a voluntary remedial action may hire a private environmental consulting or engineering firm approved by the Department to implement and oversee the voluntary remedial action. A voluntary remedial action that is implemented and overseen by a private environmental consulting or engineering firm shall be implemented in accordance with all federal and State laws, regulations, and rules that apply to remedial actions generally and is subject to rules adopted pursuant to G.S. 130A-310.12(b). The Department may revoke its approval of the oversight of a voluntary remedial action by a private environmental consulting or engineering firm and assume direct oversight of the voluntary remedial action whenever it appears to the Department that the voluntary remedial action is not being properly implemented or is not being adequately overseen. The Department may require the owner, operator, other responsible party, or private environmental consulting or engineering firm to take any action necessary to bring the voluntary remedial action into compliance with applicable requirements. (1987, c. 574, s. 2; 1989, c. 286, s. 7; 1993 (Reg. Sess., 1994), c. 598, s. 1; 1995, c. 327, s. 2; 1997-394, s. 3; 2007-107, s. 1.1(g); 2009-451, s. 13.3C(a).)

§ 130A-310.10. Annual reports.

(a) The Secretary shall report on inactive hazardous sites to the Joint Legislative Commission on Governmental Operations, the Environmental Review Commission, and the Fiscal Research Division on or before October 1 of each year. The report shall include at least the following:

(1) The Inactive Hazardous Waste Sites Priority List.

(2) A list of remedial action plans requiring State funding through the Inactive Hazardous Sites Cleanup Fund.

(3) A comprehensive budget to implement these remedial action plans and the adequacy of the Inactive Hazardous Sites Cleanup Fund to fund the cost of said plans.

(4) A prioritized list of sites that are eligible for remedial action under CERCLA/SARA together with recommended remedial action plans and a comprehensive budget to implement such plans. The budget for implementing a remedial action plan under CERCLA/SARA shall include a statement as to any appropriation that may be necessary to pay the State's share of such plan.

(5) A list of sites and remedial action plans undergoing voluntary cleanup with Departmental approval.

(6) A list of sites and remedial action plans that may require State funding, a comprehensive budget if implementation of these possible remedial action plans

is required, and the adequacy of the Inactive Hazardous Sites Cleanup Fund to fund the possible costs of said plans.

(7)   A list of sites that pose an imminent hazard.

(8)   A comprehensive budget to develop and implement remedial action plans for sites that pose imminent hazards and that may require State funding, and the adequacy of the Inactive Hazardous Sites Cleanup Fund.

(8a)   The amounts and sources of funds collected by year received under G.S. 130A-310.76, the amounts and sources of those funds paid into the Inactive Hazardous Sites Cleanup Fund established pursuant to G.S. 130A-310.11, the number of acres of contamination for which funds have been received pursuant to G.S. 130A-310.76, and a detailed annual accounting of how the funds collected pursuant to G.S. 130A-310.76 have been utilized by the Department to advance the purposes of Part 8 of Article 9 of Chapter 130A of the General Statutes.

(9)   Any other information requested by the General Assembly or the Environmental Review Commission.

(a1)   On or before October 1 of each year, the Department shall report to each member of the General Assembly who has an inactive hazardous substance or waste disposal site in the member's district. This report shall include the location of each inactive hazardous substance or waste disposal site in the member's district, the type and amount of hazardous substances or waste known or believed to be located on each of these sites, the last action taken at each of these sites, and the date of that last action.

(b)   Repealed by Session Laws 2001-452, s. 2.3, effective October 28, 2001. (1987, c. 574, s. 2; 1989, c. 286, s. 8; 1997-28, s. 1; 2001-452, s. 2.3; 2010-31, s. 13.9(b); 2011-186, s. 4; 2012-200, s. 22.)

§ 130A-310.11. Inactive Hazardous Sites Cleanup Fund created.

(a)   There is established under the control and direction of the Department the Inactive Hazardous Sites Cleanup Fund. This fund shall be a revolving fund consisting of any monies appropriated for such purpose by the General Assembly or available to it from grants, taxes, and other monies paid to it or recovered by or on behalf of the Department. The Inactive Hazardous Sites Cleanup Fund shall be treated as a nonreverting special trust fund and shall be credited with interest by the State Treasurer pursuant to G.S. 147-69.2 and G.S. 147-69.3.

(b) Funds credited to the Inactive Hazardous Sites Cleanup Fund pursuant to G.S. 130A-295.9 shall be used only as provided in G.S. 130A-295.9(1) and G.S. 130A-310.6(c). (1987, c. 574, s. 2; 1989, c. 286, s. 9; 2007-550, s. 14(d); 2009-484, s. 11; 2010-142, s. 12.)

§ 130A-310.12. Administrative procedure; adoption of rules.

(a) The provisions of Chapter 150B of the General Statutes apply to this Part. The Commission shall adopt rules for the implementation of this Part.

(b) The Commission shall adopt rules governing the selection and use of private environmental consulting and engineering firms to implement and oversee voluntary remedial actions by owners, operators, or other responsible parties under G.S. 130A-310.9(c). Rules adopted under this subsection shall specify:

(1) Standards applicable to private environmental consulting and engineering firms.

(2) Criteria and procedures for approval of firms by the Department.

(3) Requirements and procedures under which the Department monitors and audits a voluntary remedial action to ensure that the voluntary remedial action complies with applicable federal and State law, regulations, and under which the owner, operator, or other responsible party reimburses the Department for the cost of monitoring and auditing the voluntary remedial action.

(4) Any financial assurances that may be required of an owner, operator, or other responsible party.

(5) Requirements for the preparation, maintenance, and public availability of work plans and records, reports of data collection including sampling, sample analysis, and other site testing, and other records and reports that are

consistent with the requirements applicable to remedial actions generally. (1987, c. 574, ss. 2, 5; 1993 (Reg. Sess., 1994), c. 598, s. 2; 1995, c. 327, s. 3.)

§ 130A-310.13. Short title.

This Part shall be known and may be cited as the Inactive Hazardous Sites Response Act of 1987. (1991, c. 281, s. 3)

§§ 130A-310.14 through 130A-310.19. Reserved for future codification purposes.

Part 4. Superfund Program.

§ 130A-310.20. Definitions.

Unless a different meaning is required by the context, the following definitions shall apply throughout this Part:

(1) "CERCLA/SARA" or "Superfund" means the Comprehensive Environmental Response, Compensation, and Liability Act of 1980, Pub. L. No. 96-510, 94 Stat. 2767, 42 U.S.C. § 9601 et seq., as amended, and the Superfund Amendments and Reauthorization Act of 1986, Pub. L. No. 99-499, 100 Stat. 1613, as amended. (1989, c. 286, s. 10.)

§ 130A-310.21. Administration of the Superfund program.

The Department shall maintain an appropriate administrative subunit within the solid waste management unit authorized by G.S. 130A-291 to carry out those activities in which the State is authorized to engage under CERCLA/SARA. (1989, c. 286, s. 10.)

§ 130A-310.22. Contracts authorized.

(a) The Department is authorized to enter into contracts and cooperative agreements with the United States and to engage in any activity otherwise authorized by law to identify, investigate, evaluate, and clean up any site or facility covered by CERCLA/SARA including but not limited to performing preliminary assessments, site investigations, remedial investigations, and feasibility studies; preparation of records of decision; conducting emergency response, remedial, and removal actions; and engaging in enforcement activities in accordance with the provisions of CERCLA/SARA.

(b) The Department may make all assurances required by federal law or regulation including but not limited to assuring that the State will assume responsibility for the operation and maintenance of any remedial action for the anticipated duration of the remedial action; assuring that the State will provide its share of the cost of any remedial action at a site or facility which was privately owned or operated; assuring that the State will provide its share of the cost of any removal, remedial planning, and remedial action at a site or facility owned or operated by the State or a political subdivision of the State; assuring the availability of off-site treatment, storage, or disposal capacity needed to effectuate a remedial action; assuring that the State will take title to, acquire an interest in, or accept transfer of any interest in real property needed to effectuate a remedial action; assuring that the State has adequate capacity to meet the assurances required by CERCLA/SARA (42 U.S.C. § 9604(c)(9)); assuring access to the facility and any adjacent property including the securing of any right-of-way or easement needed to effectuate a remedial action; and assuring that the State will satisfy all federal, State, and local requirements for permits and approvals necessary to effectuate a remedial action.

(c) Each contract entered into by the Department under this section shall stipulate that all obligations of the State are subject to the availability of funds. Neither this section nor any contract entered into under authority of this section shall be construed to obligate the General Assembly to make any appropriation to implement this Part or any contract entered into under this section. The Department shall implement this Part and any contract entered into under this section from funds otherwise available or appropriated to the Department for such purpose. (1989, c. 286, s. 10; 1989 (Reg. Sess., 1990), c. 1004, s. 11, c. 1024, s. 30(c).)

§ 130A-310.23. Filing notices of CERCLA/SARA (Superfund) liens.

Notices of liens and certificates of notices affecting liens for obligations payable to the United States under CERCLA/SARA (Superfund) (42 U.S.C. § 9607(l)) shall be filed in accordance with Article 11A of Chapter 44 of the General

Statutes. (1989 (Reg. Sess., 1990), c. 1047, s. 1.1; 1991 (Reg. Sess., 1992), c. 890, s. 11.)

§§ 130A-310.24 through 130A-310.29. Reserved for future codification purposes.

Part 5. Brownfields Property Reuse Act.

§ 130A-310.30. Short title.

This Part may be cited as The Brownfields Property Reuse Act of 1997. (1997-357, s. 2.)

§ 130A-310.31. Definitions.

(a) Unless a different meaning is required by the context or unless a different meaning is set out in subsection (b) of this section, the definitions in G.S. 130A-2 and G.S. 130A-310 apply throughout this Part.

(b) Unless a different meaning is required by the context:

(1) "Affiliate" has the same meaning as in 17 Code of Federal Regulations § 240.12b-2 (1 April 1996 Edition).

(2) "Brownfields agreement" means an agreement between the Department and a prospective developer that meets the requirements of G.S. 130A-310.32.

(3) "Brownfields property" or "brownfields site" means abandoned, idled, or underused property at which expansion or redevelopment is hindered by actual environmental contamination or the possibility of environmental contamination and that is or may be subject to remediation under any State remedial program or that is or may be subject to remediation under the Comprehensive Environmental Response, Compensation and Liability Act of 1980, as amended (42 U.S.C. § 9601, et seq.) except for a site listed on the National Priorities List pursuant to 42 U.S.C. § 9605.

(4) "Contaminant" means a regulated substance released into the environment.

(5) "Unrestricted use standards" when used in connection with "cleanup", "remediated", or "remediation" means contaminant concentrations for each environmental medium that are considered acceptable for all uses and that comply with generally applicable standards, guidance, or established methods governing the contaminants that are established by statute or adopted, published, or implemented by the Environmental Management Commission, the Commission, or the Department instead of the site-specific contaminant levels established pursuant to this Part.

(6) "Environmental contamination" means contaminants at the property requiring remediation and that are to be remediated under the brownfields agreement including, at a minimum, hazardous waste, as defined in G.S. 130A-290; a hazardous substance, as defined in G.S. 130A-310; a hazardous substance, as defined in G.S. 143-215.77; or oil, as defined in G.S. 143-215.77.

(7) "Local government" means a town, city, or county.

(8) "Parent" has the same meaning as in 17 Code of Federal Regulations § 240.12b-2 (1 April 1996 Edition).

(9) "Potentially responsible party" means a person who is or may be liable for remediation under a remedial program.

(10) "Prospective developer" means any person with a bona fide, demonstrable desire to either buy or sell a brownfields property for the purpose of developing or redeveloping that brownfields property and who did not cause or contribute to the contamination at the brownfields property.

(11) "Regulated substance" means a hazardous waste, as defined in G.S. 130A-290; a hazardous substance, as defined in G.S. 143-215.77A; oil, as defined in G.S. 143-215.77; or other substance regulated under any remedial program implemented by the Department.

(12) "Remedial program" means a program implemented by the Department for the remediation of any contaminant, including the Inactive Hazardous Sites Response Act of 1987 under Part 3 of this Article, the Superfund Program under Part 4 of this Article, and the Oil Pollution and Hazardous Substances Control Act of 1978 under Part 2 of Article 21A of Chapter 143 of the General Statutes.

(13) "Remediation" means action to clean up, mitigate, correct, abate, minimize, eliminate, control, or prevent the spreading, migration, leaking,

leaching, volatilization, spilling, transport, or further release of a contaminant into the environment in order to protect public health or the environment.

(14) "Subsidiary" has the same meaning as in 17 Code of Federal Regulations § 240.12b-2 (1 April 1996 Edition). (1997-357, s. 2; 1997-392, ss. 4.2-4.4; 2001-384, s. 11; 2006-71, ss. 1, 2, 3; 2013-108, s. 1.)

§ 130A-310.32. Brownfields agreement.

(a) The Department may, in its discretion, enter into a brownfields agreement with a prospective developer who satisfies the requirements of this section. A prospective developer shall provide the Department with any information necessary to demonstrate that:

(1) The prospective developer, and any parent, subsidiary, or other affiliate of the prospective developer has substantially complied with:

a. The terms of any brownfields agreement or similar agreement to which the prospective developer or any parent, subsidiary, or other affiliate of the prospective developer has been a party.

b. The requirements applicable to any remediation in which the applicant has previously engaged.

c. Federal and state laws, regulations, and rules for the protection of the environment.

(2) As a result of the implementation of the brownfields agreement, the brownfields property will be suitable for the uses specified in the agreement while fully protecting public health and the environment instead of being remediated to unrestricted use standards.

(3) There is a public benefit commensurate with the liability protection provided under this Part.

(4) The prospective developer has or can obtain the financial, managerial, and technical means to fully implement the brownfields agreement and assure the safe use of the brownfields property.

(5) The prospective developer has complied with or will comply with all applicable procedural requirements.

(b) In negotiating a brownfields agreement, parties may rely on land-use restrictions that will be included in a Notice of Brownfields Property required under G.S. 130A-310.35. A brownfields agreement may provide for remediation standards that are based on those land-use restrictions.

(c) A brownfields agreement shall contain a description of the brownfields property that would be sufficient as a description of the property in an instrument of conveyance and, as applicable, a statement of:

(1) Any remediation to be conducted on the property, including:

a. A description of specific areas where remediation is to be conducted.

b. The remediation method or methods to be employed.

c. The resources that the prospective developer will make available.

d. A schedule of remediation activities.

e. Applicable remediation standards.

f. A schedule and the method or methods for evaluating the remediation.

(2) Any land-use restrictions that will apply to the brownfields property.

(3) The desired results of any remediation or land-use restrictions with respect to the brownfields property.

(4) The guidelines, including parameters, principles, and policies within which the desired results are to be accomplished.

(5) The consequences of achieving or not achieving the desired results.

(d) Any failure of the prospective developer or the prospective developer's agents and employees to comply with the brownfields agreement constitutes a violation of this Part by the prospective developer. (1997-357, s. 2; 2001-384, s. 11.)

§ 130A-310.33. Liability protection.

(a)   A prospective developer who enters into a brownfields agreement with the Department and who is complying with the brownfields agreement shall not be held liable for remediation of areas of contaminants identified in the brownfields agreement except as specified in the brownfields agreement, so long as the activities conducted on the brownfields property by or under the control or direction of the prospective developer do not increase the risk of harm to public health or the environment and the prospective developer is not required to undertake additional remediation to unrestricted use standards pursuant to subsection (c) of this section. The liability protection provided under this Part applies to all of the following persons to the same extent as to a prospective developer, so long as these persons are not otherwise potentially responsible parties or parents, subsidiaries, or affiliates of potentially responsible parties and the person is not required to undertake additional remediation to unrestricted use standards pursuant to subsection (c) of this section:

(1)   Any person under the direction or control of the prospective developer who directs or contracts for remediation or redevelopment of the brownfields property.

(2)   Any future owner of the brownfields property.

(3)   A person who develops or occupies the brownfields property.

(4)   A successor or assign of any person to whom the liability protection provided under this Part applies.

(5)   Any lender or fiduciary that provides financing for remediation or redevelopment of the brownfields property.

(b)   A person who conducts an environmental assessment or transaction screen on a brownfields property and who is not otherwise a potentially responsible party is not a potentially responsible party as a result of conducting the environmental assessment or transaction screen unless that person increases the risk of harm to public health or the environment by failing to exercise due diligence and reasonable care in performing the environmental assessment or transaction screen.

(c) If a land-use restriction set out in the Notice of Brownfields Property required under G.S. 130A-310.35 is violated, the owner of the brownfields property at the time the land-use restriction is violated, the owner's successors and assigns, and the owner's agents who direct or contract for alteration of the brownfields property in violation of a land-use restriction shall be liable for remediation to unrestricted use standards. A prospective developer who completes the remediation or redevelopment required under a brownfields agreement or other person who receives liability protection under this Part shall not be required to undertake additional remediation at the brownfields property unless any of the following apply:

(1) The prospective developer knowingly or recklessly provides false information that forms a basis for the brownfields agreement or that is offered to demonstrate compliance with the brownfields agreement or fails to disclose relevant information about contamination at the brownfields property.

(2) New information indicates the existence of previously unreported contaminants or an area of previously unreported contamination on or associated with the brownfields property that has not been remediated to unrestricted use standards, unless the brownfields agreement is amended to include any previously unreported contaminants and any additional areas of contamination. If the brownfields agreement sets maximum concentrations for contaminants, and new information indicates the existence of previously unreported areas of these contaminants, further remediation shall be required only if the areas of previously unreported contaminants raise the risk of the contamination to public health or the environment to a level less protective of public health and the environment than that required by the brownfields agreement.

(3) The level of risk to public health or the environment from contaminants is unacceptable at or in the vicinity of the brownfields property due to changes in exposure conditions, including (i) a change in land use that increases the probability of exposure to contaminants or in the vicinity of the brownfields property or (ii) the failure of remediation to mitigate risks to the extent required to make the brownfields property fully protective of public health and the environment as planned in the brownfields agreement.

(4) The Department obtains new information about a contaminant associated with the brownfields property or exposures at or around the brownfields property that raises the risk to public health or the environment associated with the brownfields property beyond an acceptable range and in a

manner or to a degree not anticipated in the brownfields agreement. Any person whose use, including any change in use, of the brownfields property causes an unacceptable risk to public health or the environment may be required by the Department to undertake additional remediation measures under the provisions of this Part.

(5)   A prospective developer fails to file a timely and proper Notice of Brownfields Development under this Part. (1997-357, s. 2; 2001-384, s. 11.)

§ 130A-310.34. Public notice and community involvement.

(a)   A prospective developer who desires to enter into a brownfields agreement shall notify the public and the community in which the brownfields property is located of planned remediation and redevelopment activities. The prospective developer shall submit a Notice of Intent to Redevelop a Brownfields Property and a summary of the Notice of Intent to the Department. The Notice of Intent shall provide, to the extent known, a legal description of the location of the brownfields property, a map showing the location of the brownfields property, a description of the contaminants involved and their concentrations in the media of the brownfields property, a description of the intended future use of the brownfields property, any proposed investigation and remediation, and a proposed Notice of Brownfields Property prepared in accordance with G.S. 130A-310.35. Both the Notice of Intent and the summary of the Notice of Intent shall state the time period and means for submitting written comment and for requesting a public meeting on the proposed brownfields agreement. The summary of the Notice of Intent shall include a statement as to the public availability of the full Notice of Intent. After approval of the Notice of Intent and summary of the Notice of Intent by the Department, the prospective developer shall provide a copy of the Notice of Intent to all local governments having jurisdiction over the brownfields property. The prospective developer shall publish the summary of the Notice of Intent in a newspaper of general circulation serving the area in which the brownfields property is located. The prospective developer shall conspicuously post a copy of the summary of the Notice of Intent at the brownfields property, and the prospective developer shall mail or deliver a copy of the summary to each owner of property contiguous to the brownfields property. The prospective developer shall submit documentation of the public notices to the Department prior to the Department entering into a brownfields agreement.

(b) Publication of the approved summary of the Notice of Intent in a newspaper of general circulation, posting the summary at the brownfields property, and mailing or delivering the summary to each owner of property contiguous to the brownfields property shall begin a public comment period of at least 30 days from the latest date of publication, posting, and mailing or delivering. During the public comment period, members of the public, residents of the community in which the brownfields property is located, and local governments having jurisdiction over the brownfields property may submit comment on the proposed brownfields agreement, including methods and degree of remediation, future land uses, and impact on local employment.

(c) Any person who desires a public meeting on a proposed brownfields agreement shall submit a written request for a public meeting to the Department within 21 days after the public comment period begins. The Department shall consider all requests for a public meeting and shall hold a public meeting if the Department determines that there is significant public interest in the proposed brownfields agreement. If the Department decides to hold a public meeting, the Department shall, at least 15 days prior to the public meeting, mail written notice of the public meeting to all persons who requested the public meeting and to each owner of property contiguous to the brownfields property. The Department shall also direct the prospective developer to publish, at least 15 days prior to the date of the public meeting, a notice of the public meeting at least one time in a newspaper having general circulation in such county where the brownfields property is located. In any county in which there is more than one newspaper having general circulation, the Department shall direct the prospective developer to publish a copy of the notice in as many newspapers having general circulation in the county as the Department in its discretion determines to be necessary to assure that the notice is generally available throughout the county. The Department shall prescribe the form and content of the notice to be published. The Department shall prescribe the procedures to be followed in the public meeting. The Department shall take detailed minutes of the meeting. The minutes shall include any written comments, exhibits, or documents presented at the meeting.

(d) Prior to entering into a brownfields agreement, the Department shall take into account the comment received during the comment period and at the public meeting if the Department holds a public meeting. The Department shall incorporate into the brownfields agreement provisions that reflect comment received during the comment period and at the public meeting to the extent practical. The Department shall give particular consideration to written comment that is supported by valid scientific and technical information and analysis and to written comment from the units of local government that have taxing jurisdiction over the brownfields property. (1997-357, s. 2; 2000-158, s. 2; 2006-71, ss. 4, 5; 2009-181, s. 1.)

§ 130A-310.35. Notice of Brownfields Property; land-use restrictions in deed.

(a) In order to reduce or eliminate the danger to public health or the environment posed by a brownfields property being addressed under this Part, a prospective developer who desires to enter into a brownfields agreement with the Department shall submit to the Department a proposed Notice of Brownfields Property. A Notice of Brownfields Property shall be entitled "Notice of Brownfields Property", shall include a survey plat of areas designated by the Department that has been prepared and certified by a professional land surveyor and that meets the requirements of G.S. 47-30, shall include a legal description of the brownfields property that would be sufficient as a description of the property in an instrument of conveyance, and shall identify all of the following:

(1) The location and dimensions of the areas of potential environmental concern with respect to permanently surveyed benchmarks.

(2) The type, location, and quantity of regulated substances and contaminants known to exist on the brownfields property.

(3) Any restrictions on the current or future use of the brownfields property or, with the owner's permission, other property that are necessary or useful to maintain the level of protection appropriate for the designated current or future use of the brownfields property and that are designated in the brownfields agreement. These land-use restrictions may apply to activities on, over, or under the land, including, but not limited to, use of groundwater, building, filling, grading, excavating, and mining. Where a brownfields property encompasses more than one parcel or tract of land, a composite map or plat showing all parcels or tracts may be recorded.

(b) After the Department approves and certifies the Notice of Brownfields Property under subsection (a) of this section, a prospective developer who enters into a brownfields agreement with the Department shall file a certified copy of the Notice of Brownfields Property in the register of deeds' office in the county or counties in which the land is located. The prospective developer shall file the Notice of Brownfields Property within 15 days of the prospective developer's receipt of the Department's approval of the notice or the prospective developer's entry into the brownfields agreement, whichever is later.

(c) Repealed by Session Laws 2012-18, s. 1.19, effective July 1, 2012.

(d) When a brownfields property is sold, leased, conveyed, or transferred, the deed or other instrument of transfer shall contain in the description section, in no smaller type than that used in the body of the deed or instrument, a statement that the brownfields property has been classified and, if appropriate, cleaned up as a brownfields property under this Part.

(e) A Notice of Brownfields Property filed pursuant to this section may, at the request of the owner of the land, be cancelled by the Secretary after the hazards have been eliminated. If requested in writing by the owner of the land and if the Secretary concurs with the request, the Secretary shall send to the register of deeds of each county where the notice is recorded a statement that the hazards have been eliminated and request that the notice be cancelled of record. The Secretary's statement shall contain the names of the owners of the land as shown in the notice and reference the plat book and page where the notice is recorded.

(f) Any land-use restriction filed pursuant to this section shall be enforced by any owner of the land. Any land-use restriction may also be enforced by the Department through the remedies provided in Part 2 of Article 1 of this Chapter or by means of a civil action. The Department may enforce any land-use restriction without first having exhausted any available administrative remedies. A land-use restriction may also be enforced by any unit of local government having jurisdiction over any part of the brownfields property by means of a civil action without the unit of local government having first exhausted any available administrative remedy. A land-use restriction may also be enforced by any person eligible for liability protection under this Part who will lose liability protection if the land-use restriction is violated. A land-use restriction shall not be declared unenforceable due to lack of privity of estate or contract, due to lack of benefit to particular land, or due to lack of any property interest in particular land. Any person who owns or leases a property subject to a land-use restriction under this section shall abide by the land-use restriction.

(g) This section shall apply in lieu of the provisions of G.S. 130A-310.8 for brownfields properties remediated under this Part. (1997-357, s. 2; 1997-443, s. 11A.119(b); 2012-18, s. 1.19.)

§ 130A-310.36. Appeals.

A decision by the Department as to whether or not to enter into a brownfields agreement including the terms of any brownfields agreement is reviewable under Article 3 of Chapter 150B of the General Statutes. (1997-357, s. 2.)

§ 130A-310.37. Construction of Part.

(a) This Part is not intended and shall not be construed to:

(1) Affect the ability of local governments to regulate land use under Article 19 of Chapter 160A of the General Statutes and Article 18 of Chapter 153A of the General Statutes. The use of the identified brownfields property and any land-use restrictions in the brownfields agreement shall be consistent with local land-use controls adopted under those statutes.

(2) Amend, modify, repeal, or otherwise alter any provision of any remedial program or other provision of this Chapter, Chapter 143 of the General Statutes, or any other provision of law relating to civil and criminal penalties or enforcement actions and remedies available to the Department, except as may be provided in a brownfields agreement.

(3) Prevent or impede the immediate response of the Department or responsible party to an emergency that involves an imminent or actual release of a regulated substance that threatens public health or the environment.

(4) Relieve a person receiving liability protection under this Part from any liability for contamination later caused by that person on a brownfields property.

(5) Affect the right of any person to seek any relief available against any party to the brownfields agreement who may have liability with respect to the brownfields property, except that this Part does limit the relief available against any party to a brownfields agreement with respect to remediation of the brownfields property to the remediation required under the brownfields agreement.

(6) Affect the right of any person who may have liability with respect to the brownfields property to seek contribution from any other person who may have

liability with respect to the brownfields property and who neither received nor has liability protection under this Part.

(7) Prevent the State from enforcing specific numerical remediation standards, monitoring, or compliance requirements specifically required to be enforced by the federal government as a condition to receive program authorization, delegation, primacy, or federal funds.

(8) Create a defense against the imposition of criminal and civil fines or penalties or administrative penalties otherwise authorized by law and imposed as the result of the illegal disposal of waste or for the pollution of the land, air, or waters of this State on a brownfields property.

(9) Relieve a person of any liability for failure to exercise due diligence and reasonable care in performing an environmental assessment or transaction screen.

(b) Notwithstanding the provisions of the Tort Claims Act, G.S. 143-291 through G.S. 143-300.1 or any other provision of law waiving the sovereign immunity of the State of North Carolina, the State, its agencies, officers, employees, and agents shall be absolutely immune from any liability in any proceeding for any injury or claim arising from negotiating, entering, monitoring, or enforcing a brownfields agreement or a Notice of Brownfields Property under this Part or any other action implementing this Part.

(c) The Department shall not enter into a brownfields agreement for a site listed on the National Priorities List pursuant to 42 U.S.C. § 9605. (1997-357, s. 2; 1997-392, s. 4.5; 2006-71, s. 6.)

§ 130A-310.38. Brownfields Property Reuse Act Implementation Account.

The Brownfields Property Reuse Act Implementation Account is created as a nonreverting interest-bearing account in the Office of the State Treasurer. The Account shall consist of fees and interest collected under G.S. 130A-310.39, moneys appropriated to it by the General Assembly, moneys received from the federal government, moneys contributed by private organizations, and moneys received from any other source. Funds in the Account shall be used by the Department to defray the costs of implementing this Part. The Department may contract with a private entity for any services necessary to implement this Part. (1997-357, s. 2; 1999-360, s. 17.2.)

§ 130A-310.39. Fees.

(a)   The Department shall collect the following fees:

(1)   A prospective developer who submits a proposed brownfields agreement for review by the Department shall pay an initial fee of two thousand dollars ($2,000).

(2)   A prospective developer who enters into a brownfields agreement with the Department shall pay a fee in an amount equal to the full cost to the Department and the Department of Justice of all activities related to the brownfields agreement, including but not limited to negotiation of the brownfields agreement, public notice and community involvement, and monitoring the implementation of the brownfields agreement. The procedure by which the amount of this fee is determined shall be established by agreement between the prospective developer and the Department and shall be set out as a part of the brownfields agreement. The fee imposed by this subdivision shall be paid in two installments. The first installment shall be due at the time the prospective developer and the Department enter into the brownfields agreement and shall equal all costs that have been incurred by the Department and the Department of Justice at that time less the amount of the initial fee paid pursuant to subdivision (1) of this subsection. The Department shall not enter into the brownfields agreement unless the first installment is paid in full when due. The second installment shall be due at the time the prospective developer submits a final report certifying completion of remediation under the brownfields agreement and shall include any additional costs that have been incurred by the Department and the Department of Justice, including all costs of monitoring the implementation of the brownfields agreement.

(b)   Fees and interest imposed under this section shall be credited to the Brownfields Property Reuse Act Implementation Account.

(c)   If a prospective developer fails to pay the full amount of any fee due under this section, interest on the unpaid portion of the fee shall accrue from the time the fee is due until paid at the rate established by the Secretary of Revenue pursuant to G.S. 105-241.21. A lien for the amount of the unpaid fee plus interest shall attach to the real and personal property of the prospective developer and to the brownfields property until the fee and interest is paid. The Department may collect unpaid fees and interest in any manner that a unit of local government may collect delinquent taxes. (1997-357, s. 2; 1999-360, s. 17.3; 2007-491, s. 44(1)(a).)

§ 130A-310.40. Legislative reports.

The Department shall prepare and submit to the Environmental Review Commission, concurrently with the report on the Inactive Hazardous Sites Response Act of 1987 required under G.S. 130A-310.10, an evaluation of the effectiveness of this Part in facilitating the remediation and reuse of existing industrial and commercial properties. This evaluation shall include any recommendations for additional incentives or changes, if needed, to improve the effectiveness of this Part in addressing such properties. This evaluation shall also include a report on receipts by and expenditures from the Brownfields Property Reuse Act Implementation Account. (1997-357, s. 2.)

§ 130A-310.41: Reserved for future codification purposes.

§ 130A-310.42: Reserved for future codification purposes.

§ 130A-310.43: Reserved for future codification purposes.

§ 130A-310.44: Reserved for future codification purposes.

§ 130A-310.45: Reserved for future codification purposes.

§ 130A-310.46: Reserved for future codification purposes.

§ 130A-310.47: Reserved for future codification purposes.

§ 130A-310.48: Reserved for future codification purposes.

§ 130A-310.49: Reserved for future codification purposes.

Part 6. Mercury Switch Removal.

§ 130A-310.50. (Effective until December 31, 2017) Definitions.

As used in this Part:

(1)   Repealed by Session Laws 2007-142, s. 1, effective June 29, 2007.

(2)   "End-of-life vehicle" means a vehicle that is sold, given, or otherwise conveyed to a vehicle crusher, vehicle dismantler, vehicle recycler, or scrap vehicle processing facility for the purpose of recycling.

(2a)   "Inaccessible", when used in connection with mercury switch, means that, due to the condition of the vehicle, the mercury switch cannot be removed from a vehicle without a significant risk of a release of mercury into the environment.

(3), (4) Repealed by Session Laws 2007-142, s. 1, effective June 29, 2007.

(4a)   "Mercury recovery performance ratio" means the ratio of the number of pounds of mercury recovered from mercury switches from the State in a calendar year to the estimated number of pounds of mercury available to be recovered from mercury switches from the State in the same calendar year.

(5)   "Mercury switch" means each capsule or assembly containing mercury that is part of a convenience light switch installed in a vehicle.

(5a)   Reserved for future codification purposes.

(5b)   "National mercury recovery performance ratio" means the ratio of the number of pounds of mercury recovered from mercury switches from the United States in a calendar year to the estimated number of pounds of mercury available to be recovered from mercury switches from the United States in the same calendar year.

(5c)   "NVMSRP" means the Memorandum of Understanding to establish the National Vehicle Mercury Switch Recovery Program dated 11 August 2006.

(6)   "Scrap vehicle processing facility" means a fixed location where machinery and equipment are used to process scrap vehicles into specification grade commodities including facilities where a shredder or fragmentizer is used to process scrap vehicles into shredded scrap and facilities where end-of-life vehicles are prepared to be shredded.

(7)   "Vehicle" means any passenger automobile or passenger car, station wagon, truck, van, or sport utility vehicle with a gross vehicle weight rating of less than 12,000 pounds.

(7a)   "Vehicle crusher" means a person who engages in the business of flattening, crushing, or otherwise processing end-of-life vehicles for recycling. Vehicle crusher includes, but is not limited to, a person who uses fixed or mobile equipment to flatten or crush end-of-life vehicles for a vehicle recycler or a scrap vehicle processing facility.

(7b)   "Vehicle dismantler" has the same meaning as "vehicle recycler."

(7c)   "Vehicle manufacturer" means a person, firm, association, partnership, corporation, governmental entity, organization, combination, or joint venture that is the last person in the production or assembly process of a motor vehicle that contains one or more mercury switches, or in the case of an imported vehicle, the importer or domestic distributor of the vehicle. "Vehicle manufacturer" does not include any person engaged in the business of selling new motor vehicles at retail or any person who converts or modifies new motor vehicles after the production or assembly process.

(8)   "Vehicle recycler" means a person or entity engaged in the business of acquiring, dismantling, or destroying six or more end-of-life vehicles in a calendar year for the primary purpose of resale of parts of the vehicle, including scrap metal. (2005-384, s. 1; 2006-255, s. 5; 2007-142, s. 1.)

§ 130A-310.50. (Effective December 31, 2017) Definitions.

As used in this Part:

(1)   "Capture rate" means the annual removal, collection, and recovery of mercury switches as a percentage of the total number of mercury switches available for removal from end-of-life vehicles.

(2)   "End-of-life vehicle" means a vehicle that is sold, given, or otherwise conveyed to a vehicle recycler or scrap metal recycling facility for the purpose of recycling.

(3) "Manufacturer" means a person, firm, association, partnership, corporation, governmental entity, organization, combination, or joint venture that is the last person in the production or assembly process of a new vehicle that utilizes mercury switches, or in the case of an imported vehicle, the importer or domestic distributor of the vehicle.

(4) "Mercury minimization plan" means a plan for removing, collecting, and recovering mercury switches from end-of-life vehicles that is prepared as provided in G.S. 130A-310.53.

(5) "Mercury switch" means each mercury-containing capsule, commonly known as a "bullet", that is part of a convenience light switch assembly installed in a vehicle.

(6) "Scrap metal recycling facility" means a fixed location where machinery and equipment are used to process scrap metal into specific grades of scrap metal for sale and whose primary product is scrap iron, scrap steel, or nonferrous metallic scrap.

(7) "Vehicle" means any passenger automobile or passenger car, station wagon, truck, van, or sport utility vehicle with a gross vehicle weight rating of less than 12,000 pounds.

(8) "Vehicle recycler" means an individual or entity engaged in the business of acquiring, dismantling, or destroying six or more end-of-life vehicles in a calendar year for the primary purpose of resale of parts of the vehicle. (2005-384, s. 1; 2006-255, s. 5; 2007-142, ss. 1, 9.)

§ 130A-310.51. (For expiration date - see note) Purpose.

The purpose of this Part is to reduce the quantity of mercury that is released into the environment by removing mercury switches from end-of-life vehicles and by creating a removal, collection, and recovery program for mercury switches that are removed from end-of-life vehicles in this State. (2005-384, s. 1; 2006-255, s. 5.)

§ 130A-310.52: Repealed by Session Laws 2007-142, s. 2, effective June 29, 2007, and expiring on December 31, 2017.

§ 130A-310.53. (Effective until December 31, 2017) Removal of mercury switches from end-of-life vehicles.

(a)   A vehicle crusher, vehicle dismantler, vehicle recycler, or scrap vehicle processing facility shall not flatten, crush, bale, or shred an end-of-life vehicle that contains accessible mercury switches. Except as provided in this subsection, a vehicle crusher, vehicle dismantler, vehicle recycler, or scrap vehicle processing facility shall remove all accessible mercury switches from end-of-life vehicles before the vehicle is flattened, crushed, baled, or shredded, or before the vehicle is conveyed to another vehicle crusher, vehicle dismantler, vehicle recycler, or scrap vehicle processing facility. If a vehicle crusher, vehicle dismantler, vehicle recycler, or scrap vehicle processing facility conveys an end-of-life vehicle to another vehicle crusher, vehicle dismantler, vehicle recycler, or scrap vehicle processing facility without removing accessible mercury switches, the receiving vehicle crusher, vehicle dismantler, vehicle recycler, or scrap vehicle processing facility must agree to accept the end-of-life vehicle and assume responsibility for the proper removal of all accessible mercury switches. The agreement to assume responsibility for the proper removal of all accessible mercury switches shall be documented on an invoice that is provided by the vehicle crusher, vehicle dismantler, vehicle recycler, or scrap vehicle processing facility to the person to whom the vehicle is conveyed.

(b)   A vehicle crusher, vehicle dismantler, vehicle recycler, or scrap vehicle processing facility that removes all accessible mercury switches from an end-of-life vehicle shall mark the vehicle to indicate that all accessible mercury switches have been removed. The vehicle crusher, vehicle dismantler, vehicle recycler, or scrap vehicle processing facility shall certify to any person to whom the vehicle is conveyed, in a form acceptable to the Department, that all accessible mercury switches have been removed from the vehicle.

(c),   (d) Repealed by Session Laws 2007-142, s. 3, effective July 1, 2007.

(e)   Mercury switches that are removed from end-of-life vehicles are considered "universal waste" as defined in 40 Code of Federal Regulations § 273.9 (July 1, 2006 Edition). Mercury switches that are removed from end-of-life vehicles shall be collected, transported, treated, stored, disposed of, and otherwise handled in accordance with rules adopted by the Commission governing universal waste.

(f) Vehicle manufacturers, in cooperation with the Department, shall develop, implement, and bear the costs of a mercury switch collection system in accordance with the NVMSRP. This system shall be developed and implemented so as to enhance vehicle recyclability, promote public education and outreach, and provide for the proper removal, collection, and disposal of mercury switches from end-of-life vehicles. (2005-384, s. 1; 2006-255, s. 5; 2007-142, s. 3.)

§ 130A-310.53. (Effective December 31, 2017) Removal of mercury switches from end-of-life vehicles.

(a) A vehicle recycler that conveys ownership of an end-of-life vehicle to a scrap metal recycling facility shall remove all mercury switches identified in the mercury minimization plan prior to delivery of the vehicle to the scrap metal recycling facility. If a mercury switch is inaccessible, the fact that the mercury switch remains in the vehicle shall be noted on the vehicle recycler's invoice.

(b) A scrap metal recycling facility that accepts an end-of-life vehicle that has not been flattened, crushed, baled, or shredded and that contains mercury switches shall remove the mercury switches before the end-of-life vehicle is flattened, crushed, baled, or shredded unless the mercury switch is inaccessible.

(c) A mercury switch is inaccessible if, due to the condition of the vehicle, the switch cannot be removed in accordance with the mercury minimization plan and removal of the switch would significantly increase the risk of a release of mercury into the environment.

(d) A vehicle recycler or scrap metal recycling facility that removes mercury switches pursuant to subsection (a) or (b) of this section shall make quarterly reports to the Department on the following:

(1) The number of vehicles that it processed for recycling.

(2) The number of vehicles from which it removed a mercury switch by make.

(3) The number of vehicles for which it could not remove the mercury switch because the switch was inaccessible.

(e) Mercury switches that are removed from end-of-life vehicles are considered "universal waste" as defined in 40 Code of Federal Regulations § 273.9 (1 July 2004 Edition). Mercury switches that are removed from end-of-life vehicles shall be collected, transported, treated, stored, disposed of, and otherwise handled in accordance with rules adopted by the Commission governing universal waste. (2005-384, s. 1; 2006-255, s. 5; 2007-142, ss. 3, 9.)

§ 130A-310.54. (Effective until December 31, 2017) Mercury Pollution Prevention Fund.

(a) The Mercury Pollution Prevention Fund is established in the Department. Revenue is credited to the Fund from the certificate of title fee under G.S. 20-85.

(b) Revenue in the Mercury Pollution Prevention Fund shall be used for the following purposes:

(1) To reimburse the Department and others for costs incurred in implementing the mercury switch removal program.

(2) To establish and implement recycling programs for products containing mercury, including at least recycling programs for light bulbs and thermostats.

(b1) The reimbursable costs under subdivision (1) of subsection (b) of this section are:

(1) Five dollars ($5.00) for each mercury switch removed by a vehicle crusher, vehicle dismantler, vehicle recycler, or scrap vehicle processing facility pursuant to this Article and sent to destination facilities in accordance with the NVMSRP for recycling or disposal.

(2) Costs incurred by the Department in administering the program.

(c) The Department shall reimburse vehicle crushers, vehicle dismantlers, vehicle recyclers, and scrap vehicle processing facilities based on a reimbursement request that attests to the number of switches sent to destination facilities for recycling or disposal in accordance with the NVMSRP. Each reimbursement request shall be verified against information posted on the Internet site provided by the vehicle manufacturers in accordance with the NVMSRP, or against other information that verifies the reimbursement requested to the satisfaction of the Department. The vehicle crusher, vehicle dismantler, vehicle recycler, or scrap vehicle processing facility shall provide the Department with any information requested by the Department to verify the accuracy of a reimbursement request. Each vehicle crusher, vehicle dismantler, vehicle recycler, or scrap vehicle processing facility shall maintain accurate records that support each reimbursement request for a minimum of three years from the date the reimbursement request is approved. (2005-384, s. 1; 2006-255, s. 5; 2007-142, s. 4; 2011-145, s. 13.10B(a).)

§ 130A-310.54. (Effective December 31, 2017) Funds to implement plan.

(a) The Mercury Pollution Prevention Fund is established in the Department. Revenue is credited to the Fund from the certificate of title fee under G.S. 20-85.

(b) Revenue in the Mercury Pollution Prevention Fund shall be used for the following purposes:

(1) To reimburse the Department and others for costs incurred in implementing the mercury minimization plan.

(2) To establish and implement recycling programs for products containing mercury, including at least recycling programs for light bulbs and thermostats.

(b1) The reimbursable costs under subdivision (1) of subsection (b) of this section are:

(1) Five dollars ($5.00) for each mercury switch removed by a vehicle recycler or scrap metal recycling facility pursuant to this Article.

(2) Costs incurred by the Department in administering the plan.

(c) The Department shall reimburse vehicle recyclers and scrap metal recycling facilities based on the quarterly reports submitted under G.S. 130A-310.53. The Department may request any information needed to determine the accuracy of the reports. (2005-384, s. 1; 2006-255, s. 5; 2007-142, ss. 4, 9; 2011-145, s. 13.10B(b).)

§ 130A-310.55. Violations of Article; enforcement.

(a) It is unlawful for a person to do any of the following:

(1) Knowingly flatten, crush, bale, shred, or otherwise alter the condition of a vehicle from which accessible mercury switches have not been removed, in any manner that would prevent or significantly hinder the removal of a mercury switch.

(2) Willfully fail to remove a mercury switch when the person is required to do so.

(3) Knowingly make a false report that a mercury switch has been removed from an end-of-life vehicle.

(4) Obtain a mercury switch from another source and falsely report that it was removed from a vehicle processed for recycling.

(b) (Effective until December 31, 2017) Any person who violates subdivision (1) or (2) of subsection (a) of this section shall be punished as provided in G.S. 14-3.

(b) (Effective December 31, 2017) This Part may be enforced as provided in Part 2 of Article 1 of this Chapter.

(c) (Expires December 31, 2017) Any person who violates subdivision (3) or (4) of subsection (a) of this section shall be guilty of a Class 2 misdemeanor and, upon conviction, shall be punished as provided in G.S. 130A-26.2.

(d) (Expires December 31, 2017) A violation of any provision of this Part, any rule adopted pursuant to this Part, or any rule governing universal waste may be enforced by an administrative or civil action as provided in Part 2 of Article 1 of this Chapter. (2005-384, s. 1; 2006-255, s. 5; 2007-142, ss. 5, 9.)

§ 130A-310.56: Repealed by Session Laws 2007-142, s. 6, effective June 29, 2007, and expiring December 31, 2017.

§ 130A-310.57: Repealed by Session Laws 2012-200, s. 21(f), effective August 1, 2012.

§ 130A-310.58. (For expiration date - see note) Adoption of rules; administrative procedure.

(a)   The Department may adopt rules to implement this Part.

(b)   Chapter 150B of the General Statutes governs implementation of this Part. (2005-384, s. 1; 2006-255, s.5.)

§ 130A-310.59: Reserved for future codification purposes.

Part 7. Management of Certain Products That Contain Mercury.

§ 130A-310.60. Recycling required by public agencies.

(a)   Each State agency, including the General Assembly, the General Court of Justice, universities, community colleges, public schools, and political subdivisions using State funds for the construction or operation of public buildings shall establish a program in cooperation with the Department of Environment and Natural Resources and the Department of Administration for the collection and recycling of all spent fluorescent lights and thermostats that contain mercury generated in public buildings owned by each respective entity. The program shall include procedures for convenient collection, safe storage, and proper recycling of spent fluorescent lights and thermostats that contain mercury and contractual or other arrangements with buyers of the recyclable materials.

(b)   Each State agency, including the General Assembly, the General Court of Justice, universities, community colleges, the Department of Public Instruction on behalf of the public schools, and political subdivisions shall submit a report on or before December 1, 2011, that documents the entity's compliance with the requirements of subsection (a) of this section to the Department of Environment and Natural Resources and the Department of Administration. The Departments shall compile the information submitted and jointly shall submit a report to the Environmental Review Commission on or before January 15, 2012, concerning the activities required by subsection (a) of this section. The information provided shall also be included in the report required by G.S. 130A-309.06(c).

(c) For purposes of this section, a political subdivision is using State funds when it receives grant funding from the State for the construction or operation of a public building. (2010-180, s. 14(a); 2011-394, s. 5.)

§ 130A-310.61. Removal and recycling of mercury-containing products from structures to be demolished.

Prior to demolition of any building or structure in the State, the contractor responsible for the demolition activity or the owner of the building or structure to be demolished shall remove all fluorescent lights and thermostats that contain mercury from the building or structure to be demolished. (2010-180, s. 14(a).)

§ 130A-310.62: Reserved for future codification purposes.

§ 130A-310.63: Reserved for future codification purposes.

§ 130A-310.64: Reserved for future codification purposes.

Part 8. Risk-Based Environmental Remediation of Industrial Sites.

§ 130A-310.65. Definitions.

As used in this Part:

(1) "Background standard" means the naturally occurring concentration of a substance in the absence of the release of a contaminant.

(2) "Commission" means the Environmental Management Commission created pursuant to G.S. 143B-282.

(3) "Contaminant" means any substance regulated under any program listed in G.S. 130A-310.67(a).

(4) "Contaminated industrial site" or "site" means any real property that meets all of the following criteria:

a. The property is contaminated and may be subject to remediation under any of the programs or requirements set out in G.S. 130A-310.67(a).

b. The property is or has been used primarily for manufacturing or other industrial activities for the production of a commercial product. This includes a property used primarily for the generation of electricity.

c. No contaminant associated with activities at the property is located off of the property at the time the remedial action plan is submitted.

d. No contaminant associated with activities at the property will migrate to any adjacent properties above unrestricted use standards for the contaminant.

(5) "Contamination" means a contaminant released into an environmental medium that has resulted in or has the potential to result in an increase in the concentration of the contaminant in the environmental medium in excess of unrestricted use standards.

(6) "Fund" means the Inactive Hazardous Sites Cleanup Fund established pursuant to G.S. 130A-310.11.

(7) "Institutional controls" means nonengineered measures used to prevent unsafe exposure to contamination, such as land-use restrictions.

(8) "Registered environmental consultant" means an environmental consulting or engineering firm approved to implement and oversee voluntary remedial actions pursuant to Part 3 of Article 9 of Chapter 130A of the General Statutes and rules adopted to implement the Part.

(9) "Remedial action plan" means a plan for eliminating or reducing contamination or exposure to contamination.

(10) "Remediation" means all actions that are necessary or appropriate to clean up, mitigate, correct, abate, minimize, eliminate, control, or prevent the spreading, migration, leaking, leaching, volatilization, spilling, transport, or further release of a contaminant into the environment in order to protect public health, safety, or welfare or the environment.

(11) "Systemic toxicant" means any substance that may enter the body and have a harmful effect other than causing cancer.

(12) "Unrestricted use standards" means contaminant concentrations for each environmental medium that are acceptable for all uses; that are protective of public health, safety, and welfare and the environment; and that comply with generally applicable standards, guidance, or methods established by statute or adopted, published, or implemented by the Commission, the Commission for Public Health, or the Department. (2011-186, s. 2.)

§ 130A-310.66. Purpose.

It is the purpose of this Part to authorize the Department to approve the remediation of contaminated industrial sites based on site-specific remediation standards in circumstances where site-specific remediation standards are adequate to protect public health, safety, and welfare and the environment and are consistent with protection of current and anticipated future use of groundwater and surface water affected or potentially affected by the contamination. (2011-186, s. 2.)

§ 130A-310.67. Applicability.

(a) This Part applies to contaminated industrial sites subject to remediation pursuant to any of the following programs or requirements:

(1) The Inactive Hazardous Sites Response Act of 1987 under Part 3 of Article 9 of Chapter 130A of the General Statutes, including voluntary actions under G.S. 130A-310.9 of that act, and rules promulgated pursuant to those statutes.

(2) The hazardous waste management program administered by the State pursuant to the federal Resource Conservation and Recovery Act of 1976, Public Law 94-580, 90 Stat. 2795, 42 U.S.C. § 6901, et seq., as amended, and Article 9 of Chapter 130A of the General Statutes.

(3) The solid waste management program administered pursuant to Article 9 of Chapter 130A of the General Statutes.

(4)   The federal Superfund program administered in part by the State pursuant to the Comprehensive Environmental Response, Compensation, and Liability Act of 1980, Public Law 96-510, 94 Stat. 2767, 42 U.S.C. § 9601, et seq., as amended, the Superfund Amendments and Reauthorization Act of 1986, Public Law 99-499, 100 Stat. 1613, as amended, and under Part 4 of Article 9 of Chapter 130A of the General Statutes.

(5)   The groundwater protection corrective action requirements adopted by the Commission pursuant to Article 21 of Chapter 143 of the General Statutes.

(6)   Oil Pollution and Hazardous Substances Control Act of 1978, Parts 1 and 2 of Article 21A of Chapter 143 of the General Statutes.

(b)   This Part shall not apply to contaminated industrial sites subject to remediation pursuant to any of the following programs or requirements:

(1)   The Leaking Petroleum Underground Storage Tank Cleanup program under Part 2A of Article 21A of Chapter 143 of the General Statutes and rules promulgated pursuant to that statute.

(2)   The Dry-Cleaning Solvent Cleanup program under Part 6 of Article 21A of Chapter 143 of the General Statutes and rules promulgated pursuant to that statute.

(3)   The pre-1983 landfill assessment and remediation program established under G.S. 130A-310.6(c) through (g).

(c)   This Part shall apply only to sites where a discharge, spill, or release of contamination has been reported to the Department prior to March 1, 2011. (2011-186, s. 2.)

§ 130A-310.68. Remediation standards.

(a)   When conducting remediation activities pursuant to this Part, a person who proposes to or is required to respond to the release of a contaminant at a contaminated industrial site shall comply with one of the following standards:

(1)   The unrestricted use standards applicable to each affected medium.

(2) The background standard, if the background standard exceeds the unrestricted use standards.

(3) A site-specific remediation standard developed in accordance with subsection (b) of this section that is approved by the Department.

(4) Any combination of remediation standards described in this subsection that is approved by the Department.

(b) Site-specific remediation standards shall be developed for each medium as provided in this subsection to achieve remediation that eliminates or reduces to protective levels any substantial present or probable future risk to human health, including sensitive subgroups, and the environment based upon the present or currently planned future use of the property comprising the site. Site-specific remediation standards shall be developed in accordance with all of the following:

(1) Remediation methods and technologies that result in emissions of air pollutants shall comply with applicable air quality standards adopted by the Commission.

(2) The site-specific remediation standard for surface waters shall be the water quality standards adopted by the Commission.

(3) The current and probable future use of groundwater shall be identified and protected. Site-specific sources of contaminants and potential receptors shall be identified. Potential receptors must be protected, controlled, or eliminated whether the receptors are located on or off the site where the source of contamination is located. Natural environmental conditions affecting the fate and transport of contaminants, such as natural attenuation, shall be determined by appropriate scientific methods.

(4) Permits for facilities located at sites covered by any of the programs or requirements set out in G.S. 130A-310.67(a) shall contain conditions to avoid exceedances of applicable groundwater standards adopted by the Commission pursuant to Article 21 of Chapter 143 of the General Statutes due to operation of the facility.

(5) Soil shall be remediated to levels that no longer constitute a continuing source of groundwater contamination in excess of the site-specific groundwater remediation standards approved under this Part.

(6) Soil shall be remediated to unrestricted use standards on residential property with the following exceptions:

a. For mixed-use developments where the ground level uses are nonresidential and where all potential exposure to contaminated soil has been eliminated, the Department may allow soil to remain on the site in excess of unrestricted use standards.

b. If soil remediation is impracticable because of the presence of preexisting structures or impracticability of removal, all areas of the real property at which a person may come into contact with soil shall be remediated to unrestricted use standards, and, on all other areas of the real property, engineering and institutional controls that are sufficient to protect public health, safety, and welfare and the environment shall be implemented and maintained.

(7) The potential for human inhalation of contaminants from the outdoor air and other site-specific indoor air exposure pathways shall be considered, if applicable.

(8) The site-specific remediation standard shall protect against human exposure to contamination through the consumption of contaminated fish or wildlife and through the ingestion of contaminants in surface water or groundwater supplies.

(9) For known or suspected carcinogens, site-specific remediation standards shall be established at exposures that represent an excess lifetime cancer risk of one in 1,000,000. The site-specific remediation standard may depart from the one-in-1,000,000 risk level based on the criteria set out in 40 Code of Federal Regulations § 300.430(e)(9)(July 1, 2003 Edition). The cumulative excess lifetime cancer risk to an exposed individual shall not be greater than one in 10,000 based on the sum of carcinogenic risk posed by each contaminant present.

(10) For systemic toxicants, site-specific remediation standards shall represent levels to which the human population, including sensitive subgroups, may be exposed without any adverse health effect during a lifetime or part of a lifetime. Site-specific remediation standards for systemic toxicants shall incorporate an adequate margin of safety and shall take into account cases where two or more systemic toxicants affect the same organ or organ system.

(11) The site-specific remediation standards for each medium shall be adequate to avoid foreseeable adverse effects to other media or the environment that are inconsistent with the risk-based approach under this Part. (2011-186, s. 2.)

§ 130A-310.69. Remedial investigation report; remedial action plans.

(a) A person who proposes to conduct remediation pursuant to this Part shall submit a remedial investigation report to the Department prior to submitting a remedial action plan. The remedial investigation report shall include, but is not limited to, a legal description of the location of the site; a map showing the location of the site; a description of the contaminants involved and their concentration in the media of the site; a narrative description of the methodology used in the investigation; a description of all on-site releases of contamination; a site map, drawn to scale, showing benchmarks, directional arrow, location of property boundaries, buildings, structures, all perennial and nonperennial surface water features, drainage ditches, dense vegetation, contaminant spill or disposal areas, underground utilities, storage vessels, and existing on-site wells; identification of adjacent property owners and adjacent land uses; description of local geologic and hydrologic conditions; an evaluation of the site and adjacent properties for the existence of environmentally sensitive areas; a description of groundwater monitoring well design and installation procedures; a map, drawn to scale, that shows all groundwater sample locations; a description of field and laboratory quality control and quality assurance procedures followed during the remedial investigation; a description of methods used to manage investigation-derived wastes; tabulation of analytical results for all sampling; copies of all laboratory reports; a description of procedures and the results of any special assessments; and any other information required by the Department or considered relevant by the investigator. The remedial investigation shall assess all contaminated areas of the site, including types and levels of contamination, and the risk that the contamination poses to public health, safety, and welfare and to the environment.

(b) A person who proposes to conduct remediation pursuant to this Part shall develop and submit a proposed remedial action plan to the Department. A remedial action plan shall provide for the protection of public health, safety, and welfare and the environment. A remedial action plan shall do all of the following:

(1) Identify actions required to remove, treat, or otherwise appropriately mitigate or isolate the source of contamination to ensure that the source will not cause unrestricted use standards to be exceeded in any medium.

(2) Address contamination that moves from one medium to another in order to prevent a violation of the remediation standards established under G.S. 130A-310.68. A more stringent remediation standard may be required for a particular medium to control impact on other media.

(3) Identify the current and anticipated future uses of property comprising the contaminated site and address any concerns raised in public comment on the proposed remedial action plan as to the proposed future uses of the property.

(4) Identify the current and anticipated future uses of groundwater in the contaminated site and address any concerns raised in public comment on the proposed remedial action plan as to the future uses of groundwater.

(5) Determine the appropriate method of remediation to achieve the site-specific remediation standards.

(6) Specify any measures that may be necessary to prevent adverse effects to the environment that may occur at levels of contamination that are lower than the standard necessary to protect human health.

(7) Specify any measures that may be necessary to prevent any discharge into surface waters during implementation of the remedial action plan that violates applicable surface water quality standards adopted by the Commission.

(8) Specify any measures that may be necessary to prevent any air emission during implementation of the remedial action plan that violates applicable air quality standards adopted by the Commission.

(9) Provide for attainment and maintenance of the remediation standards established under G.S. 130A-310.68.

(10) Provide for methods and procedures to verify that the quantity, concentration, range, or other measure of each contaminant remaining at the contaminated site at the conclusion of the contaminant-reduction phase of remediation meets the remediation standards established for the site, that an

acceptable level of risk has been achieved, and that no further remediation is required.

(11) Provide for the imposition and recordation of land-use restrictions as provided in G.S. 143B-279.9, 143B-279.10, 130A-310.3(f), 130A-310.8, 130A-310.35, 143-215.84(f), and 143-215.85A if the remedial action plan allows contamination in excess of the greater of unrestricted use standards or background standards to remain on any real property or in groundwater that underlies any real property.

(12) Provide for submission of an annual certification to the Department by the property owner that land use at the site is in compliance with land-use restrictions recorded pursuant to this Part and that the land-use restrictions are still properly recorded in the chain of title for the property.

(13) Provide a detailed description of the proposed remedial action to be taken; the results of any treatability studies and additional site characterization needed to support the proposed remedial action; plans for postremedial and confirmatory sampling; a project schedule; a schedule for progress reports to the Department; and any other information required by the Department or considered relevant by the person who submits the proposed remedial action plan.

(14) Provide a description of measures that will be employed to ensure that the safety and health of persons on properties in the vicinity of the site and persons visiting or doing business on the site will not be adversely affected by any remediation activity.

(15) Provide a reasonable estimate of the probable cost of the remedial action sufficient for the Department to determine an acceptable level of financial assurance.

(16) Provide proof of financial assurance as required by G.S. 130A-310.72.

(c) A remedial action plan shall also include an analysis of each of the following factors:

(1) Long-term risks and effectiveness of the proposed remediation, including an evaluation of all of the following:

a. The magnitude of risks remaining after completion of the remediation.

b. The type, degree, frequency, and duration of any postremediation activity that may be required, including, but not limited to, operation and maintenance, monitoring, inspection, reports, and other activities necessary to protect public health, safety, and welfare and the environment.

c. Potential for exposure of human and environmental receptors to contaminants remaining at the site.

d. Long-term reliability of any engineering and voluntary institutional controls, including repair, maintenance, or replacement of components.

e. Time required to achieve remediation standards.

(2) Toxicity, mobility, and volume of contaminants, including the amount of contaminants that will be removed, contained, treated, or destroyed; the degree of expected reduction in toxicity, mobility, and volume; and the type, quantity, toxicity, and mobility of contaminants that will remain after implementation of the remedial action plan.

(3) Short-term risks and effectiveness of the remediation, including the short-term risks that may be posed to the community, workers, or the environment during implementation of the remedial action plan, and the effectiveness and reliability of protective measures to address short-term risks.

(4) The ease or difficulty of implementing the remedial action plan, including commercially available remedial measures; expected operational reliability; available capacity and location of needed treatment, storage, and disposal services for wastes; time to initiate remediation; and approvals necessary to implement the remediation.

(d) The development of a remedial action plan may require supplemental submissions and revisions based on Department review, remedial action pilot studies, and public comment from local government and citizens. (2011-186, s. 2.)

§ 130A-310.70. Notice of intent to remediate.

In addition to the public participation requirements of the individual programs listed in G.S. 130A-310.67(a), the person who proposes to remediate a site under this Part shall send a notice of intent to remediate to all local governments having taxing or land-use jurisdiction over the site, and to all adjoining landowners. The notice shall include all of the information required in G.S. 130A-310.69(a) and include a statement of intent to clean up the site to site-specific remediation standards. The person shall submit to the Department a copy of the notice of intent provided to local governments and adjoining landowners, a certification that the notice of intent to remediate was so provided to those parties, and all information and comments that the person received in response to the notice. In addition, the person shall, when appropriate, describe how the remedial action plan was modified to address comments received in response to the notice. (2011-186, s. 2.)

§ 130A-310.71. Review and approval of proposed remedial action plans.

(a)   The Department shall review and approve a proposed remedial action plan consistent with the remediation standards set out in G.S. 130A-310.68 and the procedures set out in this section. In its review of a proposed remedial action plan, the Department shall do all of the following:

(1)   Determine whether site-specific remediation standards are appropriate for a particular contaminated site. In making this determination, the Department shall consider proximity of the contamination to water supply wells or other receptors; current and probable future reliance on the groundwater as a water supply; current and anticipated future land use; environmental impacts; and the feasibility of remediation to unrestricted use standards.

(2)   Determine whether the party conducting the remediation has adequately demonstrated through modeling or other scientific means acceptable to the Department that no contamination will migrate to adjacent property at levels above unrestricted use standards.

(3)   Determine whether the proposed remedial action plan meets the requirements of G.S. 130A-310.69.

(4)   Determine whether the proposed remedial action plan meets the requirements of any other applicable remediation program except those pertaining to remediation standards.

(5) Establish the acceptable level or range of levels of risk to public health, safety, and welfare and to the environment.

(6) Establish, for each contaminant, the maximum allowable quantity, concentration, range, or other measures of contamination that will remain at the contaminated site at the conclusion of the contaminant-reduction phase of the remediation.

(7) Consider the technical performance, effectiveness, and reliability of the proposed remedial action plan in attaining and maintaining compliance with applicable remediation standards.

(8) Consider the ability of the person who proposes to remediate the site to implement the proposed remedial action plan within a reasonable time and without jeopardizing public health, safety, or welfare or the environment.

(9) Determine whether the proposed remedial action plan adequately provides for the imposition and maintenance of engineering and institutional controls and for sampling, monitoring, and reporting requirements necessary to protect public health, safety, and welfare and the environment.

(10) Approve the circumstances under which no further remediation is required.

(b) The person who proposes a remedial action plan has the burden of demonstrating with reasonable assurance that contamination from the site will not migrate to adjacent property above unrestricted use levels and that the remedial action plan is protective of public health, safety, and welfare and the environment by virtue of its compliance with this Part. The demonstration shall (i) take into account actions proposed in the remedial action plan that will prevent contamination from migrating off the site; and (ii) use scientifically valid site-specific data.

(c) The Department may require a person who proposes a remedial action plan to supply any additional information necessary for the Department to approve or disapprove the plan.

(d) In making a determination on a proposed remedial action plan, the Department shall consider the information provided by the person who proposes the remedial action plan as well as information provided by local governments and adjoining landowners pursuant to G.S. 130A-310.70. The Department shall disapprove a proposed remedial action plan unless the Department finds that the plan is protective of public health, safety, and welfare and the environment and complies with the requirements of this Part. If the Department disapproves a proposed remedial action plan, the person who submitted the plan may seek review as provided in Article 3 of Chapter 150B of the General Statutes. If the Department fails to approve or disapprove a proposed remedial action plan within 120 days after a complete plan has been submitted, the person who submitted the plan may treat the plan as having been disapproved at the end of that time period. (2011-186, s. 2.)

§ 130A-310.72. Financial assurance requirement.

The person conducting remediation of a contaminated industrial site pursuant to the provisions of this Part shall establish financial assurance that will ensure that sufficient funds are available to implement and maintain the actions or controls specified in the remedial action plan for the site. The person conducting remediation of a site may establish financial assurance through one of the following mechanisms, or any combination of the following mechanisms, in a form specified or approved by the Department: insurance products issued from entities having no corporate or ownership association with the person conducting the remediation; funded trusts; surety bonds; certificates of deposit; letters of credit; corporate financial tests; local government financial tests; corporate guarantees; local government guarantees; capital reserve funds; or any other financial mechanism authorized for the demonstration of financial assurance under (i) 40 Code of Federal Regulations Part 264, Subpart H (July 1, 2010 Edition) and (ii) Section .1600 of Subchapter B of Chapter 13 of Title 15A of the North Carolina Administrative Code. Proof of financial assurance shall be provided in the remedial action plan and annually thereafter on the anniversary date of the approval of the plan. (2011-186, s. 2.)

§ 130A-310.73. Attainment of the remediation standards.

(a) Compliance with the approved remediation standards is attained for a site or portion of a site when a remedial action plan approved by the Department has been implemented and applicable soil, groundwater, surface water, and air emission standards have been attained. The remediation standards may be attained through a combination of remediation activities that can include treatment, removal, engineering, or institutional controls, except that the person conducting the remediation may not demonstrate attainment of an unrestricted use standard or a background standard through the use of institutional controls alone. When the remedial action plan has been fully implemented, the person conducting the remediation shall submit a final report to the Department, with notice to all local governments with taxing and land-use jurisdiction over the site, that demonstrates that the remedial action plan has been fully implemented, that any land-use restrictions have been certified on an annual basis, and that the remediation standards have been attained. The final report shall be accompanied by a request that the Department issue a determination that no further remediation beyond that specified in the approved remedial action plan is required.

(b) The person conducting the remediation has the burden of demonstrating that the remedial action plan has been fully implemented and that the remediation standards have been attained in compliance with the requirements of this Part. The Department may require a person who implements the remedial action plan to supply any additional information necessary for the Department to determine whether the remediation standards have been attained.

(c) The Department shall review the final report, and, upon determining that the person conducting the remediation has completed remediation to the approved remediation standard and met all the requirements of the approved remedial action plan, the Department shall issue a determination that no further remediation beyond that specified in the approved remedial action plan is required at the site. Once the Department has issued a no further action determination, the Department may require additional remedial action by the responsible party only upon finding any of the following:

(1) Monitoring, testing, or analysis of the site subsequent to the issuance of the no further action determination indicates that the remediation standards and objectives were not achieved or are not being maintained.

(2) One or more of the conditions, restrictions, or limitations imposed on the site as part of the remediation have been violated.

(3) Site monitoring or operation and maintenance activities that are required as part of the remedial action plan or no further action determination for the site are not adequately funded or are not adequately implemented.

(4)   A contaminant or hazardous substance release is discovered at the site that was not the subject of the remedial investigation report or the remedial action plan.

(5)   A material change in the facts known to the Department at the time the written no further action determination was issued, or new facts, cause the Department to find that further assessment or remediation is necessary to prevent a significant risk to human health and safety or to the environment.

(6)   The no further action determination was based on fraud, misrepresentation, or intentional nondisclosure of information by the person conducting the remediation.

(7)   Installation or use of wells would induce the flow of contaminated groundwater off the site.

(d)   The Department shall issue a final decision on a request for a determination that remediation has been completed to approved standards and that no further remediation beyond that specified in the approved remedial action plan is required within 180 days after receipt of a complete final report. Failure of the Department to issue a final decision on a no further remediation determination within 180 days after receipt of a complete final report and request for a determination of no further remediation may be treated as a denial of the request for a no further remediation determination. The responsible person may seek review of a denial of a request for a release from further remediation as provided in Article 3 of Chapter 150B of the General Statutes. (2011-186, s. 2.)

§ 130A-310.74. Compliance with other laws.

Where a site is covered by an agreement under the Brownfields Property Reuse Act of 1997, as codified as Part 5 of Article 9 of Chapter 130A of the General Statutes, any work performed by the prospective developer pursuant to that agreement is not required to comply with this Part, but any work not covered by such agreement and performed at the site by another person not a party to that agreement may be performed pursuant to this Part. (2011-186, s. 2.)

§ 130A-310.75. Use of registered environmental consultants.

The Department may approve the use of a registered environmental consultant to provide oversight for the assessment and remediation of a site under this Part. If remediation under this Part is not undertaken voluntarily, the Department may not require the use of a registered environmental consultant to provide oversight for the assessment and remediation of a site under this Part. (2011-186, s. 2.)

§ 130A-310.76. Fees; permissible uses of fees.

(a) A person who undertakes remediation of environmental contamination under site-specific remediation standards as provided in G.S. 130A-310.68 shall pay a fee to the Fund in an amount equal to four thousand five hundred dollars ($4,500) for each acre or portion of an acre of contamination, including any area that will become contaminated as a result of the release; however, no person shall be required to pay more than one hundred twenty-five thousand dollars ($125,000) to the Fund for any individual site, regardless of its size. This one-time fee shall be payable at the time the person undertaking remediation submits the remedial action plan to the Department.

(b) Funds collected pursuant to subsection (a) of this section may be used only for the following purposes:

(1) To pay for administrative and operating expenses necessary to implement this Part.

(2) To establish, administer, and maintain a system for the tracking of land-use restrictions recorded at sites that are remediated pursuant to this Part. (2011-186, s. 2.)

§ 130A-310.77. Construction of Part.

This Part shall not be construed or implemented in any of the following ways:

(1) In any manner that would jeopardize federal authorization under any of the federal statutes, programs, or requirements set out in G.S. 130A-310.67(a)

or would otherwise conflict with federal authority under those statutes, programs, and requirements. This Part is supplemental to the programs and requirements set out in G.S. 130A-310.67(a) that would otherwise govern the remediation of a contaminated industrial site. Where the definitions, provisions, or requirements of this Part conflict with the definitions, provisions, or requirements of an otherwise applicable remediation program, this Part shall control, unless expressly stated to the contrary.

(2) To limit the authority of the Department to require investigation, initial response, or remediation of environmental contamination under any other provision of State or federal law necessary to address an imminent threat to public health, safety, or welfare or the environment.

(3) To alter the requirements of programs to prevent or mitigate the release or discharge of contaminants to the environment, including permitting requirements that regulate the handling of hazardous substances or wastes.

(4) To supersede or otherwise affect or prevent the enforcement of any land-use or development regulation or ordinance adopted by a municipality pursuant to Article 19 of Chapter 160A of the General Statutes or adopted by a county pursuant to Article 18 of Chapter 153A of the General Statutes. The use of a site and any land-use restrictions imposed as part of a remedial action plan shall comply with land-use and development controls adopted by a municipality pursuant to Article 19 of Chapter 160A of the General Statutes or adopted by a county pursuant to Article 18 of Chapter 153A of the General Statutes. (2011-186, s. 2.)

§ 130A-310.78: Reserved for future codification purposes.

§ 130A-310.79: Reserved for future codification purposes.

§ 130A-310.80: Reserved for future codification purposes.

Article 10.

North Carolina Drinking Water Act.

§ 130A-311. Short title.

This Article shall be cited as the "North Carolina Drinking Water Act." (1979, c. 788, s. 1; 1983, c. 891, s. 2.)

§ 130A-312. Purpose.

The purpose of this Article is to regulate water systems within the State which supply drinking water that may affect the public health. (1979, c. 788, s. 1; 1983, c. 891, s. 2.)

§ 130A-313. Definitions.

The following definitions shall apply throughout this Article:

(1) "Administrator" means the Administrator of the United States Environmental Protection Agency.

(2) "Certified laboratory" means a facility for performing bacteriological, chemical or other analyses on water which has received interim or final certification by either the Environmental Protection Agency or the Department.

(3) "Contaminant" means any physical, chemical, biological or radiological substance or matter in water.

(3a) "Department" means the Department of Environment and Natural Resources.

(4) "Drinking water rules" means rules adopted pursuant to this Article.

(5) "Federal act" means the Safe Drinking Water Act of 1974, P.L. 93-523, as amended.

(6) "Federal agency" means any department, agency or instrumentality of the United States.

(7) "Maximum contaminant level" means the maximum permissible level of a contaminant in water which is delivered to any user of a public water system.

(8) "National primary drinking water regulations" means primary drinking water regulations promulgated by the Administrator pursuant to the federal act.

(9) "Person" means an individual, corporation, company, association, partnership, unit of local government, State agency, federal agency or other legal entity.

(10) "Public water system" means a system for the provision to the public of water for human consumption through pipes or other constructed conveyances if the system serves 15 or more service connections or which regularly serves 25 or more individuals. The term includes:

a. Any collection, treatment, storage or distribution facility under control of the operator of the system and used primarily in connection with the system; and

b. Any collection or pretreatment storage facility not under the control of the operator of the system that is used primarily in connection with the system.

A public water system is either a "community water system" or a "noncommunity water system" as follows:

a. "Community water system" means a public water system that serves at least 15 service connections used by year-round residents or regularly serves at least 25 year-round residents.

b. "Noncommunity water system" means a public water system that is not a community water system.

A connection to a system that delivers water by a constructed conveyance other than a pipe is not a connection within the meaning of this subdivision under any one of the following circumstances:

a. The water is used exclusively for purposes other than residential uses. As used in this subdivision, "residential uses" mean drinking, bathing, cooking, or other similar uses.

b. The Department determines that alternative water to achieve the equivalent level of public health protection pursuant to applicable drinking water rules is provided for residential uses.

c. The Department determines that the water provided for residential uses is centrally treated or treated at the point of entry by the provider, a pass-through entity, or the user to achieve the equivalent level of protection provided by the applicable drinking water rules.

(10a) "Secretary" means the Secretary of Environment and Natural Resources.

(11) "Supplier of water" means a person who owns, operates or controls a public water system.

(12) "Treatment technique requirement" means a requirement of the drinking water rules which specifies a specific treatment technique for a contaminant which leads to reduction in the level of the contaminant sufficient to comply with the drinking water rules. (1979, c. 788, s. 1; 1983, c. 891, s. 2; 1987, c. 704, s. 2; 1993 (Reg. Sess., 1994), c. 776, s. 14; 1997-30, s. 1; 1997-443, s. 11A.81A; 2012-200, s. 10.)

§ 130A-314. Scope of the Article.

(a) The provisions of this Article shall apply to each public water system in the State unless the public water system meets all of the following conditions:

(1) Consists only of distribution and storage facilities and does not have any collection and treatment facilities;

(2) Obtains all of its water from, but is not owned or operated by, a public water system to which the drinking water rules apply;

(3) Does not sell water to any person; and

(4) Is not a carrier which conveys passengers in interstate commerce.

(b) A provision of any charter granted to a public water system in conflict with the provisions of this Article is repealed. (1979, c. 788, s. 1; 1983, c. 891, s. 2.)

§ 130A-315. Drinking water rules; exceptions; limitation on implied warranties.

(a) The Commission shall adopt and the Secretary shall enforce drinking water rules to regulate public water systems. The rules may distinguish between community water systems and noncommunity water systems.

(b) The rules shall:

(1) Specify contaminants which may have an adverse effect on the public health;

(2) Specify for each contaminant either:

a. A maximum contaminant level which is acceptable in water for human consumption, if it is feasible to establish the level of the contaminant in water in public water systems; or

b. One or more treatment techniques which lead to a reduction in the level of contaminants sufficient to protect the public health, if it is not feasible to establish the level of the contaminants in water in a public water system; and

(3) Establish criteria and procedures to assure a supply of drinking water which dependably complies with maximum contaminant levels and treatment techniques as determined in paragraph (2) of this subsection. These rules may provide for:

a. The minimum quality of raw water which may be taken into a public water system;

b. A program of laboratory certification;

c. Monitoring and analysis;

d. Record-keeping and reporting;

e. Notice of noncompliance, failure to perform monitoring, variances and exemptions;

f. Inspection of public water systems; inspection of records required to be kept; and the taking of samples;

g. Criteria for design and construction of new or modified public water systems;

h. Review and approval of design and construction of new or modified public water systems;

i. Siting of new public water system facilities;

j. Variances and exemptions from the drinking water rules; and

k. Additional criteria and procedures as may be required to carry out the purpose of this Article.

(b1) The rules may also establish criteria and procedures to insure an adequate supply of drinking water. The rules may:

(1) Provide for record keeping and reporting.

(2) Provide for inspection of public water systems and required records.

(3) Establish criteria for the design and construction of new public water systems and for the modification of existing public water systems.

(4) Establish procedures for review and approval of the design and construction of new public water systems and for the modification of existing public water systems.

(4a) Limit the number of service connections to a public water system based on the quantity of water available to the public water system, provided that the number of service connections shall not be limited for a public water system operating in accordance with a local water supply plan that meets the requirements of G.S. 143-355(l).

(5) Establish criteria and procedures for siting new public water systems.

(6) Provide for variances and exemptions from the rules.

(7) Provide for notice of noncompliance in accordance with G.S. 130A-324.

(b2) Two or more water systems that are adjacent, that are owned or operated by the same supplier of water, that individually serve less than 15 service connections or less than 25 persons but that in combination serve 15 or more service connections or 25 or more persons, and that individually are not public water systems shall meet the standards applicable to public water systems for the following contaminants: coliform bacteria, nitrates, nitrites, lead, copper, and other inorganic chemicals for which testing and monitoring is required for public water systems on 1 July 1994. The standards applicable to these contaminants shall be enforced by the Commission as though the water systems to which this subsection applies were public water systems.

(b3)	The Department shall not certify or renew a certification of a laboratory under rules adopted pursuant to subdivision (3)b. of subsection (b) of this section unless the laboratory offers to perform composite testing of samples taken from a single public water supply system for those contaminants that the laboratory is seeking certification or renewal of certification to the extent allowed by regulations adopted by the United States Environmental Protection Agency.

(c)	The drinking water rules may be amended as necessary in accordance with required federal regulations.

(d)	When a person that receives water from a public water system is authorized by the Utilities Commission, pursuant to G.S. 62-110(g), to charge for the costs of providing water or sewer service, that person shall not be subject to regulation under this Article solely as a result of submetering and billing for water service. The supplying water system shall perform the same level of monitoring, analysis, and record keeping that the supplying system would perform if the providing water system had not been authorized to charge for the costs of providing water or sewer service pursuant to G.S. 62-110(g).

(e)	When a public water system supplies water through a master meter to a water system not regulated by this Article, the supplying water system is not responsible for operation, maintenance, or repair of the providing water system. The supplying water system shall not be responsible for contamination that is confined to the providing water system if the supplying water system meets applicable requirements for water quality, treatment, and system operation for that contaminant. The supplying water system may monitor the water within the providing water system for contamination pursuant to rules adopted under this Article. The supplying water system and the Department shall have access to the providing water system to investigate water quality problems and to determine whether any contamination is confined to the providing water system and whether the quality of the water supplied by the supplying water system is contributing contamination to the providing water system.

(f) If water in the providing water system exceeds the maximum contaminant levels established pursuant to this Article and the Department determines that the supplying water system is not responsible, the supplying water system must notify the providing water system owner in writing within one day of determining that the contamination is confined solely to the providing water system for bacteria, nitrate, and nitrite, and within 30 days for all other contaminants.

(g) A supplier of water regulated under this Article shall not be deemed to provide any warranty under Article 2 of Chapter 25 of the General Statutes, including an implied warranty of merchantability or an implied warranty of fitness for a particular purpose. (1979, c. 788, s. 1; 1983, c. 891, s. 2; 1985, c. 417, ss. 1, 2; 1991 (Reg. Sess., 1992), c. 826, s. 1; 1993 (Reg. Sess., 1994), c. 776, s. 15; 1995, c. 25, s. 1; 2000-172, s. 1.1; 2001-502, s. 6; 2004-143, s. 8; 2008-140, s. 1.)

§ 130A-316. Department to examine waters.

The Department shall examine all waters and their sources and surroundings which are used as, or proposed to be used as, sources of public water supply to determine whether the waters and their sources are suitable for use as public water supply sources. (1979, c. 788, s. 1; 1983, c. 891, s. 2.)

§ 130A-317. Department to provide advice; submission and approval of public water system plans.

(a) The Department shall advise all persons and units of local government locating, constructing, altering or operating or intending to locate, construct, alter or operate a public water system of the most appropriate source of water supply and the best practical method of purifying water from that source having regard to the present and prospective needs and interests of other persons and units of local government which may be affected. The Department shall also advise concerning accepted engineering practices in the location, construction, alteration and operation of public water systems.

(b) All persons and units of local government constructing or altering a public water system shall give prior notice and submit plans, specifications and other information to the Department. The Commission shall adopt rules providing for the amount of prior notice required to be given and the nature and detail of the plans, specifications and other information required to be submitted. The Commission shall take into consideration the complexity of the construction or alteration which may be involved and the resources of the Department to review the plans, specifications and other information. The Department shall review the plans, specifications and other information, and notify the person, Utilities Commission and unit of local government of compliance or lack of compliance with applicable statutes and rules of the Commission.

(c)   No person or unit of local government shall begin construction or alteration of a public water system or award a contract for construction or alteration unless all of the following conditions are met:

(1)   The plans for construction or alteration have been prepared by an engineer licensed by this State.

(2)   The Department has determined that the system, as constructed or altered, will be capable of compliance with the drinking water rules.

(3)   The Department has determined that the system is capable of interconnection at an appropriate time with an expanding municipal, county or regional system.

(4)   The Department has determined that adequate arrangements have been made for the continued operation, service and maintenance of the public water system.

(5)   The Department has approved the plans and specifications.

(d)   Municipalities, counties, local boards or commissions, water and sewer authorities, or groups of municipalities and counties may establish and administer within their utility service areas their own approval program in lieu of State approval of water system plans required in subsection (c) of this section for construction or alteration of the distribution system of a proposed or existing public water system, subject to the prior certification of the Department. For purposes of this subsection, the service area of a municipality shall include only that area within the corporate limits of the municipality and that area outside a municipality in its extraterritorial jurisdiction where water service is already being provided to the permit applicant by the municipality or connection to the municipal water system is immediately available to the applicant; the service areas of counties and the other entities or groups shall include only those areas where water service is already being provided to the applicant by the permitting authority or connection to the permitting authority's system is immediately available. No later than the 180th day after the receipt of an approval program and statement submitted by any local government, commission, authority, or board, the Department shall certify any local program that meets all of the following conditions:

(1) Provides by ordinance or local law for requirements compatible with those imposed by this Article, and the standards and rules adopted pursuant to this Article.

(2) Provides that the Department receives notice and a copy of each application for approval and that the Department receives copies of approved plans.

(3) Provides that plans and specifications for all construction and alterations be prepared by or under the direct supervision of an engineer licensed to practice in this State.

(4) Provides for the adequate enforcement of the program requirements by appropriate administrative and judicial process.

(5) Provides for the adequate administrative organization, engineering staff, financial and other resources necessary to effectively carry out its plan review program. A local government, commission, authority, or board may either employ an engineer licensed under Chapter 89C of the General Statutes to practice as a professional engineer in the State or contract with an engineer licensed under Chapter 89C of the General Statutes to practice as a professional engineer in the State in order to provide for adequate engineering staff under this subdivision.

(6) Provides that the system is capable of interconnection at an appropriate time with an expanding municipal, county, or regional system.

(7) Provides for the adequate arrangement for the continued operation, service, and maintenance of the public water system.

(8) Provides that an approved system, as constructed or altered, will be capable of compliance with the drinking water rules.

(9)   Is approved by the Department as adequate to meet the requirements of this Article and any applicable rules adopted pursuant to this Article.

(e)   The Department may deny, suspend, or revoke the certification of a local program upon a finding that a violation of the provisions in subsection (d) of this section has occurred. A local government administering an approval program shall be given notice that there has been a tentative decision to deny, suspend, or revoke certification and that an administrative hearing will be held in accordance with Chapter 150B of the General Statutes where the decision may be challenged. If a violation of the provisions in subsection (d) of this section presents an imminent hazard, certification may be suspended or revoked immediately. The Department shall give notice of the immediate suspension or revocation and notice that an administrative hearing will be held in accordance with Chapter 150B of the General Statutes where the decision may be challenged.

(f)   Notwithstanding any other provisions of subsection (d) of this section, if the Department determines that a public water system is violating plan approval requirements of a local program and that the local government has not acted to enforce those approval requirements, the Department may, after written notice to the local government, take enforcement action in accordance with the provisions of this Article. (1979, c. 788, s. 1; 1983, c. 891, s. 2; 1985, c. 697, s. 1; 1987, c. 827, s. 1; 2006-238, s. 1.)

§ 130A-318. Disinfection of public water systems.

(a)   The Department is authorized to require disinfection of:

(1)   Public water systems introduced on or after January 1, 1972; and

(2)   All public water systems, regardless of the date introduced, whenever:

a.   The maximum microbiological contaminant level is exceeded; or

b.   Conditions exist which make continued use of the water potentially hazardous to public health.

(b)   Public water systems shall employ disinfection methods and procedures approved by the Department. (1979, c. 788, s. 1; 1983, c. 891, s. 2.)

§ 130A-319. Condemnation of lands for public water systems.

All units of local government operating public water systems and all water companies operating under franchise from the State or units of local government, may acquire by condemnation lands and rights in lands and water necessary for the successful operation and protection of their systems. Condemnation proceedings under this section shall be the same as prescribed by law under Chapter 40A of the General Statutes. (1979, c. 788, s. 1; 1981, c. 919, s. 14; 1983, c. 891, s. 2.)

§ 130A-320. Sanitation of watersheds; rules; inspections.

(a)   The Commission shall adopt rules governing the sanitation of watersheds from which public drinking water supplies are obtained. In adopting these rules the Commission is authorized to consider the different classes of watersheds, taking into account general topography, nature of watershed development, density of population and need for frequency of sampling of raw water. The rules shall govern the keeping of livestock, operation of recreational areas, maintenance of residences and places of business, disposal of sewage, establishment of cemeteries or burying grounds, and any other factors which would endanger the public water supply.

(b)   Any person operating a public water system and furnishing water from unfiltered surface supplies shall inspect the watershed area at least quarterly, and more often when the Department determines that more frequent inspections are necessary. (1979, c. 788, s. 1; 1983, c. 891, s. 2.)

§ 130A-321. Variances and exemptions; considerations; duration; condition; notice and hearing.

(a)   The Secretary may authorize variances from the drinking water rules.

(1)   The Secretary may grant one or more variances to a public water system from any requirement respecting a maximum contaminant level of an applicable drinking water rule upon a finding that:

a. Because of characteristics of the raw water sources reasonably available to the system, the system cannot meet the requirements respecting the maximum contaminant levels of the drinking water rules after application of the best technology, treatment techniques, or other means which the Secretary finds are available (taking costs into consideration); and

b. The granting of a variance will not result in an unreasonable risk to public health when considering the population exposed, the projected duration of the requested variance and the degree to which the maximum contaminant level is being or will be exceeded.

(2) The Secretary may grant one or more variances to a public water system from any requirement of a specified treatment technique of an applicable drinking water rule upon a finding that the public water system applying for the variance has demonstrated that the treatment technique is not necessary to protect the public health because of the nature of the raw water source of the system.

(3) In consideration of whether the public water system is unable to comply with a contaminant level required by the drinking water rules because of the nature of the raw water sources, the Secretary shall consider factors such as:

a. The availability and effectiveness of treatment methods for the contaminant for which the variance is requested; and

b. Costs of implementing the best treatment(s), improving the quality of the raw water by the best means or using an alternate source.

(4) In consideration of whether a public water system should be granted a variance from a required treatment technique because the treatment is unnecessary to protect the public health, the Secretary shall consider factors such as:

a. Quality of the water source including water quality data and pertinent sources of pollution; and

b. Source protection measures employed by the public water system.

(5) In order to implement sub-subdivision a. of subdivision (1) of this subsection, the Commission shall adopt by rule a list of the best available

technologies, treatment techniques, or other means available, to deal with each contaminant for which a maximum contaminant level is established.

(b) The Secretary may authorize exemptions from the drinking water rules.

(1) The Secretary may exempt a public water system from any requirement respecting a maximum contaminant level or any treatment technique requirement, or from both, of an applicable drinking water rule upon a finding that:

a. Due to compelling factors, including economic factors, the public water system is unable to comply with the contaminant level or treatment technique requirement;

b. The public water system was in operation on the effective date of the contaminant level or treatment technique requirement or, for a system that was not in operation on that date, only if no reasonable alternative source of drinking water is available to the new system; and

c. The granting of the exemption will not result in an unreasonable risk to public health when considering the population exposed, the projected duration of the requested exemption and the degree to which the maximum contaminant level is being or will be exceeded.

(2) In consideration of whether the public water system is unable to comply due to compelling factors, the Secretary shall consider factors such as:

a. Construction, installation or modification of treatment equipment or systems;

b. The time needed to put into operation a new treatment facility to replace an existing system which is not in compliance; and

c. Economic feasibility of immediate compliance.

(c) As a condition of issuance of either a variance or an exemption, the Secretary shall issue a schedule of compliance for the public water system, including increments of progress for each drinking water rule for which the variance or exemption was issued. As a further condition of a variance or exemption, the Secretary shall require the public water system to implement any necessary control measures prescribed by the Secretary during the period of the variance or exemption. The compliance schedule for an exemption shall require compliance as expeditiously as practical but no later than June 19, 1987, for existing maximum contaminant levels and treatment techniques, or no later than one year from the issuance of the exemption for any newly adopted maximum contaminant level or treatment technique. The final date for compliance provided in any exemption schedule may be extended up to three years after the date of the issuance of the exemption if the water system establishes:

(1) The water system cannot meet the standard without capital improvements which cannot be completed within the period of exemption, or

(2) The system needs financial assistance for necessary improvements and has entered into an agreement to obtain such assistance, or

(3) The system has entered into an enforceable agreement to become part of a regional public water system and the system is taking all practical steps to meet the standard.

If a public water system serves 500 or fewer service connections and needs financial assistance for necessary improvements, an exemption may be renewed for one or more additional two-year periods if the system establishes it meets the requirements set forth in subdivisions (1) and (2) of this section.

(d) The Secretary shall provide notice and opportunity for public hearing on proposed variances and proposed variance and exemption schedules. (1979, c. 788, s. 1; 1981, c. 353, ss. 1, 2; 1983, c. 891, s. 2; 1987, c. 704, ss. 3-5.)

§ 130A-322. Imminent hazard; power of the Secretary.

(a) The Secretary shall judge whether an imminent hazard exists concerning a present or potential condition in a public water system.

(b) In order to eliminate an imminent hazard, the Secretary may, without notice or hearing, issue an order requiring the person or persons involved to immediately take action necessary to protect the public health. A copy of the order shall be delivered by certified mail or personal service. The order shall become effective immediately and shall remain in effect until modified or rescinded by the Secretary or by a court of competent jurisdiction. (1979, c. 788, s. 1; 1983, c. 891, s. 2.)

§ 130A-323. Emergency plan for drinking water; emergency circumstances defined.

(a) The Secretary shall develop and implement an adequate plan for the provision of drinking water under emergency circumstances. When the Secretary determines that emergency circumstances exist with respect to a need for drinking water, the Secretary may take action in accordance with the plan as necessary in order to provide drinking water.

(b) Emergency circumstances shall exist whenever the available supply of drinking water is inadequate. (1979, c. 788, s. 1; 1983, c. 891, s. 2.)

§ 130A-324. Notice of noncompliance; failure to perform monitoring; variances and exemptions.

Whenever a public water system:

(1) Is not in compliance with the drinking water rules;

(2) Fails to perform an applicable testing procedure or monitoring required by the drinking water rules;

(3) Is subject to a variance granted for inability to meet a maximum contaminant level requirement;

(4) Is subject to an exemption; or

(5) Fails to comply with the requirements prescribed by a variance or exemption,

the supplier shall as soon as possible, but not later than 48 hours after discovery, notify the Department and give public notification as prescribed by the drinking water rules. (1979, c. 788, s. 1; 1983, c. 891, s. 2.)

§ 130A-325. Prohibited acts.

The following acts are prohibited:

(1)   Failure by a supplier of water to comply with this Article, an order issued under this Article, or the drinking water rules;

(2)   Failure by a supplier of water to comply with the requirements of G.S. 130A-324 or the dissemination by a supplier of any false or misleading information with respect to remedial actions being undertaken to achieve compliance with the drinking water rules;

(3)   Refusal by a supplier of water to allow the Department or local health department to inspect a public water system as provided for in G.S. 130A-17;

(4)   The willful defiling by any person of any water supply of a public water system or the willful damaging of any pipe or other part of a public water system;

(5)   The discharge by any person of sewage or other waste above the intake of a public water system, unless the sewage or waste has been passed through a system of purification approved by the Department ; and

(6)   The failure by a person to maintain a system approved by the Department for collecting and disposing of all accumulations of human excrement located on the watershed of a public water system. (1979, c. 788, s. 1; 1983, c. 891, s. 2; 1985, c. 462, s. 2; 1989, c. 727, s. 146.)

§ 130A-326. Powers of the Secretary.

To carry out the provisions of this Article, the Secretary is authorized to:

(1)   Administer and enforce the provisions of this Article, the drinking water rules and orders issued under this Article;

(2)   Enter into agreements or cooperative arrangements with, or participate in related programs of other states, other state agencies, federal or interstate agencies, units of local government, educational institutions, local health departments or other organizations or individuals;

(3) Receive financial and technical assistance from the federal government and other public or private agencies;

(4) Require public water systems to take actions or make modifications as necessary to comply with the requirements of this Article or the drinking water rules;

(5) Prescribe policies and procedures necessary or appropriate to carry out the Secretary's function under this Article;

(6) Establish and collect fees to recover the costs of laboratory analyses performed for compliance with this Article. The fees shall not exceed two hundred dollars ($200.00) for each analysis; and

(7) Establish and collect fees for certification and certification renewal of laboratories to perform analyses for compliance under this Article. The fees shall not exceed twenty dollars ($20.00) per analyte certified. The minimum fee for certification or certification renewal shall be two hundred fifty dollars ($250.00) per analyte category. The maximum fee for certification or certification renewal shall be six hundred dollars ($600.00) per analyte category. The fees collected under this subdivision shall be used to administer blind performance evaluation samples to certified laboratories to determine compliance with certification requirements. (1979, c. 788, s. 1; 1981, c. 562, s. 9; 1983, c. 891, s. 2; 1987, c. 471; 1991 (Reg. Sess., 1992), c. 1039, s. 10.)

§ 130A-327. Construction.

This Article shall be interpreted as giving the State the authority needed to assume primary enforcement responsibility under the federal act. (1979, c. 788, s. 1; 1983, c. 891, s. 2.)

§ 130A-328. Public water system operating permit and permit fee.

(a) No person shall operate a community or non transient non-community water system who has not been issued an operating permit by the Department. A community or non transient non-community water system operating permit shall be valid from January 1 through December 31 of each year unless suspended or revoked by the Department for cause. The Commission shall adopt rules concerning permit issuance and renewal and permit suspension and revocation. The annual fees in subsection (b) shall be prorated on a monthly basis for permits obtained after January 1 of each year.

(b) The following fees are imposed for the issuance or renewal of a permit to operate a community or non transient non-community water system; the fees are based on the number of persons served by the system:

Non Community Water Systems:
Fee

Base Fee:

Non transient non-community
$150

Community Water Systems:

Number of Persons Served

50 or fewer
$255

More than 50 but no more than 100
$270

More than 100 but no more than 200
$330

More than 200 but no more than 300
$350

More than 300 but no more than 400
$385

More than 400 but no more than 500
$420

More than 500 but no more than 750
$780

More than 750 but no more than 1000
$810

More than 1000 but no more than 2000
$840

More than 2000 but no more than 3000
$870

More than 3000 but no more than 4000
$1350

More than 4000 but no more than 5000
$1460

More than 5000 but no more than 7500
$1925

More than 7500 but no more than 10,000
$2065

More than 10,000 but no more than 25,000
$2600

More than 25,000 but no more than 50,000
$2925

More than 50,000 but no more than 75,000
$4250

More than 75,000 but no more than 100,000
$4675

More than 100,000 but no more than 250,000
$5100

More than 250,000 but no more than 500,000
$5525

More than 500,000
$5950

(c) The following fees are imposed for the review of plans, specifications, and other information submitted to the Department for approval of construction or alteration of a public water system. The fees are based on the type of constructions or alteration proposed:

Distribution system:
Fee

Construction of water lines, less than 5000 linear feet
$150

Construction of water lines, 5000 linear feet or more
$200

Other construction or alteration to a distribution system
$75

Ground water system:

Construction of a new ground water system or adding a new well
$200

Alteration to an existing ground water system
$100

Surface Water system:

Construction of a new surface water treatment facility
$250

Alteration to an existing surface water treatment facility
$150

Water System Management Plan review
$75

Miscellaneous changes or maintenance not covered above
$50

(d) The Department may charge an administrative fee of up to one hundred fifty dollars ($150.00) for failure to pay the permit fee by January 31 of each year.

(e) All fees collected under this section shall be applied to the costs of administering and enforcing this Article. (1991, c. 576, s. 1; 1991 (Reg. Sess., 1992), c. 811, s. 6; c. 1039, s. 11; 2006-66, s. 11.7(a).)

§ 130A-329. Reporting.

Reports required to be submitted under this Article or under rules adopted by the Commission shall be submitted electronically on a form specified by the Department. The Department may waive the requirement for electronic submission of a report if the water system demonstrates that it lacks the technical capability to report electronically. (2008-143, s. 12.)

§ 130A-330. Reserved for future codification purposes.

§ 130A-331 Reserved for future codification purposes.

§ 130A-332 Reserved for future codification purposes.

Article 11.

Wastewater Systems.

§ 130A-333. Purpose.

The General Assembly finds and declares that continued installation, at a rapidly and constantly accelerating rate, of septic tank systems and other types of wastewater systems in a faulty or improper manner and in areas where unsuitable soil and population density adversely affect the efficiency and functioning of these systems, has a detrimental effect on the public health and environment through contamination of land, groundwater and surface waters. Recognizing, however, that wastewater can be rendered ecologically safe and the public health protected if methods of wastewater collection, treatment and disposal are properly regulated and recognizing that wastewater collection, treatment and disposal will continue to be necessary to meet the needs of an expanding population, the General Assembly intends to ensure the regulation of wastewater collection, treatment and disposal systems so that these systems may continue to be used, where appropriate, without jeopardizing the public health. (1973, c. 452, s. 3; 1981, c. 949, s. 3; 1983, c. 891, s. 2; 1991 (Reg. Sess., 1992), c. 944, ss. 1, 2.)

§ 130A-334. Definitions.

The following definitions shall apply throughout this Article:

(1)   "Construction" means any work at the site of placement done for the purpose of preparing a residence, place of business or place of public assembly for initial occupancy, or subsequent additions or modifications which increase sewage flow.

(1a)   "Department" means the Department of Health and Human Services.

(2)   Repealed by Session Laws 1985, c. 462, s. 18.

(2a)   "Industrial process wastewater" means any water-carried waste resulting from any process of industry, manufacture, trade, or business.

(3)   "Location" means the initial placement for occupancy of a residence, place of business or place of public assembly.

(3a)   "Maintenance" means normal or routine maintenance including replacement of broken pipes, cleaning, or adjustment to an existing wastewater system.

(4), (5) Repealed by Session Laws 1985, c. 462, s. 18.

(6)   "Place of business" means a store, warehouse, manufacturing establishment, place of amusement or recreation, service station, office building or any other place where people work.

(7)   "Place of public assembly" means a fairground, auditorium, stadium, church, campground, theater or any other place where people assemble.

(7a) "Plat" means a property survey prepared by a registered land surveyor, drawn to a scale of one inch equals no more than 60 feet, that includes: the specific location of the proposed facility and appurtenances, the site for the proposed wastewater system, and the location of water supplies and surface waters. "Plat" also means, for subdivision lots approved by the local planning authority and recorded with the county register of deeds, a copy of the recorded subdivision plat that is accompanied by a site plan that is drawn to scale.

(7b) "Pretreatment" means any biological, chemical, or physical process or system for improving wastewater quality and reducing wastewater constituents prior to final treatment and disposal in a subsurface wastewater system and includes, but is not limited to aeration, clarification, digestion, disinfection, filtration, separation, and settling.

(8) "Public or community wastewater system" means a single system of wastewater collection, treatment and disposal owned and operated by a sanitary district, a metropolitan sewage district, a water and sewer authority, a county or municipality or a public utility.

(9) "Relocation" means the displacement of a residence or place of business from one site to another.

(9a) "Repair" means the extension, alteration, replacement, or relocation of existing components of a wastewater system.

(10) "Residence" means a private home, dwelling unit in a multiple family structure, hotel, motel, summer camp, labor work camp, manufactured home, institution or any other place where people reside.

(10a) "Secretary" means the Secretary of Environment and Natural Resources.

(11) Repealed by Session Laws 1992, c. 944, s. 3.

(12) "Septic tank system" means a subsurface wastewater system consisting of a settling tank and a subsurface disposal field.

(13) "Sewage" means the liquid and solid human body waste and liquid waste generated by water-using fixtures and appliances, including those associated with foodhandling. The term does not include industrial process wastewater or sewage that is combined with industrial process wastewater.

(13a) "Site plan" means a drawing not necessarily drawn to scale that shows the existing and proposed property lines with dimensions, the location of the facility and appurtenances, the site for the proposed wastewater system, and the location of water supplies and surface waters.

(14) "Wastewater" means any sewage or industrial process wastewater discharged, transmitted, or collected from a residence, place of business, place of public assembly, or other places into a wastewater system.

(15) "Wastewater system" means a system of wastewater collection, treatment, and disposal in single or multiple components, including a privy, septic tank system, public or community wastewater system, wastewater reuse or recycle system, mechanical or biological wastewater treatment system, any other similar system, and any chemical toilet used only for human waste. (1973, c. 452, s. 4; 1981, c. 949, s. 3; 1983, c. 891, s. 2; 1985, c. 462, s. 18; c. 487, s. 9; 1987, c. 435; 1991, c. 256, s. 1; 1991 (Reg. Sess., 1992), c. 944, s. 3; c. 1028, s. 4; 1995, c. 285, s. 1; 1995 (Reg. Sess., 1996), c. 585, s. 1; 1996, 2nd Ex. Sess., c. 18, ss. 27.31(a), (b); 1997-443, s. 11A.82; 2011-145, s. 13.3(bbb).)

§ 130A-335. Wastewater collection, treatment and disposal; rules.

(a) A person owning or controlling a residence, place of business or a place of public assembly shall provide an approved wastewater system. Except as may be allowed under another provision of law, all wastewater from water-using fixtures and appliances connected to a water supply source shall discharge to the approved wastewater system. A wastewater system may include components for collection, treatment and disposal of wastewater.

(b) All wastewater systems shall be regulated by the Department under rules adopted by the Commission except for the following wastewater systems that shall be regulated by the Department under rules adopted by the Environmental Management Commission:

(1) Wastewater collection, treatment, and disposal systems designed to discharge effluent to the land surface or surface waters.

(2) Wastewater systems designed for groundwater remediation, groundwater injection, or landfill leachate collection and disposal.

(3) Wastewater systems designed for the complete recycle or reuse of industrial process wastewater.

(4)   Gray water systems as defined in G.S. 143-350.

(c)   A wastewater system subject to approval under rules of the Commission shall be reviewed and approved under rules of a local board of health in the following circumstances:

(1)   The local board of health, on its own motion, has requested the Department to review its proposed rules concerning wastewater systems; and

(2)   The local board of health has adopted by reference the wastewater system rules adopted by the Commission, with any more stringent modifications or additions deemed necessary by the local board of health to protect the public health; and

(3)   The Department has found that the rules of the local board of health concerning wastewater collection, treatment and disposal systems are at least as stringent as rules adopted by the Commission and are sufficient and necessary to safeguard the public health.

(d)   The Department may, upon its own motion, upon the request of a local board of health or upon the request of a citizen of an affected county, review its findings under subsection (c) of this section.

The Department shall review its findings under subsection (c) of this section upon modification by the Commission of the rules applicable to wastewater systems. The Department may deny, suspend, or revoke the approval of local board of health wastewater system rules upon a finding that the local wastewater rules are not as stringent as rules adopted by the Commission, are not sufficient and necessary to safeguard the public health, or are not being enforced. Suspension and revocation of approval shall be in accordance with G.S. 130A-23.

(e)   The rules of the Commission and the rules of the local board of health shall address at least the following: Wastewater characteristics; Design unit; Design capacity; Design volume; Criteria for the design, installation, operation, maintenance and performance of wastewater collection, treatment and disposal systems; Soil morphology and drainage; Topography and landscape position; Depth to seasonally high water table, rock and water impeding formations; Proximity to water supply wells, shellfish waters, estuaries, marshes, wetlands, areas subject to frequent flooding, streams, lakes, swamps and other bodies of surface or groundwaters; Density of wastewater collection, treatment and disposal systems in a geographical area; Requirements for issuance, suspension and revocation of permits; and Other factors which affect the effective operation and performance of wastewater collection, treatment and disposal systems. The rules regarding required design capacity and required design volume for wastewater systems shall provide that exceptions may be granted upon a showing that a system is adequate to meet actual daily water consumption.

(f) The rules of the Commission and the rules of the local board of health shall classify systems of wastewater collection, treatment and disposal according to size, type of treatment and any other appropriate factors. The rules shall provide construction requirements, including pretreatment and system control requirements, standards for operation, maintenance, monitoring, reporting, and ownership requirements for each classification of systems of wastewater collection, treatment and disposal in order to prevent, as far as reasonably possible, any contamination of the land, groundwater and surface waters. The Department and local health departments may impose conditions on the issuance of permits and may revoke the permits for failure of the system to satisfy the conditions, the rules, or this Article. Permits other than improvement permits shall be valid for a period prescribed by rule. Improvement permits shall be valid upon a showing satisfactory to the Department or the local health department that the site and soil conditions are unaltered, that the facility, design wastewater flow, and wastewater characteristics are not increased, and that a wastewater system can be installed that meets the permitting requirements in effect on the date the improvement permit was issued. Improvement permits for which a plat is provided shall be valid without expiration. Improvement permits for which a site plan is provided shall be valid for five years. The period of time for which the permit is valid and a statement that the permit is subject to revocation if the site plan or plat, whichever is applicable, or the intended use changes shall be displayed prominently on both the application form for the permit and the permit.

(f1) A preconstruction conference with the owner or developer, or an agent of the owner or developer, and a representative of the local health department shall be required for any authorization for wastewater system construction issued with an improvement permit under G.S. 130-336 when the authorization is greater than five years old. Following the conference, the local health department shall issue a revised authorization for wastewater system construction that includes current technology that can reasonably be expected to improve the performance of the system.

(f2)   For each septic tank system that is designed to treat 3,000 gallons per day or less of sewage, rules adopted pursuant to subsection (f) of this section shall require the use of an effluent filter to reduce the total suspended solids entering the drainfield and the use of an access device for each compartment of the septic tank to provide access to the compartment in order to facilitate maintenance of the septic tank. The Commission shall not adopt specifications for the effluent filter and access device that exceed the requirements of G.S. 130A-335.1. Neither this section nor G.S. 130A-335.1 shall be construed to prohibit the use of an effluent filter or access device that exceeds the requirements of G.S. 130A-335.1. The Department shall approve effluent filters that meet the requirements of this section, G.S. 130A-335.1, and rules adopted by the Commission.

(g)   Prior to denial of an improvement permit, the local health department shall advise the applicant of possible site modifications or alternative systems, and shall provide a brief description of those systems. When an improvement permit is denied, the local health department shall issue the site evaluation in writing stating the reasons for the unsuitable classification. The evaluation shall also inform the applicant of the right to an informal review by the Department, the right to appeal under G.S. 130A-24, and to have the appeal held in the county in which the site for which the improvement permit was requested is located.

(h)   Except as provided in this subsection, a chemical or portable toilet may be placed at any location where the chemical or portable toilet can be operated and maintained under sanitary conditions. A chemical or portable toilet shall not be used as a replacement or substitute for a water closet or urinal where a water closet or urinal connected to a permanent wastewater treatment system is required by the North Carolina State Building Code, except that a chemical or portable toilet may be used to supplement a water closet or urinal during periods of peak use. A chemical or portable toilet shall not be used as an alternative to the repair of a water closet, urinal, or wastewater treatment system. It shall be unlawful to discharge sewage or other waste from a chemical or portable toilet used for human waste except into a wastewater system that has been approved by the Department under rules adopted by the Commission or by the Environmental Management Commission or at a site that is permitted by the Department under G.S. 130A-291.1. (1957, c. 1357, s. 1; 1973, c. 471, s. 1; c. 476, s. 128; c. 860; 1977, c. 857, s. 1; 1979, c. 788, s. 2; 1981, c. 949, s. 3; c. 1127, s. 47; 1983, c. 891, s. 2; 1987, c. 267, ss. 1, 2; 1989, c. 727, s. 147; c. 764, ss. 6, 7; 1989 (Reg. Sess., 1990), c. 1075, s. 2; 1991 (Reg. Sess., 1992), c. 944, s. 4; 1993, c. 173, s. 5; 1995, c. 285, s. 1; 1995 (Reg. Sess., 1996), c.

585, s. 2; 1996, 2nd Ex. Sess., c. 18, s. 27.31(c); 1998-126, s. 1; 1998-217, s. 46(a); 2008-143, s. 13; 2011-394, s. 12(c).)

§ 130A-335.1. Effluent filters and access devices for certain septic tank systems.

(a) The person who manufactures, installs, repairs, or pumps any septic tank to be installed in this State as a part of a septic tank system that is designed to treat 3,000 gallons per day or less of sewage shall provide an effluent filter approved by the Department pursuant to the requirements of G.S. 130A-335, this section, and rules adopted by the Commission. Any person who manufactures, installs, repairs, or pumps systems described in this section may purchase and install any approved filters on the systems. The person who installs the effluent filter shall install the effluent filter as a part of the septic tank system in accordance with the specifications provided by the manufacturer of the effluent filter. An effluent filter shall:

(1) Be made of materials that are capable of withstanding the corrosives to which septic tank systems are normally subject.

(2) Prevent solid material larger than one-sixteenth of an inch, as measured along the shortest axis of the material, from entering the drainfield.

(3) Be designed and constructed to allow for routine maintenance.

(4) Be designed and constructed so as not to require maintenance more frequently than once in any three-year period under normally anticipated use.

(b) The access device required by G.S. 130A-335(f) shall provide access to each compartment of a septic tank for inspection and maintenance either by means of an opening in the top of the septic tank or by a riser assembly and shall include an appropriate cover. The access device shall:

(1) Be of sufficient size to facilitate inspection and service.

(2) Be designed and constructed to equal or exceed the minimum loading specifications applicable to the septic tank.

(3) Prevent water entry.

(4) Come to within six inches of the finished grade.

(5) Be visibly marked so that the access device can be readily located. (1998-126, s. 2; 2006-255, s. 4; 2006-264, s. 63(a).)

§ 130A-336. Improvement permit and authorization for wastewater system construction required.

(a) Any proposed site for a residence, place of business, or place of public assembly in an area not served by an approved wastewater system shall be evaluated by the local health department in accordance with rules adopted pursuant to this Article. An improvement permit shall be issued in compliance with the rules adopted pursuant to this Article. An improvement permit shall include:

(1) For permits that are valid without expiration, a plat or, for permits that are valid for five years, a site plan.

(2) A description of the facility the proposed site is to serve.

(3) The proposed wastewater system and its location.

(4) The design wastewater flow and characteristics.

(5) The conditions for any site modifications.

(6) Any other information required by the rules of the Commission.

The improvement permit shall not be affected by change in ownership of the site for the wastewater system provided both the site for the wastewater system and the facility the system serves are unchanged and remain under the ownership or control of the person owning the facility. No person shall commence or assist in the construction, location, or relocation of a residence, place of business, or place of public assembly in an area not served by an approved wastewater system unless an improvement permit and an authorization for wastewater system construction are obtained from the local health department. This requirement shall not apply to a manufactured residence exhibited for sale or stored for later sale and intended to be located at another site after sale.

(b) The local health department shall issue an authorization for wastewater system construction authorizing work to proceed and the installation or repair of a wastewater system when it has determined after a field investigation that the system can be installed and operated in compliance with this Article and rules adopted pursuant to this Article. This authorization for wastewater system construction shall be valid for a period equal to the period of validity of the improvement permit, not to exceed five years, and may be issued at the same time the improvement permit is issued. No person shall commence or assist in the installation, construction, or repair of a wastewater system unless an improvement permit and an authorization for wastewater system construction have been obtained from the Department or the local health department. No improvement permit or authorization for wastewater system construction shall be required for maintenance of a wastewater system. The Department and the local health department may impose conditions on the issuance of an improvement permit and an authorization for wastewater system construction.

(c) Unless the Commission otherwise provides by rule, plans, and specifications for all wastewater systems designed for the collection, treatment, and disposal of industrial process wastewater shall be reviewed and approved by the Department prior to the issuance of an authorization for wastewater system construction by the local health department.

(d) If a local health department repeatedly fails to issue or deny improvement permits for conventional septic tank systems within 60 days of receiving completed applications for the permits, then the Department of Environment and Natural Resources may withhold public health funding from that local health department. (1973, c. 452, s. 5; c. 476, s. 128; 1981, c. 949, s. 3; 1983, c. 891, s. 2; 1985, c. 273; 1991, c. 256, s. 2; 1991 (Reg. Sess., 1992), c. 944, s. 5; 1995, c. 285, s. 1; 1995 (Reg. Sess., 1996), c. 585, s. 3; 1996, 2nd Ex. Sess., c. 18, s. 27.31(d)-(f); 1997-443, ss. 11A.83, 11A.119(a).)

§ 130A-337. Inspection; operation permit required.

(a) No system of wastewater collection, treatment and disposal shall be covered or placed into use by any person until an inspection by the local health department has determined that the system has been installed or repaired in accordance with any conditions of the improvement permit, the rules, and this Article.

(b) Upon determining that the system is properly installed or repaired and that the system is capable of being operated in accordance with the conditions of the improvement permit, the rules, this Article and any conditions to be imposed in the operation permit, as applicable, the local health department shall issue an operation permit authorizing the residence, place of business or place of public assembly to be occupied and for the system to be placed into use or reuse.

(c) Upon determination that an existing wastewater system has a valid operation permit and is operating properly in a manufactured home park, the local health department shall issue authorization in writing for a manufactured home to be connected to the existing system and to be occupied. Notwithstanding G.S. 130A-336, an improvement permit is not required for the connection of a manufactured home to an existing system with a valid operation permit in a manufactured home park.

(d) No person shall occupy a residence, place of business or place of public assembly, or place a wastewater system into use or reuse for a residence, place of business or place of public assembly until an operation permit has been issued or authorization has been obtained pursuant to G.S. 130A-337(c). (1973, c. 452, s. 6; 1981, c. 949, s. 3; 1983, c. 891, s. 2; 1985, c. 487, s. 9; 1991 (Reg. Sess., 1992), c. 944, s. 6; 1995, c. 285, s. 1.)

§ 130A-338. Authorization for wastewater system construction required before other permits to be issued.

Where construction, location or relocation is proposed to be done upon a residence, place of business or place of public assembly, no permit required for electrical, plumbing, heating, air conditioning or other construction, location or relocation activity under any provision of general or special law shall be issued until an authorization for wastewater system construction has been issued under G.S. 130A-336 or authorization has been obtained under G.S. 130A-337(c). (1973, c. 452, s. 7; 1981, c. 949, s. 3; 1983, c. 891, s. 2; 1995, c. 285, s. 1.)

§ 130A-339. Limitation on electrical service.

No person shall allow permanent electrical service to a residence, place of business or place of public assembly upon construction, location or relocation until the official electrical inspector with jurisdiction as provided in G.S. 143-143.2 certifies to the electrical supplier that the required improvement permit authorization for wastewater system construction and an operation permit or authorization under G.S. 130A-337(c) has been obtained. Temporary electrical service necessary for constructing a residence, place of business or place of public assembly can be provided upon compliance with G.S. 130A-338. (1973, c. 452, s. 8; 1981, c. 949, s. 3; 1983, c. 891, s. 2; 1995, c. 285, s. 1.)

§ 130A-340. Review procedures and appeals.

The Department, upon request by an applicant for an improvement permit, shall provide a technical review of any scientific data and system design submitted by the applicant. The data and system design shall be evaluated by professional peers of those who prepared the data and system design. The results of the technical review shall be available prior to a decision by the local health department and shall not affect an applicant's right to a contested hearing under Chapter 150B of the General Statutes. (1989, c. 764, s. 5.)

§ 130A-341. Consideration of a site with existing fill.

Upon application to the local health department, a site that has existing fill, including one on which fill material was placed prior to July 1, 1977, and that has sand or loamy sand for a depth of at least 36 inches below the existing ground surface, shall be evaluated for an on-site wastewater system. The Commission shall adopt rules to implement this section. (1989, c. 764, s. 8; 1991 (Reg. Sess., 1992), c. 944, s. 7.)

§ 130A-342. Residential wastewater treatment systems.

(a) Individual residential wastewater treatment systems that are approved and listed in accordance with the standards adopted by the National Sanitation Foundation, Inc. for Class I residential wastewater treatment systems, as set out in Standard 40 of the National Sanitation Foundation, Inc., (as approved 13 January 2001) as amended, shall be permitted under rules adopted by the

Commission. The Commission may establish standards in addition to those set by the National Sanitation Foundation, Inc.

(b) A permitted system shall be operated and maintained by a certified wastewater treatment facility operator.

(c) Each county, in which one or more residential wastewater treatment systems permitted pursuant to this section are in use, shall document the performance of each system and report the results to the Department annually. (1989, c. 727, s. 223(b); c. 764, s. 9; 1989 (Reg. Sess., 1990), c. 1004, ss. 12, 37; 1991 (Reg. Sess., 1992), c. 944, s. 8; 1995, c. 285, s. 1; 1997-443, ss. 11A.84, 11A.119(a); 2001-505, s. 2.1.)

§ 130A-343. Approval of on-site subsurface wastewater systems.

(a) Definitions. - As used in this section:

(1) "Accepted wastewater system" means any wastewater system, other than a conventional wastewater system, or any technology, device, or component of a wastewater system that: (i) has been previously approved as an innovative wastewater system by the Department; (ii) has been in general use in this State as an innovative wastewater system for more than five years; and (iii) has been approved by the Commission for general use or use in one or more specific applications. An accepted wastewater system may be approved for use in applications for which a conventional wastewater system is unsuitable. The Commission may impose any design, operation, maintenance, monitoring, and management requirements on the use of an accepted wastewater system that it determines to be appropriate.

(2) "Controlled demonstration wastewater system" means any wastewater system or any technology, device, or component of a wastewater system that, on the basis of acceptable research, is approved by the Department for research, testing, or trial use under actual field conditions in this State pursuant to a protocol that has been approved by the Department.

(3) "Conventional wastewater system", "conventional sewage system", or "conventional septic tank system" means a wastewater system that consists of a traditional septic or settling tank and a gravity-fed subsurface disposal field that

uses washed gravel or crushed stone to distribute effluent to soil in one or more nitrification trenches and that does not include any other appurtenance.

(4) "Experimental wastewater system" means any wastewater system or any technology, device, or component of a wastewater system that is approved by the Department for research, testing, or limited trial use under actual field conditions in this State pursuant to a protocol that has been approved by the Department.

(5) "Innovative wastewater system" means any wastewater system, or any technology, device, or component of a wastewater system that: (i) has been demonstrated to perform in a manner equal or superior to a conventional wastewater system; (ii) is constructed of materials whose physical and chemical properties provide the strength, durability, and chemical resistance to allow the system to withstand loads and conditions as required by rules adopted by the Commission; and (iii) has been approved by the Department for general use or for one or more specific applications. An innovative wastewater system may be approved for use in applications for which a conventional wastewater system is unsuitable. The Department may impose any design, operation, maintenance, monitoring, and management requirements on the use of an innovative wastewater system that it determines to be appropriate.

(b) Adoption of Rules Governing Approvals. - The Commission shall adopt rules for the approval and permitting of experimental, controlled demonstration, innovative, and accepted wastewater systems. The rules shall address the criteria to be considered prior to issuing a permit for a system, requirements for preliminary design plans and specifications that must be submitted, methodology to be used, standards for monitoring and evaluating the system, research evaluation of the system, the plan of work for monitoring system performance and maintenance, and any additional matters the Commission deems appropriate.

(c) Approved Systems. - The Department may modify, suspend, or revoke the approval of a wastewater system if the Department determines that the approval is based on false, incomplete, or misleading information or if the Department finds that modification, suspension, or revocation is necessary to protect public health, safety, or welfare. The Department shall provide a listing of all approved experimental, controlled demonstration, innovative, and accepted wastewater systems to the local health departments annually, and more frequently, when the Department makes a final agency decision related to the approval of a wastewater system or the Commission adopts rules related to the approval of a wastewater system.

(d)   Evaluation Protocols. - The Department shall approve one or more nationally recognized protocols for the evaluation of on-site subsurface wastewater systems. Any protocol approved by the Department shall specify a minimum number of sites that must be evaluated and the duration of the evaluation period. At the request of a manufacturer of a wastewater system, the Department may approve an alternative protocol for use in the evaluation of the performance of the manufacturer's wastewater system. A protocol for the evaluation of an on-site subsurface wastewater system is a scientific standard within the meaning of G.S. 150B-2(8a)h.

(e)   Experimental Systems. - A manufacturer of a wastewater system that is intended for on-site subsurface use may apply to the Department to have the system evaluated as an experimental wastewater system as provided in this subsection. The manufacturer shall submit a proposal for evaluation of the system to the Department. The proposal for evaluation shall include the design of the system, a description of any laboratory or field research or testing that will be used to evaluate the system, a description of the research or testing protocol, and the credentials of the independent laboratory, consultant, or other entity that will be conducting the research or testing on the system. The proposal may include an evaluation of research and testing conducted in other states to the extent that the research and testing involves soil types, climate, hydrology, and other relevant conditions that are comparable to conditions in this State and if the research or testing was conducted pursuant to a protocol acceptable to the Department. The manufacturer shall enter into a contract for an evaluation of the performance of the experimental wastewater system with an independent laboratory, consultant, or other entity that has expertise in the evaluation of wastewater systems and that is approved by the Department. The manufacturer may install up to 50 experimental systems pursuant to a protocol approved by the Department on sites that are suitable for a conventional wastewater system and that have a repair area of sufficient size to allow installation of a conventional wastewater system, an approved innovative wastewater system, or an accepted wastewater system if the experimental wastewater system fails to perform properly.

(f)   Controlled Demonstration Systems. - A manufacturer of a wastewater system intended for on-site subsurface use may apply to the Department to have the system evaluated as a controlled demonstration wastewater system as provided in this subsection. The manufacturer shall submit a proposal for evaluation of the system to the Department. The proposal for evaluation shall include the design of the system, a description of any laboratory or field research or testing that will be used to evaluate the system, a description of the research or testing protocol, and the credentials of the independent laboratory, consultant, or other entity that will be conducting the research or testing on the system. If the system was evaluated as an experimental system under subsection (e) of this section, the proposal shall include the results of the evaluation. The proposal may include an evaluation of research and testing conducted in other states to the extent that the research and testing involves soil types, climate, hydrology, and other relevant conditions that are comparable to conditions in this State and if the research or testing was conducted pursuant to a protocol acceptable to the Department. The manufacturer shall enter into a contract for an evaluation of the performance of the controlled demonstration wastewater system with an independent laboratory, consultant, or other entity that has expertise in the evaluation of wastewater systems and that is approved by the Department. The manufacturer may install up to 200 controlled demonstration wastewater systems pursuant to a protocol approved by the Department on sites that are suitable for a conventional wastewater system and that have a repair area of sufficient size to allow installation of a conventional wastewater system, an approved innovative wastewater system, or an accepted wastewater system if the controlled demonstration wastewater system fails to perform properly. If the controlled demonstration wastewater system is intended for use on sites that are not suitable, or that are provisionally suitable, for a conventional wastewater system, the Department may approve the installation of the controlled demonstration wastewater system if the Department determines that the manufacturer can provide an acceptable alternative method for collection, treatment, and disposal of the wastewater.

(g)   Innovative Systems. - A manufacturer of a wastewater system for on-site subsurface use that has been evaluated as an experimental wastewater system as provided in subsection (e) of this section or that has been evaluated as a controlled demonstration wastewater system as provided in subsection (f) of this section may apply to the Department to have the system approved as an innovative wastewater system as provided in this subsection. A manufacturer of a wastewater system for on-site subsurface use that has not been evaluated as an experimental wastewater system or as a controlled demonstration wastewater system may also apply to the Department to have the system approved as an innovative wastewater system on the basis of research and testing conducted in other states. The manufacturer shall provide the Department with the data and findings of all evaluations of the performance of the system that have been conducted in any state by or on behalf of the manufacturer. The manufacturer shall also provide the Department with a summary of the data and findings of all other evaluations of the performance of the system that are known to the manufacturer. The Department shall publish a notice that the manufacturer has submitted an application under this subsection in the North Carolina Register and may provide additional notice to the public via the Internet or by other means. The Department shall receive public comment on the application for at least 30 days after the date the notice is published in the North Carolina Register. In making a determination under this subsection, the Department shall consider the data, findings, and recommendations submitted by the manufacturer and all public comment. The Department may also consider any other information that the Department determines to be relevant. The Department shall determine: (i) whether the system performs in a manner equal or superior to a conventional wastewater system; (ii) whether the system is constructed of materials whose physical and chemical properties provide the strength, durability, and chemical resistance to allow the system to withstand loads and conditions as required by rules adopted by the Commission; (iii) the circumstances in which use of the system is appropriate; and (iv) any conditions and limitations related to the use of the system. The Department shall make the determinations required by this subsection and approve or deny the application within 180 days after the Department receives a complete application from a manufacturer. If the Department fails to act on the application within 180 days, the manufacturer may treat the application as denied and challenge the denial by filing a contested case as provided in Article 3 of Chapter 150B of the General Statutes. If the Department approves an innovative wastewater system, the Department shall specify the circumstances in which use of the system is appropriate and any conditions and limitations related to the use of the system.

(g1)   Approval of Functionally Equivalent Trench Systems as Innovative Systems. - A manufacturer of a wastewater trench system may petition the Commission to have the wastewater trench system approved as an innovative wastewater system as provided in this subsection.

(1)   The Commission shall approve a wastewater trench system as an innovative wastewater system if it finds that there is clear, convincing, and cogent evidence that the wastewater trench system is functionally equivalent to a wastewater trench system that is approved as an accepted wastewater system. A wastewater trench system shall be considered functionally equivalent to an accepted wastewater trench system if the performance characteristics of the wastewater trench system satisfy all of the following requirements:

a. The physical properties and chemical durability of the materials from which the wastewater trench system is constructed are equal to or superior to the physical properties and chemical durability of the materials from which the accepted wastewater trench system is constructed.

b. The permeable sidewall area and bottom infiltrative area of the wastewater trench system are equal to or greater than the permeable sidewall area and bottom infiltrative area of the accepted wastewater trench system at a field-installed size.

c. The wastewater trench system utilizes a similar method and manner of function for the conveyance and application of effluent as the accepted wastewater trench system.

d. The structural integrity of the wastewater trench system is equal to or superior to the structural integrity of the accepted wastewater trench system.

e. The wastewater trench system shall provide a field installed system storage volume equal to or greater than the field installed system storage volume of the accepted wastewater trench system.

(2) As part of its petition, the manufacturer shall provide to the Commission all of the following information:

a. Specifications of the wastewater trench system.

b. Data necessary to demonstrate that the wastewater trench system is functionally equivalent to a wastewater trench system that is approved as an accepted wastewater system.

c. A certified statement from an independent, third-party professional engineer or testing laboratory that, based on verified documentation, the wastewater trench system is functionally equivalent to an accepted wastewater system.

(3) Approval of a wastewater trench system as an innovative wastewater system shall not be conditioned on the manufacturer of the wastewater trench system having operational systems installed in the State.

(4) The Commission shall authorize the use of a wastewater trench system as an innovative wastewater system in the same applications as the accepted wastewater trench system.

(5) The Commission shall not include conditions and limitations in the approval of a wastewater trench system as an innovative wastewater system that are not included in the approval of the accepted wastewater trench system.

(h) Accepted Systems. - A manufacturer of an innovative wastewater system that has been in general use in this State for more than five years may petition the Commission to have the system designated as an accepted wastewater system as provided in this subsection. The manufacturer shall provide the Commission with the data and findings of all prior evaluations of the performance of the system. In addition, the manufacturer shall provide the Commission with information sufficient to enable the Commission to fully evaluate the performance of the system in this State for at least the five-year period immediately preceding the petition. The Commission shall designate a wastewater system as an accepted wastewater system only if it finds that there is clear, convincing, and cogent evidence (i) to confirm the findings made by the Department at the time the Department approved the system as an innovative wastewater system and (ii) that the system performs in a manner that is equal or superior to a conventional wastewater system under actual field conditions in this State. The Commission shall specify the circumstances in which use of the system is appropriate and any conditions and limitations related to the use of the system.

(i) Miscellaneous Provisions. -

(1) In evaluating applications for approval under this section, the Department may consult with persons who have special training and experience related to on-site subsurface wastewater systems and may form a technical advisory committee for this purpose. However, the Department is responsible for making timely and appropriate determinations under this section.

(2) The Department may initiate a review of a nonproprietary wastewater system and approve the system for on-site subsurface use as an experimental wastewater system, a controlled demonstration wastewater system, or an innovative wastewater system without having received an application from a manufacturer. The Department may recommend that the Commission designate a nonproprietary wastewater system as an accepted wastewater system without having received a petition from a manufacturer.

(j)   Warranty Required in Certain Circumstances. - The Department shall not approve a reduction of the total nitrification trench length for an innovative wastewater system or accepted wastewater system handling untreated septic tank effluent of more than twenty-five percent (25%) as compared to the total nitrification trench length required for a 36-inch-wide conventional wastewater system unless the manufacturer of the innovative wastewater system or accepted wastewater system provides a performance warranty for the nitrification trench system to each owner or purchaser of the system for a warranty period of at least five years from the date on which the wastewater system is placed in operation. The warranty shall provide that the manufacturer shall provide all material and labor that may be necessary to provide a fully functional wastewater system. The Commission shall establish minimum terms and conditions for the warranty required by this subsection. This subsection shall not be construed to require that a manufacturer warrant a wastewater system that is not properly sized to meet the design load required for a particular use, that is improperly installed, or that is improperly operated and maintained.

(k)   Fees. - The Department shall collect the following fees under this section:

(1)   Review of an alternative protocol

        under subsection (d) of this section
$1,000.00

(2)   Review of an experimental system
$3,000.00

(3)   Review of a controlled demonstration system
$3,000.00

(4)   Review of an innovative system
$3,000.00

(5)   Review of an accepted system
$3,000.00

(6)   Review of a residential wastewater treatment

system pursuant to G.S. 130A-342 $1,500.00

(7)　　Review of a component of a system　　　　　　　　　　　　$ 100.00

(8)　　Modification to approved innovative system $1,000.00

(l)　　On-Site Wastewater System Account. - The On-Site Wastewater System Account is established as a nonreverting account within the Department. Fees collected pursuant to this section shall be placed in the On-Site Wastewater System Account and shall be applied only to the costs of implementing this section. (1989, c. 764, s. 10; 1991 (Reg. Sess., 1992), c. 944, s. 9; 1995, c. 285, s. 1; 2001-505, s. 2.2; 2011-261, s. 1.)

§ 130A-343.1. Transfer of ownership of provisionally approved septic tanks and innovative septic tank systems to joint agency in certain counties; inspection fees in those counties.

(a)　　As used in this section, "provisionally approved septic tank or innovative septic tank system" means a septic tank system located in soil that is classified as provisionally suitable or an innovative septic tank system, as those terms are used in Subchapter 18A of Chapter 18 of Title 15A of the North Carolina Administrative Code, G.S. 130A-343, and any applicable local rules or ordinances.

(b)　　As used in this subsection, "unit of local government" has the same meaning as in G.S. 160A-460. One or more units of local government located in the Counties of Camden, Chowan, Currituck, Gates, Hertford, Pasquotank, Perquimans, Tyrrell, and Washington may establish a joint agency for the purpose of owning and operating a provisionally approved septic tank or innovative septic tank system as provided in Article 20 of Chapter 160A of the General Statutes. Bertie County may join any joint agency established under this subsection. The owner of any provisionally approved septic tank or innovative septic tank system may, upon acceptance by a joint agency established under this subsection, transfer ownership of any real or personal property or interest therein that is a part of or used in connection with the provisionally approved septic tank or innovative septic tank system to the joint agency. Notwithstanding G.S. 160A-462(a), a joint agency created pursuant to this subsection may hold real property necessary to the undertaking. Any county named in this subsection may accept real or personal property described in this subsection from the owner of the property for transfer to a joint agency established as provided in this subsection.

(c) The Counties of Bertie, Camden, Chowan, Currituck, Gates, Hertford, Pasquotank, Perquimans, Tyrrell, and Washington may adopt an ordinance providing that any fee for the inspection, maintenance, and repair of a provisionally approved septic tank or other innovative septic tank system may be billed as property taxes, may be payable in the same manner as property taxes, and in the case of nonpayment, may be collected in any manner by which property taxes can be collected. If the ordinance states that delinquent fees can be collected in the same manner as delinquent real property taxes, the delinquent fees are a lien on the real property described on the bill that includes the fee. (1999-288, ss. 1-3; 2001-78, ss. 1-3.)

§ 130A-344: Repealed by Session Laws 1995, c. 285, s. 2.

§ 130A-345. Reserved for future codification purposes.

Article 12.

Mosquito and Vector Control.

Part 1. Mosquito and Vector Control Program.

§ 130A-346: Repealed by Session Laws 2011-145, s. 13.3(j), effective July 1, 2011.

§ 130A-347: Repealed by Session Laws 2011-145, s. 13.3(j), effective July 1, 2011.

§ 130A-348: Repealed by Session Laws 2011-145, s. 13.3(j), effective July 1, 2011.

§ 130A-349: Repealed by Session Laws 2011-145, s. 13.3(j), effective July 1, 2011.

§ 130A-350: Reserved for future codification purposes.

§ 130A-351: Reserved for future codification purposes.

Part 2. Mosquito Control Districts.

§ 130A-352. Creation and purpose of mosquito control districts.

For the purpose of protecting and promoting the public health and welfare by providing for the control of mosquitoes and other arthropods of public health significance, mosquito control districts may be created in accordance with the provisions of this Part. A mosquito control district may be comprised of one or more contiguous counties or contiguous parts of one or more counties. (1957, c. 1247, s. 1; 1983, c. 891, s. 2.)

§ 130A-353. Nature of district; procedure for forming districts.

(a)   A mosquito control district shall be a body politic and corporate and a political subdivision of the State. A mosquito control district may sue and be sued in its corporate name.

(b)   If the proposed district lies wholly within a county, ten percent (10%) or more of the resident freeholders within the proposed district may petition the board of commissioners of the county in which the proposed district lies setting forth the boundaries of the district and a suggested name for the district. For the purposes of this Part, the term "freeholders" shall mean persons holding a deed to a tract of land within the district or proposed district, and also shall mean a person who has entered into a contract to purchase a tract of land within the district or proposed district, is making payments pursuant to a contract, and will receive a deed upon completion of the contractual payments. If the county board of commissioners considers the formation of the district to be in the interest of the public health, the board shall forward the petition to the Department. If the Department considers the formation of the district to be in the interest of the public health, the Department shall notify the county board of commissioners. Upon notification, the board shall give notice of a public hearing on the question of the formation of the district by advertising the time, place and purpose of the hearing once a week for four successive weeks prior to the hearing in a newspaper either published in the county or having a general circulation in the county. The public hearing shall be presided over by the chairman of the county board of commissioners and shall be attended by a representative of the Department. The hearing may be continued as may be necessary to hear the proponents and opponents of the formation of the district. If after the hearing, the county board of commissioners deem it advisable that the district be created, the board shall submit the question of whether or not the district shall be created to the voters residing within the proposed district at an election called for that purpose. Upon determining that the district should be created and established, and prior to the submission of the question of the formation of the district to the voters of the proposed district, the county board of commissioners may determine the maximum amount of special tax to be levied for mosquito control purposes should the formation of the district be approved by the voters. In no event shall the maximum authorized levy exceed thirty-five cents (35¢) upon the one hundred dollar ($100.00) assessed valuation. If the county board of commissioners determines that the maximum amount of special tax to be levied for mosquito control purposes is to be less than thirty-five cents (35¢) on the one hundred dollar ($100.00) valuation, the maximum amount must appear on the ballot to be used by the voters on the question of the creation of the district.

(c)   Prior to the election, the county board of commissioners may make minor deviations in defining the boundaries of the proposed district if: (1) the board determines that minor deviation from the boundaries described in the petition is in the interest of public health; and (2) ten percent (10%) of the resident freeholders within the revised boundaries have signed the petition proposing the creation of the district or additional resident freeholders within the revised boundaries of the proposed district sign the petition to bring the total number of petitioners within the proposed revised boundaries to not less than ten percent (10%) of the voters therein.

(d)   The county board of commissioners shall request the county board of elections to hold the election and shall pay the expense of the election. The election shall be held in accordance with the applicable provisions of Chapter 163 of the General Statutes. Notice shall be given as provided in G.S. 163-33(8).

(e)   The form of the question to be stated on the ballot shall be in substantially the following words:

"[] FOR creation of the (here insert name) Mosquito Control District and the levy of a special tax (here insert the words "not to exceed" and the maximum amount of special tax to be levied for mosquito control purposes if the county board of commissioners has determined that the maximum authorized amount is to be less than thirty-five cents (35¢) on the one hundred dollar ($100.00) assessed valuation) for mosquito control purposes.

[] AGAINST creation of the (here insert name) Mosquito Control District and the levy of a special tax (here insert the words "not to exceed" and the maximum amount of special tax to be levied for mosquito control purposes if the county board of commissioners has determined that the maximum authorized amount is to be less than thirty-five cents (35¢) on the one hundred dollar ($100.00) assessed valuation) for mosquito control purposes."

The affirmative and negative forms shall be printed on one ballot and the voters shall make a mark of an "X" in one of the squares preceding the form.

(f) If a majority of the voters voting at the election vote in favor of creation of the district and the levy of the special tax, the county board of commissioners shall declare the district created and shall adopt a resolution to that effect.

(g) In the event the proposed mosquito control district shall embrace lands lying in two or more counties, the petition signed by the requisite number of resident freeholders within the proposed district shall be addressed to the Department. If the Department deems the formation of the proposed district to be in the interest of the public health, the Department shall hold public hearings within the proposed district after first giving notice of the time and place of the hearings by publication once a week for four successive weeks in a newspaper published or circulated in the proposed district. A public hearing shall be held in the courthouse of each of the counties in which any part of the proposed district is situated. After the hearing, if the Department deems the formation of the district to be in the interest of the public health, the Department shall order an election to be held upon the question of the formation of the district after first advertising the time of the election in the manner provided in subsection (d). At the request of the Commission, the county commissioners of the counties in which the proposed district lies shall request the county board of elections to hold an election on the question with substantially the same form of ballot set forth in subsection (e). Each county shall bear the expense of the election held in that county. The board of elections shall certify the results to the county commissioners and the Commission. If a majority of the votes cast favor creation of the district and the levy of the special tax, the Commission shall declare the district created and the county commissioners shall enter the certification upon the minutes of the board. Registration shall be in accordance with G.S. 163-288.2. (1957, c. 1247, s. 2; 1959, c. 622, s. 1; 1973, c. 476, s. 128; 1981, c. 188, ss. 1, 2; 1983, c. 891, s. 2.)

§ 130A-354. Governing bodies for mosquito control districts.

(a)   A mosquito control district shall be governed by a board of commissioners. In the case of a district lying wholly within a single county, the board shall be composed of five members, all of whom shall be residents of the district. Three of the members shall be appointed by the county board of commissioners, one for an initial term of one year, one for an initial term of two years and one for an initial term of three years. All subsequent appointments made by the county board of commissioners shall be for terms of three years. One member shall be appointed by the Secretary and one member by the Director of the Wildlife Resources Commission. These two appointees shall serve at the pleasure of the appointing authority. A vacancy shall be filled by the authority which appointed the member creating the vacancy.

(b)   In the case of a district lying in two or more counties, the Secretary shall appoint one member and the Director of the Wildlife Commission shall appoint one member. The board of commissioners of each county in which any part of the district lies shall appoint one member. In the event the district lies in only two counties, the board of commissioners of the county in which a majority of the acreage of the district lies shall appoint two members, one for an initial term of one year and the other for an initial term of two years. The other county shall appoint one member for an initial term of three years. All succeeding terms of county appointees shall be for three years. A vacancy shall be filled by the authority which appointed the member creating the vacancy, and the appointees of the Secretary and the Director of the Wildlife Resources Commission shall hold office at the pleasure of the appointing authority.

(c)   At its first meeting, the board shall elect a chairman, a vice-chairman, a secretary and a treasurer. The office of secretary and treasurer may be held by the same member. All official acts done by the board shall be entered in a book of minutes to be kept by the secretary. The board shall meet at least quarterly and may meet in a special meeting at any time upon call of the chairman or any two members, and upon notice of the time, place and purpose of the meeting of not less than three days. Before entering upon the discharge of their duties, each member shall take and subscribe an oath of office as follows and the oath shall be entered in the minute book:

"I, _____, do solemnly swear that I will well and truly perform my duties as a Commissioner of the _____ Mosquito Control District.

_____ Signature

Affirmed and subscribed before me this ____ day of _____ _____

_____

Signature of Officer Administering Oath."

(1957, c. 1247, s. 3; 1973, c. 476, s. 128; 1983, c. 891, s. 2; 1999-456, s. 59.)

§ 130A-355. Corporate powers.

A mosquito control district created in accordance with the provisions of this Part shall have and exercise through its board of commissioners the following corporate powers in addition to any incidental powers as may be necessary in order to discharge its corporate functions:

(1) To levy ad valorem taxes upon all the taxable property within the district at a rate not to exceed thirty-five cents (35¢) upon the adjusted one hundred dollar ($100.00) assessed valuation, except as provided in subdivision (a) of this subsection.

a. Where a mosquito control district lies solely within a single county and includes the entire county, the county board of commissioners may levy and determine the rate of ad valorem tax to be levied at a rate not to exceed thirty-five cents (35¢) upon the adjusted one hundred dollar ($100.00) assessed valuation. Where a mosquito control district lies wholly within a single county and the maximum authorized special tax approved by the voters at the time of voting on the creation of the district was less than thirty-five cents (35¢) on the one hundred dollar assessed valuation, the ad valorem tax levy shall not exceed the lesser amount.

b. In the case of a district lying wholly within a single county, the valuations assessed by the county tax authorities shall be used by the mosquito control district or the county board of commissioners as the basis for its tax assessment. The mosquito control district or the county board of commissioners shall certify its tax rate to the county tax collector or supervisor in time to have the rate and the amount of tax due upon the valuation entered upon the official county tax receipts and stubs or duplicates. The county tax collector shall collect the taxes at the same time as county taxes are collected and shall deposit the receipts to the credit of the mosquito control district in a depository or depositories designated by the governing board of the district.

    c.   In the case of a district lying in two or more counties, the commissioners of the mosquito control district shall horizontally equalize the assessed valuations of the property in all counties in which the district lies by adjusting the ratio of assessed valuation in the counties to the true values of the taxable property in the counties. From the adjusted and equalized valuations, any county board of commissioners may appeal to the Department of Revenue using the procedures set forth in Subchapter II of Chapter 105 of the General Statutes.

    d.   The board of commissioners of the mosquito control district shall levy a tax based upon the equalized assessed valuations and shall certify the amount of the levy against each taxpayer to the appropriate county tax collector or supervisor in time for the amount of the mosquito control district tax to be entered upon the county tax receipts and stubs or duplicates. The county tax collectors shall collect the tax and deposit the receipts to the credit of the mosquito control district in a depository or depositories designated by the commissioners of the district.

    e.   The taxes levied according to this Part shall become due; shall be subject to the same discounts, penalties and interest; and shall have the same remedies for the collection and refund of the taxes as provided for county and municipal ad valorem taxation by Chapter 310 of the Session Laws of 1939 as amended. These taxes shall constitute a lien to the same extent and with the same force and effect as county and municipal ad valorem taxes and shall have equal priority with those taxes;

(2)   To accept gifts or endowments and to receive federal and State grants-in-aid. All money or property acquired under this section or any other source, shall be deposited in a separate fund to be used solely for the purpose of carrying out the provisions of this Part. The deposited funds shall be withdrawn by warrants signed by the chairperson of the governing board of the district and countersigned by the secretary;

(3) To take all necessary and proper steps to prevent the breeding of mosquitoes and other arthropods of public health significance within the district, and to destroy adult mosquitoes and other arthropods of public health significance found within the district;

(4) To conduct arthropod control measures in cooperation with individuals, firms and corporations, and federal, State and local governmental agencies;

(5) To enter all places both publicly and privately owned within the district to inspect, survey and treat with proper means all places where mosquitoes or other arthropods of public health significance are breeding and to take other actions as may be necessary;

(6) To acquire by purchase, condemnation or otherwise, and to hold real and personal property, easements, rights-of-way or other property necessary or convenient for accomplishing the purpose of this Part. Any land which has been acquired by the board and improved by drainage, filling, diking or other treatment, and other real property held by the board may be sold or leased through competitive bidding. All condemnation proceedings are to be in accordance with the provisions of Chapter 40A of the General Statutes;

(7) To employ necessary personnel; fix salaries; purchase equipment, supplies and materials; make contracts; rent office or storage space; and perform other administrative functions necessary for the purpose of carrying out this Part;

(8) To borrow money in anticipation of tax collection and to execute and deliver its notes or bonds. Money shall be borrowed in gross amounts not to exceed the anticipated tax receipts for the fiscal year;

(9) To reimburse members and employees of the board for actual expenditures incurred in authorized travel; and

(10) To employ a district superintendent who is an engineer, entomologist or otherwise qualified as an arthropod control specialist. The professional qualifications of the superintendent must be approved by the Secretary. (1957, c. 1247, s. 4; 1959, c. 622, s. 2; 1973, c. 476, ss. 128, 193; 1981, c. 919, s. 15; 1983, c. 891, s. 2.)

§ 130A-356. Adoption of plan of operation.

(a) At least 60 days prior to the initiation of operations, the governing board of each mosquito control district must submit to the Secretary, a plan of procedure and operation in a form and manner prescribed by the Secretary. The Secretary shall have authority to approve, modify or take other appropriate action in regard to the plans. No contract may be entered into, program commenced or work begun prior to the approval of the plan by the Secretary.

(b) At least 60 days prior to the expiration of each fiscal year, the governing board of each mosquito control district must submit to the Secretary a plan of procedure and operation for the next fiscal year in a form and manner prescribed by the Secretary. The Secretary shall have authority to approve, modify or take other appropriate action in regard to the plans. No contract may be entered into, program commenced or work begun or continued prior to the approval of the plan by the Secretary. (1957, c. 1247, s. 5; 1973, c. 476, s. 128; 1983, c. 891, s. 2.)

§ 130A-357. Bond issues.

A mosquito control district shall have power to issue bonds and notes under the Local Government Bond Act. (1957, c. 1247, s. 6; 1971, c. 780, s. 25; 1983, c. 891, s. 2.)

§ 130A-358. Dissolution of certain mosquito control districts.

Fifty-one percent (51%) or more of the resident freeholders of a mosquito control district which has no outstanding indebtedness may submit a petition for dissolution to the county board of commissioners in which all or the greater portion of the resident freeholders of the district are located. The county board of commissioners shall notify the Department and the county board of commissioners of any other county or counties in which any portion of the district lies, of the receipt of the petition, and shall request the Department to hold a joint public hearing with the county commissioners concerning the dissolution of the district. The Department and the chairperson of the county board of commissioners shall name a time and place within the district for the public hearing. The chairperson of the county board of commissioners of the county in which all or the greater portion of the resident freeholders of the district are located shall give prior notice of the hearing by posting a notice at the courthouse door of each county and also by publication in a newspaper or newspapers published in the county or counties at least once a week for four successive weeks. In the event that all matters pertaining to the dissolution of the mosquito control district cannot be concluded at the hearing, the hearing may be continued to a time and place determined by the Department. If after the hearing, the Commission and the county commissioners shall deem it advisable to comply with the request of the petition, the Commission shall adopt a resolution dissolving the district. (1959, c. 622, s. 3; 1973, c. 476, s. 128; 1983, c. 891, s. 2.)

§ 130A-359. Reserved for future codification purposes.

§ 130A-360. Reserved for future codification purposes.

Article 13.

Nutrition.

§ 130A-361. Department to establish nutrition program.

(a) The Department shall establish and administer a nutrition program to promote the public health by achieving and maintaining optimal nutritional status in the population through activities such as nutrition screening and assessment; dietary counseling and treatment; nutrition education; follow-up; referral; and the direct provision of food. The program may also include, but shall not be limited to, establishing policies and standards for nutritional practices; monitoring and surveillance of nutritional status; promoting interagency cooperation, professional education and consultation; providing technical assistance; conducting and supporting field research; providing direct care; and advising State and private institutions and other State and local agencies and departments in the establishment of food, nutrition and food service management standards.

(b) The Commission for Public Health shall adopt rules necessary to implement the program. (Resolution 112, 1973, p. 1413; 1983, c. 891, s. 2; 1989, c. 204; 1991, c. 188, s. 1; 2007-182, s. 2.)

§§ 130A-362 through 130A-365. Reserved for future codification purposes.

Article 14.

Dental Health.

§ 130A-366. Department to establish dental health program.

(a)   The Department shall establish and administer a dental health program for the delivery of preventive, educational and dental care services to preschool children, school-age children, and adults. The program shall include, but not be limited to, providing teacher training, adult and child education, consultation, screening and referral, technical assistance, community coordination, field research and direct patient care. The primary emphasis of the program shall be the delivery of preventive, educational, and dental care services to preschool children and school-age children.

(b)   The Commission shall adopt rules necessary to implement the program. (1983, c. 891, s. 2; 1993, c. 321, s. 269.)

§ 130A-367. Dental providers for problem access areas.

The State's dental public health program shall encourage the expansion of current educational and training programs for dentists, dental hygienists, and dental assistants targeted to serve citizens' unmet needs, particularly in the rural and low-income areas that have traditionally had problems in accessing dental care. The program shall also promote and encourage the recruitment of in-State and out-of-state private sector dental personnel to work in these dental health professional shortage areas. (2002-37, s. 1.)

§§ 130A-368 through 130A-370. Reserved for future codification purposes.

Article 15.

State Center for Health Statistics.

§ 130A-371. State Center for Health Statistics established.

A State Center for Health Statistics is established within the Department. (1983, c. 891, s. 2.).

§ 130A-372. Definitions.

The following definitions shall apply throughout this Article:

(1) "Health data" means information relating to the health status of individuals, the availability of health resources and services, and the use and cost of these resources and services. The term shall not include vital records registered under the provisions of Article 4 of this Chapter.

(2) "Medical records" means health data relating to the diagnosis or treatment of physical or mental ailments of individuals. (1983, c. 891, s. 2.)

Vision Books Order Form

Fax Orders:	1-980-299-5965
Phone Orders:	1-704-898-0770
E-mail Orders:	www.visionbooks.org
Mail Orders:	Vision Books, LLC P.O. Box 42406 Charlotte, NC 28215

Shipp To:
Name_____
Address_____
City_____State_____Zip_____
Phone_____Fax_____
Email_____@_____

Bill To: We can bill a third party on your behalf.
Name_____
Address_____
City_____State_____Zip_____
Phone   (   )   Fax_____
Email_____@_____

Pamphlet Number ($15.00 Each)	Qty	Total Cost
_____	_____	_____
_____	_____	_____
_____	_____	_____
_____	_____	_____
_____	_____	_____
_____	_____	_____
_____	_____	_____
_____	_____	_____
<u>Full Volume Set 1-92</u>	<u>92 Pamphlets</u>	<u>1,380.00</u>

Free Shipping & Handling on Full Volume Orders
Add $1.00 Shipping & Handling Per Pamphlet $_____

Total Cost $_____

Thank you for your support. Management!

DID YOU ENJOY THIS BOOK?

Vision Books, LLC would like to hear from you! If you or someone you know has been fasely imprisoned, we would like to hear your story. If the 'North Carolina Criminal Law and Procedure' has had an effect in your life or if you have suggestions, we would like to hear from you. Send your letters to:

Vision Books, LLC
Attn: Staff Writers
P.O. Box 42406
Charlotte, NC 28215
Email: staff@visionbooks.org

Order Additional Copies:

Fax Orders:	1-980-299-5965
Phone Orders:	1-704-898-0770
E-mail Orders:	www.visionbooks.org
Mail Orders:	Vision Books, LLC P.O. Box 42406 Charlotte, NC 28215

www.ingramcontent.com/pod-product-compliance
Lightning Source LLC
Chambersburg PA
CBHW051631170526
45167CB00001B/138